Tuesday's Child

A Reader for Christian Educators

D0230868

**A P ect i the
Consultative Group nistry
among Children, a network of
Churches Together in Britain and Ireland**

Developed and edited by John Sutcliffe

CHRIS✝IAN education PUBLISHING

Reverend Doctor John M Sutcliffe is a minister of the United Reformed Church and for a short time was its Education Secretary. He has been General Secretary of the Christian Education Movement and worked in the second of two pastorates before becoming Director of the Manchester Christian Institute. He is a past President of the National Christian Education Council and has served on a number of Syllabus Committees. For over ten years he chaired the *Partners In Learning* editorial group. He retired in 2000 from the post of President of the Partnership for Theological Education, Manchester, an affiliated institution of the University of Manchester.

Published by:
Christian Education Publications
1020 Bristol Road
Selly Oak
Birmingham
B29 6LB

ISBN: 1-904024-00-9

First published: 2001

Designed and typeset by Christian Education Publications

Printed and bound in the UK by Herald Forms Group

**'Monday's child is fair of face,
Tuesday's child is full of grace...'**

Contents

Introduction

The purpose of this collection of quotations is to help readers to explore the developments in thinking about childhood and children, their spirituality and faith development, their place and role in the Church and their challenge to the Church. It is also a modest contribution to the telling of the story of change in Christian education in the churches during the twentieth century. This is a complex story in which approaches in Religious Education in schools, the influence of psychology and sociology on education, the implications of a renewal in liturgical studies and a broadening interest in worship, the development of new ways of doing theology, the study of human groups, and community development theory and practice all played a part.

The Consultative Group on Ministry Among Children, a network of Churches Together in Britain and Ireland whose members made a first selection of texts that might be included, generated the idea for this anthology. They then asked me to develop and edit the work. It has been a stimulating task, not least because in one way or another, for over forty years, I have participated in the upheavals in Christian education both in the churches and in day schools implicit in the quotations and I know or have known many of the people who are quoted. Deciding whose work should be left out has been painful.

I have continued to receive advice from members of the Consultative Group on Ministry Among Children, Judy Jarvis in particular; from Ian Birnie and other members of the Christian Education Movement; and from Rachel Eichhorn, the Learning Resources Tutor, and other former staff colleagues in the Partnership for Theological Education, Manchester.

The decision to tell the story in chronological order, rather than thematically, was made both by members of the Consultative Group and by myself. I have contributed introductory comments and arranged the quotations in the order in which they were published, in the hope that readers will gain a better sense of the movement of ideas throughout the century; practice most often lagged behind. I hope, too, that the inclusion of quotations of varying length and weightiness will help to make the anthology useful to as wide a range of readers as possible. What is not here, but is necessary for a fuller understanding of the quotations, is a historical commentary on the social, international, technological, political, medical, religious and broader educational life of the century.

In spite of the limitations of space and, no doubt, my failure to grasp the significance of some publications, **I hope the collection will be a valuable resource to all who work with children in the churches, to Christian teachers in day schools, students of theology and people preparing for lay and ordained ministries in the churches**.

John Sutcliffe
2001

1900–2000
Tuesday's Child

British children born into the world of empire, heavy industry and international commerce of 1900 would hardly be able to comprehend the world into which children were born in the year 2000 with its freedoms, rights, self-expression and technology. Nor has the position of children in the churches remained static during that time. The crowds attending churches and Sunday Schools in 1900 – albeit a significantly reducing proportion of the population in industrial cities – with their formality and their style, authority and conviction in teaching, all gradually evaporated. Where in many Sunday Schools at the beginning of the century children attended in their hundreds, by the end of it there was only a handful of children and many of the Sunday Schools' buildings had been demolished. Two world wars, rapid scientific and technological progress, the development of relatively cheap international travel and of a global economy, mass news and other communications media, and the presence in Britain of many people of Muslim, Hindu, Sikh and other faiths each played a part in changing attitudes towards public religion.

It would be easy to describe the position of the churches in 2000 in negative terms. They were perceived not to have met the intellectual and moral challenges of the century. They appeared to be stuck in a rut. Their traditional styles of beauty had become the taste of the few. Evangelical or Pentecostal churches had increased in number and had grown in size but their numerical successes in no way made up for the decline in the numbers associated with the older denominations. Relatively few children attended church; Sunday Schools had entered upon a seemingly terminal decline, though in some places the decline of the Sunday School was the result of careful and theologically motivated planning.

It is also possible to see the century as one in which very considerable positive thought was given to the role of the Church in society and to the place and role of children in the Church. The 1900s child would be astonished to discover that in 2000 children were listened to in many churches, that they were deemed to be teachers as well as learners, that the language of 'school', 'teacher' and 'scholar' was judged to be inappropriate and that as well as being regarded as 'the future of the Church', children were also recognised as being 'the Church of today', communicant members in their own right.

One of the central differences between the Church in 2000 and the Church in the earlier decades of the century was that, earlier in the century, many scholars and Church leaders were committed to helping to reform and develop Christian education in both church and day school. For instance, Dr A E Garvie, Principal of New College, London, took a leading role and drew several colleagues into the work of the International Lessons Committee.

Theologians and church leaders, including university professors, principals of theological colleges, archbishops and bishops, also contributed through direct participation and, for instance, through articles in *Religion in Education* and early issues of *Learning for Living* (both predecessors of the *British Journal of Religious Education*). Distinguished scholars addressed questions about the nature of Christian education and Christian community in relation to day schools. Key among them later in the century were John Macmurray (*Reason and Emotion,* Faber, 1935, republished 1961), Spencer Leeson (*Christian Education,* the 1947 Bampton Lectures, published by Longman), W R Niblett (*Christian Education in a Secular Setting,* Oxford University Press, 1959) and Ninian Smart (*The Teacher and Christian Belief,* James Clark, 1966). They were generally concerned with the values and moral ethos of the school, the quality of teachers who could see and communicate fundamental questions of truth and meaning implicit in their disciplines, and the ways in which disciplines related to each other and to daily life and to the aims of the school (see the quotation on pages 100–105 from Ian T Ramsey). The failure of the Churches and Christian thinkers of standing now to address such issues – the hidden secular and theological agenda of education – leaves the input of the Churches into debates about public education at the level of fairly mundane comment on the practicalities of Government proposals. In 2000 the Churches with valuable historic involvement in day school education seemed concerned only with their own systems and ignored the value-laden nature of the National Curriculum, which was and is in many respects antipathetic to Christian values.

1900–1940
The Beginnings of
a Child-Centred Approach

Hamilton Archibald inspired the first significant development in Christian education in Protestant churches in the new century. One inheritance of the twentieth century was large Sunday Schools in which children and people of all ages were taught together. Archibald questioned this approach. He was a Canadian who came to Britain in 1902, having become well-known in his home country and the United States for pioneering work with Sunday Schools. In lectures to Sunday School teachers, which became extremely popular, he emphasised the centrality of the child and asked teachers to approach Bible teaching through the eyes and experience of a child. Gradually Sunday School teachers in most parts of the country were influenced and teacher training classes based on his insights and new teaching material became common practice. Archibald's work led to the formation of the British Lessons Council in 1916 and Westhill College, Birmingham. (West Hill weeks, residential courses for Sunday School teachers, began in 1907.) The new enthusiasm in Britain for genuinely educational approaches and to teaching in age-groups was also strengthened through the World Sunday School Association founded in 1907 (to become the World Council of Christian Education in 1948). The emphasis on child-centredness, grounded in the growingly important psychology of childhood and of education, can be seen in the quotations from Archibald, Dorothy Wilson and Basil Yeaxlee. Yeaxlee's work and that of L W Grensted, who wrote about the psychology of religion, later gave psychological foundations to the work of H A Hamilton.

The momentum created by these new approaches lasted until the Second World War, but was tempered by the loss of young men from the churches during the 1914–18 war and other consequences of war, and then the depressing effects of industrial and economic recession in the 1930s. A paper on the 'Foundation of a True Social Order' presented to the Yearly Meeting of the Religious Society of Friends in 1918 sums up the liberal aspiration of its period:

'The opportunity of full development, physical, moral and spiritual should be assured to every member of the community...'

During the first several decades of the century, in which the teaching of children in the Roman Catholic Church was almost exclusively the responsibility of priests and church schools, there was little ecumenical contact between Christian educators. The Catholic Church gave basic teaching to a majority of its children through the document popularly known as the 'Penny Catechism'. Through a series of questions and answers children were told 'all they needed to know about the faith'. Because this was a distinct and separated activity of the Church, the majority of the earlier quotations are from Protestant sources, though it could be argued there were parallel developments in the Roman Catholic Church. Canon Drinkwater of the Birmingham Diocese, who in 1928 founded a monthly review *The Sower*, probably took the first initiative that led to a departure from the Penny Catechism. Drinkwater's experiences as an army chaplain in the First World War had taught him that Catholic young men needed more than abstract questions and answers. He argued against 'parrot learning' and encouraged the use of ordinary language in relating faith and life. In 1929 the 'Sower Scheme' was introduced in Catholic schools in his diocese. The fact that the Roman Catholic Church in Britain is part of a universal church determines its approach to catechetics in ways that are not part of the experience of other communions and which, some might think, are potentially both strengthening and limiting. The story of catechetics is told by Liam Kelly in *Catechetics Revisited* (Darton, Longman and Todd, 2000).

The Eastern Orthodox Churches' approach to children and their education is fundamentally different from those of all the other major denominations. Babies are baptised into the Church, receive the sacrament and become active participants in the Church. The purpose of education in the Church is not to inform children about what will eventually be theirs, but to interpret and deepen understanding of what is already theirs, that is, what children are already experiencing through being the Church. It was the logic as well as the practice of this important ecclesiological, psychological and educational difference that drew the attention of H A Hamilton and to which he tried to give expression in the very different Free Church context. See the chapter on the 1940s.

A 'Joint Commission of the (then) three Methodist Churches on Sunday-school Work', presented to Conference in 1931, drew attention to the net decreases in children attending Sunday School. In 1930, the figure was calculated to be 12,905. Of the 100,000–150,000 who had grown through their Sunday School years each year, it was said that only 20% remained in contact with the church. The Report made strong cases for the better training of teachers, that children's work should be part of the education of ordinands and that more resources should be spent on children's work to make possible a properly graded approach. The Commission's paragraphs on the 'Strategical Importance of Sunday-school work' are quoted below.

Archibald's message was summarised:

I.   All education begins, not with the lesson, not with the teacher, but with the child.
II. The child's love of Nature must be recognised.
III. The child must be taught largely through his senses and his activities.
IV. The appeal must be made principally through the child's imagination and his emotions rather than through his intellect.
V.   The Sunday school of the future must be decentralised.

From the 1913–14 report of the Durham Diocesan Board of Education. For further reading see *The Rise and Development of the Sunday School Movement in England 1780–1980*, Philip Cliff, NCEC, 1986.

Archibald's influence was considerable but he was not alone in seeing the need for change. In 1907 many leaders in Christian education met with theologians and Biblical scholars in London as the International Lesson Committee. Their aim was to:

- embrace the best in **Biblical criticism**
- encourage interdenominational **cooperation** and Christian unity
- stand for steady **self-evaluation** and **improvement** in S.S. work
- adopt **cycles** for curriculum to provide coherence and essentials

- practice **grading** to suit the capacities of different ages
- stress in-service **training** of teachers
- emphasize **service** to men as integral to accepting Christ
- teach for **peace** and international efforts for understanding
- make **missions** not a special Sunday but a constant in teaching
- face unmet **educational needs**, identify with **developing nations,** implement a **teaching vision** for the whole world.

From the *WCCE Family Album 1889–1971*, World Council of Christian Education, 1971

The child is a pragmatist; he judges values by results. Religion for children must be presented as something to live by; more even than something to die by. Generally speaking, the Church is finding itself more and more concerned with man's social environment; with his unclean face, his scanty clothing, and his ravenous appetite. The Sunday school teacher of to-day is dealing with a far wider circle of need than the teacher of yesterday. Therefore the Sunday school leader must have his aim clear, and that aim must be stated most concretely. It is not enough to talk about sin and salvation in general. Make religion concrete and the abstract will take care of itself. Boys and girls must be prepared specifically to meet every situation that they are likely to have to face...

The curriculum must be constructed with the home and family life of the child in mind: this not only to affect and improve his conduct in the home, but also to prepare him ultimately for parental obligations. The home is the heart of the community, and the school can do much to cultivate a clean and wholesome atmosphere; the destiny of the race is here at stake.

Nor is all this a counsel of perfection. I know how easy it is to say what *ought* to be, but I suggest that we have wasted much time and effort in attempting to deal with religion almost wholly in the abstract and general. The right and successful way is to deal with it in the concrete and particular. Remember we are dealing with the immature...

... but the point of view at the present day is that all religious education must begin with the child. In the olden days childhood was looked upon as a misfortune, something to be pitied, and the object of the parent and teacher was to rescue the child from himself. The idea was to press him, push him, hurry him into being a man. The argument was, there's only one life worth living, and that is the life of maturity; immaturity is something to escape from with all possible speed. But the new point of view is that life in all its beauty is to be found in the child. Not life in embryo only, but glad, happy, full, free life. Life, young or old, is a growth, and the joy of living is the joy of growing. When we look at the religious life from this point of view we see that the object of the teacher is to help each individual to live out its growing, developing life to the full, and to supply it with nurture that is needed not only for the future but primarily for the present stage of development...

In the last analysis it is better models rather than better teachers that immature children or primitive nations most need. Perhaps this explains the comparative powerlessness of the Church. She has taught her children to feel and to know without developing sufficiently the power to do. Now if this error in method is ever to be rectified, there must be a large place in religious education for expression. We learn, not by *memorizing*, not by *thinking*, but by doing; for, as one has said: 'All truth dies in the mind that is not lived out in practice.' The Catechism must have been invented to help indolent fathers and mothers to free themselves from the real task of training their children. It certainly was never written by sympathetic lovers of child life who appreciated the 'learning by doing' principle...

What, then, is wrong with the functioning of our Sunday schools? Indeed, with the functioning of much religious education? And what is the line of reform and progress? The Sunday school is not organized along sufficiently practical lines. I mean that religious education for the most part is too 'preachy' and 'talky-talky.' It aims to instruct and inspire, but fails to furnish opportunity for completing the teaching through expression. To be good one must be good for something. It is better to practise goodness than it is to either talk about it or think about it.

Perhaps the Sunday school benefits the teachers more than it does the scholars, for it is by teaching we learn. *Docere est discere.* The modern Sunday school excels in that it provides work for many more workers than the old-fashioned school did, but it still falls far short of the ideal. It must provide not only lessons for all stages of development, but it must become an institution for learning, and for learning by doing. The more advanced schools already provide opportunities for expressing the lesson in various ways...

And what shall we say of play, its place, its power, and its possibilities in the functioning of the life of the child and youth in the Sunday school? Day-school education is recognizing its value. Sunday schools and churches are following their lead, though, truth to tell, somewhat reluctantly. The significance of play as a recreation has long been recognized, but play as a unique, useful, and efficient ally in religious education is a different thing. Great teachers work *with* nature, and recognize play not only as a recreation but as an educational method, with roots as deep as instinct is deep. The tendency to express oneself in play is nearly as old as heredity. As hunger and thirst express a physiological need, so play is the expression of a psychological necessity, and its authoritative demand must be heeded.

In the Sunday school of to-morrow, the teacher will plan his work so that the influence of his Sunday teaching will extend into weekday play activities.

The play activities of the child change with his developing life. It is a fascinating study to note the different forms of interest in games. The child of three or four is happier with his bricks alone than in any co-operative play. A little child's tea-party always results in each individual playing his own game. The co-operative interest does not awaken till later. Children are often induced to play such games before they are really ready for them. There is a significant difference in the child's value of a cricket score from that of his elder brother's. Members of the lower school team start by asking, 'How many runs did I make?' And the lad is satisfied if he has made top score, even if his side has been defeated. The idea of playing for one's side comes later.

But let us look deeper into the meaning of play, for it has a wide significance. As long ago as the seventeenth century the poet Schiller wrote: 'Deep meaning oft lies hid in childish play.' Poets are seers. They glimpse into the dim and distant future and blaze the trail for the scientists. Except by the seer the value of play was not appreciated in the olden days, and it is only beginning to be realized in the twentieth century. The love of play is something comparable to the love of a story or, on the negative side, to the repulsion one feels in the presence of a serpent.

Why does the child love a story? Why does the human being shrink from crawling creatures? Why have these instinctive reactions become so deeply imbedded in human nature? Doubtless the cause dates back at least to the time when our forefathers lived among trees. There they were safe from the attack of the larger animals; lions and tigers and elephants had comparatively little terror for them. But the serpent and the creatures that crept and crawled had access to their habitations. For ages these preyed upon the offspring of the tree-dwellers; the serpent was one of the few creatures who could steal the babe from the mother's arms, and the peculiar terror that is inborn in female life, though not wholly confined to the female, is comprehensible. The stories of the Garden of Eden picture sin as a serpent. The terror of the serpent was known or at any rate felt by primitive folk, consequently the figure was a perfect one to make vivid the awfulness of sin.

Children love stories because in the olden days, when there were no newspapers, no books, no printing, not even writing, all knowledge was passed on from generation to generation by means of tales handed down from father to child...

The work of the Sunday school and of other kindred agencies of the Church must be organized and conducted in such a manner as will nurture rather than repress the highest and holiest impulses of the child's soul. Good motive on the part of those who are responsible is not enough; there must be efficiency in operation as well as purity of purpose. A reverent atmosphere is absolutely essential to Sunday school work.

But what is atmosphere? Atmosphere is like the air that the child breathes as contrasted with the food that he eats. He thrives just as much upon what he unconsciously inhales as upon that with which he is consciously fed. Since atmosphere is something felt, rather than known, it cannot be adequately described. It is not order only; nor is it silence. It is not something forced or mechanical. It is only present when there is spontaneity, freedom, and yet unity. It arises out of environment, setting, personality, prestige, music, beauty. The very walls of the room, the colour scheme, the voice of the leader, the vestment, the ritual, or the lack of ritual – all foster it; but the greatest of all is the personality of the leader.

From *The Modern Sunday School: its psychology and method*, G H Archibald, Pilgrim Press, 1926

The child's freedom

AUTHORITY, it has been argued, holds a necessary place in child-life and training, but in all education worthy of the name obedience to it is a stage which must be largely outgrown. A man or woman who will not think, who follows slavishly the will of the majority and the judgment of the herd, is an uneducated man or woman. Teachers should not be satisfied until their pupils can keep an open mind, exercise an independent judgment, and, if necessary, be sufficiently courageous to stand alone in action. Such men and women are moral pioneers who lead their fellows forward into rich and undiscovered countries, who hear the high call of

This main miracle that thou art thou,
With power on thine own act and on the world.

The necessary condition of such an attitude and such a work is freedom of the spirit; freedom to seek for, recognize and express truth, beauty and goodness as the individual himself sees them. In doing this he will not reject all the past experience of the human race, but instead of coming to him as heavy-handed and soul-deadening authority, it will come as wellnigh over-whelming evidence. One of the most difficult things a teacher has to do is to stand aside when the time comes for this free expression of his pupil's spiritual activities; it is so much easier to tell what he wishes to be true, than to help the pupil to judge for himself what really is true. Here the emphasis of our modern education on the training and development of something within, rather than on the imposition of something from without, is a wholesome and even a religious one; 'out of the heart are the issues of life.'

Such free faculties and activities of the spirit will not spring up in one moment mature and ready-armed. They must develop and be trained and nourished from the earliest days; the freedom must be progressive. Because it is freedom of the spirit it need not clash with authority, for such freedom is not licence to do as one pleases, but to express the deeper demands of the soul. No one can do this without obedience, and self-restraint of lower impulses and desires. Where authority allies itself with the demands of the spirit it may encourage freedom instead of curtailing it, and its restraint will pass over into self-restraint. The teacher will aim at helping the child to choose the true, the good and the beautiful for their own sake, because he really prefers them. This builds up self-respect and makes use of the powerful self-regarding sentiment. The child rejoices to use the faculties which he is taught to believe he really possesses.

This principle has an important bearing on the question of religious education. Since the general abandonment of the idea of the inborn depravity of all children, men have felt a new reverence for the natural and spontaneous tendencies for good in the souls of these little ones. They believe now that these tendencies can be fostered, that it is possible to help towards a growing spiritual appreciation, a developing insight into religious truth, a strengthening of will and character. How may this best be done?

It has been noted already that although growth comes from within it receives its nourishment from without. Hence it is necessary that the inward and the outward should be brought into contact, that the inner faculties should be stimulated to attend to outer things, to absorb them, to act upon them. The teacher's business is the provision of such stimulus, the encouragement of such attention, assimilation and expression. These will now be considered in this order.

Nature herself provides one great stimulus to attention to outer things and that is the stimulus of curiosity. Without this impulse to investigate what is new the child would never learn; in this sense Plato's saying that 'Curiosity is the mother of all knowledge' is true. It produces attention, or concentration of activity, and interest, the feeling which accompanies it. It is practically certain that if no curiosity can be aroused in a new subject, all study of it will be futile. Curiosity is the force which urges the child on to fresh intellectual activity, to the satisfaction of an intellectual hunger. The teacher's first step, then, in teaching anything new, is to try to arouse the child's curiosity about it. The progressive stages of curiosity in children have been classified as follows:

(a) *The Apperceptive.*	'What is it?'
(b) *The Utilitarian.*	'What is it for?'
(c) *The Scientific.*	'How does it do it?'
(d) *The Philosophical.*	'Why does it do it?'

Sully thinks that the child first makes really vigorous attempts to understand the things about him somewhere about the end of the third year and the beginning of the fourth. Certainly the age of incessant and pertinacious questioning begins about this time. Many parents have shared Kipling's experience of his little daughter:

She sends 'em abroad on her own affairs,
From the second she opens her eyes –
One million Hows, two million Whens,
And seven million Whys!

Mothers and nurses often consider such ceaseless questioning to be done by the child as a studied means of annoyance. Undoubtedly there are times when it is a symptom of restless peevishness and is best dispelled by a romp or walk out of doors. This point of view, however, is less vividly held than formerly. The questions are now recognized to be the outcome of a form of mental craving, of demand for intellectual satisfaction. The demand is largely for fact, but often, too, a search for general laws or for origin and purpose. Where this is so it is best met by an open, patient and sincere response, which not only gives a satisfying answer to an immediate problem, but also leads to a right relationship between parent and child. Children will often ask questions which would puzzle the greatest sages; in such cases nothing is lost by the honest reply 'I do not know.' This is far better than the insincerity which gives a false answer, or the conceit which refuses to admit ignorance.

The search for origins, causes and purpose leads nearly all children to a theological curiosity. Here are some actual questions which express it: 'Who made God?' 'What was there before God?' 'If I'd gone upstairs could God make it that I hadn't?' 'Why doesn't God kill the devil?' 'Did God get to Heaven in an aeroplane?' 'Who pours the water over Niagara Falls?' If no answer in the least degree satisfying is forthcoming to such questions the beginnings of religious doubt may be seen, even in very young children. It has been noted as early as the third and fourth years, and in later childhood it is frequently found. One instance may be given:

'I was in my eighth year when, one evening, a song which
my grandmother had sung before going to bed roused
such thoughts that I could not sleep all night... The most
refined atheistic notions coursed through my soul.'

Miracles and other supernatural stories cause widespread doubt among older children, especially when the age of imagination is passing and a wider experience of life is showing what does or does not pass beyond the bounds of probability. Such a period of doubt is frequent between about eight and twelve years of age, when the old faith in fairies and Santa Claus has passed and before the capacity to see the truth underlying such stories has developed. These children need much patient sympathy and understanding, encouragement to talk over their difficulties frankly. Above all they must be shown now that it is their duty to think as hard as they can and that no one will shrink from telling them the truth. Any deception or evasion at this time may be fatal to a reasoned and truth-loving faith later. It is probably wiser to omit, as far as possible, at this time, stories containing much of the supernatural element. This cannot, however, be entirely banished or postponed. After many a Bible story the child will ask: 'Is that story true?' 'Did it really happen like that?' While it is hardly possible to explain the full critical interpretation and conclusions to a child of nine or ten years of age who has, as yet, insufficient mental equipment for their understanding, it is possible to give the right point of view and the right method of approach; free, unfettered and expectant. One can show how God taught men as the children themselves are taught, by degrees and as they were able to bear it. In answer to the question, 'Is that a true story?' some such answer as this may be given: 'Do you know *The Pilgrim's Progress*? Is it true? Things did not happen just like that, and yet it is one of the truest stories in the world. Jesus told many stories like that, 'The Good Samaritan,' 'The Lost Sheep,' 'The Prodigal Son,' and others. Were they true? Which part of them is true? *The meaning is true.* Let us see what is the true meaning of this story.'

Children taught in this way will have nothing to unlearn, the truth will make them free. Religious education must be of the kind which makes them seek truth and pursue it, for its own sake, because only in truth can their souls rest. It must aim at developing those reasoning powers which can think God's thoughts after Him, albeit afar off; which see the effect in the cause, discern the great principle of continuity running through life, so that one can say, not only with faith but also with some degree of insight, that all things work together for good to those that love God.

While curiosity is the stimulus which stirs children to take notice of outer things, and interest the emotion which accompanies it, attention is the outcome of them both. It is necessary to distinguish between the two kinds of attention; involuntary or spontaneous attention which we give apart altogether from our wills, and voluntary attention which we give in order to reach some end. For example, a student may be writing a difficult essay on a subject in which he is not naturally interested. The front-door bell rings, and immediately his thoughts wander from the essay to the person at the door; the voluntary attention has given place to the involuntary. If, however, he sticks to his work until he grasps the principle behind it, or sees it from some new and fascinating standpoint, the voluntary attention may become spontaneous and he will be so much absorbed that next time the front-door bell rings he will not even hear it. Interest is thus the condition of whole-hearted attention. The interest, however, need not be of the immediate and obvious kind. The essay may be a necessary step in getting a degree and fitting the student for his life-work, in which case interest in a remote end will make prolonged attention possible, even when the immediate work is difficult and uncongenial. This habit of concentration, for the sake of a remote end, is only gradually formed. A small child finds it difficult to work for anything but an immediate end, although the teacher will aim at helping him to place his aims at an ever-increasing distance, to widen continually the circle of his interests. While attention is not possible without some kind of interest, the interest which has any educational value is not that which simply amuses the child, but the kind which makes him put forth some real effort to attain a definite end. The child must be trained to attend to unattractive things; this does not mean, however, that attention can be divorced from interest, but only that the interest is of a deeper and more remote kind, the child henceforth 'takes an interest' in that subject. In infancy and early childhood, it must be admitted, this capacity is practically non-existent. Attention can only be gained by spontaneous interest, which has its origin in the instincts, such as imitation, sense-satisfaction, imagination, curiosity, desire for recognition, self-assertion and self-preservation, desire for love, and so on. In gaining the child's attention the teacher must begin by exciting these instinctive interests, and by building on these lead him on to wider interests connected with them, associating the new with the old in some natural and telling way. Some teachers oppose this idea of education through the interests because they believe it makes things so easy that all necessity for effort is abolished and so character suffers. But in practice this is not so; it is the uninterested children, not the interested ones, who dawdle over their work and put no effort into it. Study of the lives of great men suggests that those work hardest and go farthest whose work has for them an absorbing interest. Where children are taken from the work which naturally interests them not only is there grave danger of the psychological disorders which follow repression, but men of genius may be lost to the world, for whom a number of persevering 'machine-minds' are but a poor substitute.

As an instance of the high degree of concentration which an intense interest will cause in children Sully tells of a little boy, only two years and eleven months old, much interested in railways, who travelled on two railways in the one day and then asked his mother if she had noticed the difference in the make of the rails on the two lines, a difference which existed in fact, but which was hardly noticeable even when pointed out. Such interests are usually connected with the child's abilities. We like the things we can do best. The wise teacher will utilize such interests, striving always to widen them, to make them purposive and persistent, even in face of difficulties, so that neither native ability nor strength of character shall suffer. These principles hold good in religious as in general education...

Another side of the question must now be noted. Where interests are assured and emotions kindled, unless they can find some practical outlet they are not only useless but positively harmful. At some time they should express themselves in action. Our Lord taught that it is not the man who hears His words alone, but the man who hears and *does* them who builds his house on a rock. The exercise of a function is a necessary part of its training; apart from this it will atrophy. Such exercise should be real self-activity, entered into with spontaneity and zest. Of late years many interesting educational experiments by Montessori, MacMunn, Dewey, and others have shown the astonishing progress that children will make when left free to express themselves in their own way. The freedom is not absolute, in so much as it is freedom in a controlled environment, but that is its only limitation. MacMunn tells his boys that they are free to walk about and get things, to choose the subject at which they will work. He tells them that he believes that work and play are the same thing, that they must help him to prove it. His boys write and act their own plays and make their own scenery. Montessori provides elaborate sets of apparatus by which little children largely teach themselves; the teacher sits quietly in the room until individual children come and appeal for help or information. There can be no doubt that these methods encourage native ability and initiative. Because they are allied with the child's interests they call forth all his energies. Those who have had any experience of these self-teaching methods can have little doubt that they should find some place in every educational scheme. But not every one would feel that they should have exclusive possession; that all external influence or interference should be abolished. Is the teacher to exercise no restraint over selfish, cruel or sensual impulses? Some followers of Freud, with their fear of repression, would go as far as this; further than Freud himself would go. But the unrestrained expression of all the lower impulses causes repression of a more serious kind, repression of the moral sense, of the spirit in man. There is ample evidence of the hysteria and neuroses following such a line of action. And apart altogether from the question of restraint, there must always be a place in education for impression, for leadership and for the influence of the mature mind upon the immature.

In religious education the importance of impression has long been recognized, that of expression has been overlooked. Sermons and lessons have been impressive; they have often failed to stir those who heard them to apply the truth they contained. This has been one of the greatest weaknesses of preaching and of religious education in general. Attempts are now being made, by reformers interested in this work, to remedy this defect. Self-teaching methods have been introduced into the Sunday School, by means of pictures, study-cards and self-teaching guides. They have met with marked success. Other schools have put aside the part of the session which follows the lesson as 'Expression-Time,' when the children, by drawing, writing, handwork or dramatization, express, at any rate partially, the truth they have heard. I have been convinced by a wide experience of the very great value of such work, for purposes of re-impression, revision, correction and expression.

From *Child Psychology and Religious Education*, Dorothy Wilson, SCM Press, 1928

I. The Aim and The Task

We begin by claiming that 'the Sunday-school is the Church engaged in teaching and training the young in spiritual things.' To this end it used the process of educational evangelism, with a view to (1) nurturing the religious life of little children; (2) leading them to awareness of definite fellowship with God in Christ, and into full membership of the Church; and (3) securing their progressive training for Christian living and service throughout life.

II. The Mind of the Church

We believe that once this definition of the Sunday-school and its aim is fully recognized by the Church, far reaching changes will become inevitable, both in the mind of the Church and its accepted methods of work. It is recognized that in prosecuting its divinely-appointed task of spreading the Kingdom of God, the Church must necessarily seek to evangelise the present generation of adults, but it should also endeavour to accomplish its task by helping the rising generation to find God.

(a)   Strategical Importance of Sunday-school work.

It is obvious that the possibilities of success are vastly greater with the rising generation than with the adults. The Commission would, therefore, draw the attention of the Church to the situation that still persists, in which the bulk of the resources of the Church are expended on the much less productive work among adults, while the work amongst the young is inadequately provided for and is left almost entirely in the hands of untrained though devoted teachers.

Consequently it cannot be wondered at that the three Methodist Churches write off over 100,000 young people from their Sunday-school registers each year, though this appalling fact is disguised by the number of new scholars added. The fact that 80 percent of the present members of the Church have been secured to it through the Sunday-school also has a bearing on the point, since it demonstrates beyond question that the proportion of attention and resources devoted to these two sides of the Church's work needs to be completely revised. To make real progress in that direction, however, a complete change of mind on the part of the whole Church is demanded.

From the *Report of the Joint Commission of the Three Methodist Churches on Sunday-school Work* to Conference, 1931

The most accurate classification of religion, psychologically, is indeed to speak of it as a sentiment. The technical use of this term is of course not to be confused with the popular. A sentiment is formed by the grouping of emotional tendencies round an object in consciousness so that when one of them is aroused it tends to call the others into activity also. Inasmuch as the emotions are closely connected with propensities (*i.e.* 'instincts') the latter also are stimulated, and thus action along the line of the abilities is instigated. Reason, intelligence, choice, purpose and other factors in personality will play a large part in deciding which abilities are exercised. Habit, character and will are involved. The bodily energies are brought into play as well as those of the mind and spirit. Moreover, sentiments, while each consisting of a grouping of emotions and propensities round lesser objects, may themselves be grouped round a greater by means of a dominant, integrating sentiment. Family life, school and college, sport, vocation, political party and Church may all be objects about which a man has built up sentiments, but all these sentiments may enter into the composition of his patriotism, which in certain circumstances may become dominant. In this sense, then, religion is regarded as a sentiment, and, apart from adherence to a particular creed or committal to the cause of one religious community rather than another, there are ample psychological reasons for holding that religion not only may, but must, become the dominating sentiment for us all if our individual and corporate life is to achieve wholeness, if security and freedom as well as health of body and mind are to be established, and if our life is to be at once conservative of all the treasures that humanity has won and creative of that which has enduring worth.

Religion thus involves and expresses the whole person in all his relationships. Thought, feeling and will, reasonable belief, disciplined and directed emotion, purposive conduct – all are bound up with it. 'Religion,' as Jung has said, 'is the fruit and the culmination of the completeness of life.' It is the response of the complete man to what is supreme in his universe. Thus at every stage from birth to maturity our developing propensities, abilities and capacities are to our ripening religion as warp to woof. This book seeks to trace out that connection. The human and scientific interest of doing so would in itself make such a study worth while. If it be true that religion is not only the one dominant sentiment which touches every aspect of human personality and society but is also the sentiment most surely centred in the ultimate Reality of all existence, the practical importance of knowing how it unifies and directs all our natural energies of body and mind at once becomes evident. For then we have in our hands, by cultivation of it in our own lives and by educating children in accordance with our own knowledge and experience, nothing less than the reshaping of our world, beginning from within ourselves by that worship of God which issues in service of men. We become ever-growing and genuinely creative persons.

From *Religion and the Growing Mind*, Basil Yeaxlee, SCM Press, 1939

1940s
Family Church and
the Conflict of Values
in Wartime

The first decades of the century brought the move from all-age Sunday Schools to teaching and learning in peer groups, or departments, and to a style of Bible teaching which, along with the claim to be child-centred, persisted until the late 1960s. Whereas this early period of change was built on the insights of educational psychology, from the 1940s onwards sociology and an understanding of the importance and interaction of human groups began to come to the fore.

Sunday Schools were associated with churches but in many places had developed a separate identity. Relatively few children progressed through the Sunday School to become members of the Church. One development which built on Archibald's educational initiative was inspired by a Congregational minister, H A Hamilton, who in turn also drew on the burgeoning ecumenism, the work of the Faith and Order and Life and Work Movements, the new emphasis on liturgy (Gregory Dix's *The Shape of the Liturgy* was published in 1945) and the debate about religion in public education which led to the (child-centred) 1944 Education Act. Other influences on Hamilton were his experience as a soldier in the First World War, the philosophers John Macmurray and Martin Buber, and his experience of the Orthodox Church. Hamilton saw that the social experience of the child in the church – what the church was, what it did with the child, and how people behaved towards the child (how love was expressed) – were at least as important as what was taught in nurturing a child. The church could be a vital social experience that could lead to religious awareness. He adopted T S Eliot's dictum, spoken by Harry in *The Family Reunion* (Faber, 1939, page 70):

> I think that the things that are taken for granted
> At home, make a deeper impression on children
> Than what they are told.

Hamilton posited the idea of the church as a family. He encouraged a number of churches to follow his suggested lines of experimentation and in 1941 published *The Family Church in Theory and Practice*.

It is our faith, based on the work of Christ and vindicated in Christian history, that God has chosen, as the instrument of His loving purpose, the community of men and women who, because they love Christ, are drawn to one another and, through their fellowship, become in fact a redeeming community...

If, then, Christian Education must take place within the life of a community, it follows that there will be no single factor more important than the potential influence of that community's life. Most of us are irretrievably in debt to the Christian community, either through a Christian home, or a group of Christian friends, or the Church itself, or more probably all of them. We are therefore disposed to see this work as a question of making available the resources of Christian community life in the most direct and creative ways possible.

The Fellowship and Worship and Work of a Church are indispensable agencies; they are the living expressions of the faith we want to teach. Each and all of them should be ways in which the power of the Spirit of Christ is set forth; indeed, it is not too much to say that it is not what we teach about the Church which will determine the decision which people make about it, it is what the Church in fact *is* and *does* in their lives. There is abundant evidence that it is our failure in that sphere which has allowed so many adults in this generation to feel that the Church is irrelevant. It is, I believe, even more true that it is our failure to make the word 'Church' mean something desirable and desired in the experience of the children we teach that has made them so reluctant to join its membership.

There is, of course, no doubt that the primary agency in Christian Education is a Christian home. There is no substitute for it in the early years of life. Nor can it be too clearly said that by a Christian home we mean much more than a home in which parents have Christian opinions and attend public worship. We mean supremely a home in which a man and a woman have a love for each other which is true and trusting, which they know is a gift of God to them. A growing child needs the security of that background; it is every bit as important as the parents' loving relationship with the child. It is in that atmosphere that the child is disposed towards or away from faith in God. Who can tell how many young people are disposed to cynicism because of that inability to trust love where it should have been most trustworthy?...

WHAT are our present means for dealing with this new situation? In the main the Churches rely on the work of the Sunday-school or similar smaller organisations with different names. It may fairly be said that most of the larger of these schools have adopted some form of Graded work and worship and use a regular syllabus of instruction: there are still, however, far too many Sunday-schools that have neither Grading nor organised instruction. Yet the menacing question which thrusts itself at us remains. How is it that despite improved methods and a well-ordered curriculum, the Sunday-school has so frequently failed to lead young people into the Church?

Is the answer, in part, because it *is* Sunday-school? We have inherited this institution, which has been honoured through 180 years by devoted service, and more than any other single agency has been productive of Christian character in the young people of the country. Even so, may it not unwittingly be itself partly responsible for the problem which we are facing? The Sunday-school has a separate existence, meets at a different time, in a different organisation. Its relationship to the Church varies from one of close co-operation to one of complete independence, conditioned, in the main, by personal factors. But whether such relationship is close or distant, to the children it is largely non-existent. As far as most of them are concerned the Church is 'the other place', 'where the other people go,' at the other time.

The majority of the teachers are members of the Church, but to the children they are 'teacher' and to the children's homes they are 'teacher'; in other words, during the formative years of the child's life he comes to associate religion with the Sunday-school. With the transfer from Primary to Secondary School at the age of 10+ the boy (or girl) feels superior to the younger children and soon tends to regard Sunday-school as 'beneath' him. As he approaches adolescence he is beginning to have done with school in his own mind; and very often he is sufficiently free to please himself to ensure that his contact with one school, at least, is prematurely cut! Does not the existence of the Sunday-school as a separate body constitute part of our difficulty? The reiterated question 'How shall we build a bridge between the Sunday-school and the Church?' compels the answer: 'The need to build a bridge only exists because there *are* two organisations to be bridged.'...

...the Church is neither a building, nor a service, it is a community of Christian people.

One of the great tasks of Christian Education is to discover how to develop the sense of Christian family life between the 80 per cent of children who come to us from homes which have no connection with the Church and the members of the Christian community we want them to enter. At the moment the vast majority of those whom we do have the joy of bringing into church membership have either a Christian home background, or have had the personal friendship of some Christian man or woman in the Sunday-school or week-night organisation. Can these not be vastly multiplied? Can we not mobilise the resources of the whole Christian fellowship in this task of winning for Christ and His Church a generation beset on every side by pagan forces?

From *The Family Church in Principle and Practice*, H A Hamilton, REP, 1941

The great danger of all planning about the future is that we are prone to make a leap of the imagination from where we are to where we would be. Such planning is nothing but an escape into Utopianism. Today we are setting our minds to *real* planning for the future, and therefore we must start from where we are and build a solid road towards where we would be.

We must start, then, with the children of the present. Our task is to get as true a picture as we can of the real life of children in this country and to study that picture squarely. And here let me ask – Do any of us really know what the life of children in this modern society is like? Our own favoured few in Christian homes – yes, we know something about them. But what about the vast mass of children? Their lives are parcelled out between Home, School, Street, perhaps Sunday School and Club. Different aspects of them are known to different people – one may find that in the course of a day the parent, teacher, school-doctor, club-leader, policeman, have all handled the same child 'departmentally.' But what adult has *all* the data? Who can see the child *whole*? Because we as Christians believe in the integrity of persons, an urgent Christian duty at the moment is to withstand this departmentalism. We must be concerned, not with aspects of children – the Sunday School scholar, the Day School pupil, the member of our week-night organisation – but with *whole children* – whole persons. We could well set ourselves the task of trying to collect all the data we can for the children with which we deal. I should like to see in different localities Christian groups springing up to study in wholeness the child-life of that district, and to frame policies. in the light of that total picture. Such groups might bring together to share their knowledge parents, teachers, ministers, youth-leaders, employers, and many others responsible for the young.

Let us turn now directly to the consideration of the children of today. What are the forces moulding their lives? The main point I want to make is that the basic forces with which we should be concerning ourselves are not on the whole intellectual but emotional. I think we tend to under-estimate emotional factors. What matters is not so much what children learn with their minds but the values and attitudes which they pick up from the society in which they live. By values I mean 'goods' – those things which the individual regards as good in themselves, worth having or doing, which he will choose in preference to other things, for which he will strive with effort, or give up other desirable things. Some common values are bodily comfort, material possessions, pleasure, money, power. From values follow attitudes to all kinds of things – to work, to other people, to the future, and so on. Now children are catching these values and attitudes all the time from the older people with whom they find themselves. They are being continually educated in their emotions by these things. For in every social situation a choice of values is implicit – a choice between this or that 'good,' and when we make the choices of daily life, or when we react with enthusiasm or disgust to different social occurrences, we express our real values. What matters is not what we *say* we believe in, not the careful statement of our faith which we make to our children, but our *real* beliefs, those values which really determine our day-to-day choices and which children will pick up in spite of ourselves. Take a typical family conversation on the child's career: job is weighed against job: this is safe, that has money in it, another may lead to the top of the tree: what the child is really learning is the 'faith' of his family. We adults, in fact, cannot avoid influencing the children who are with us all the time, not just in our studied and conscious moments, but in our unstudied attitudes, indeed even in our gestures and facial expressions, as our true values come out.

What sort of values are the mass of children today imbibing from the societies in which they grow up? What are they learning to regard as things worth having and doing and being? We have to picture the typical home-life – its relationships, conversations, choices; the life of the street and the shops, with its push and clamour and competition; the cinema, glorifying pleasure, glamour, sensation; the attitudes and conversations of factory, office, and shop where the young work. We have to think of children nurtured in the life of this great city, imbibing its values with the breath they draw. What view of life, what 'faith,' are they drawing from this industrial, mass-producing civilisation?

I can only illustrate here what seem to me to be some of the prevailing values and attitudes:

(i)   The happiest person is he who possesses the most material possessions; the chief satisfaction in life is to get and get, more and more; when you've got a bicycle you must have a car, if you've achieved a wireless you must get a gramophone, and then a piano and then maybe another.

(ii) The law of the world is competition; the only sensible way to act is to get on, to climb up, to push someone else down.

(iii) Work is a nuisance to be avoided by every device possible; the less work you do the more lucky you are; the farther up the tree you climb the less work you do, whilst the 'big toff' at the top of the tree does no work at all.

(iv) The powers that rule this world – known as 'they' – are untrustworthy and arbitrary, to be tricked and outwitted as often as possible and obeyed as seldom as possible.

These and other similar values shout at the young today; they are blazoned forth in advertisement, film, and cheap reading.

In the midst of this clamour some children hear what must seem the tiny Christian voice upraised, maybe at home, or school, or church. It says the dead opposite of what the world is saying:

(i)   It is more blessed to give than to receive.

(ii) We are members one of another.

(iii) He that is greatest among you let him be the servant of all.

(iv) God rules this world and God is Love.

Thus there is a direct conflict between the values of the world – the values experienced in ordinary life – and those taught by the Christian Church. It is hardly surprising that for the majority the conclusion is: the Christian faith is irrelevant to real life; this sort of stuff just doesn't work, for life is not like that at all. We must remember here that this Christian teaching is so often a predominantly intellectual lesson, a matter of *words*, not of experience embodied in the relationships of a group, like the life of home or street. Also, it usually occupies minute portions of time, whilst against it all the time you have the pull of continual living experience.

The predominant experience of the young today seems to me to be one of conflict in values and chaos in purpose. The life of the community is nurturing them in no clear pattern of life which teaches them what is good and guides their experience. Out of a welter of experience a multitude of conflicting voices arise – voices of materialist values, or of competing political faiths, and amongst these the Church's is only one, adding to rather than resolving the conflict. Their life in society offers them no guide to a predominating 'good' and challenges them to no great overriding purposes. Chaos without pattern breeds emotional insecurity. The fundamental need of each child is to 'belong,' to belong in a society which is trustworthy, loving and consistent, which has its own laws and pattern of relationships, and its own accepted values. Here he is secure because he is 'at home,' and this security is the basis of his freedom, for he cannot adventure out confidently unless he has first felt at home and is able to trust life. On the other hand, confused experience, untrustworthy relationships, clash of purposes, produce a deep insecurity, a fear of life and what it may do to you which makes it impossible to go forth freely into wider life. When experience becomes too chaotic and the conflict unbearable, one way out is to take refuge in inertia, which is a psychological defence against confusion; that is to say, to make up your mind that there is no great purpose or meaning in life at all, that nothing is worth pursuing at all except immediate pleasure and quick returns in sensation. This seems to me to be true of many of the young today: the conflict of purposes has produced such insecurity that they are unable or unwilling to commit themselves to any long-term purposes or embrace any causes with continued enthusiasm and wholehearted effort. Not only do they not care about work (cf. the problem of absenteeism among the young), they do not join organisations – even political ones – nor take up causes; some cannot even use effort to organise their own amusements in youth clubs. They are bored with the prospect of activity, cynical about all enthusiasms, disillusioned about purposes. Will and effort seem to be dying just when they should be coming most alive, and life, instead of challenging them to fresh and larger commitments, leaves them unable to give them-selves to the service of anything but the next sensation.

The root cause of this, as I see it, is that the young are not being nurtured in a community which expresses right through its whole life a common set of true values, and which guides them by their very experience of living into the great community faith and purposes.

We have to think, then, of *Christian education in this chaotic semi-pagan society*. But let us not be dismayed. Again and again at this time one is driven back to think of the early Church. How did it succeed in bringing up its young in that confused and conflicting pagan society? So far as one can see, by nurture in a closely-knit community where all the relationships of persons sought to express Christian values, where the great common purposes and attitudes were experienced emotionally before they were taught to the mind, and where the society of the Church held the young so closely within it that his life received its pattern from the fellowship and its meaning was integrated with experience. The young could face the clash of pagan values outside because they were established and secure within the fellowship...

The importance of bringing together in a unity intellectual instruction in the faith with emotional activity in expressing it. We must remember that the Bible is a *living* word, and although instruction in the Bible is of vital importance, to divorce teaching it from living, active expression is to make of it an arid, formal thing irrelevant to real life. This is the danger of a Sunday School which is conceived of as a lesson with 'opening and closing exercises' tacked on fore and aft. We need rather to develop our Sunday Schools into true services of worship, *planned and led by the children*, in which the lesson (taken by adults) is only one, though an integral part. A group of children, planning out a service of worship beforehand with their adult leader, can, in fact, learn a great deal in discussion about worship, about great Bible hymns and prayers, etc., but this will be part of an activity they are offering to God. For worship children need many varied symbols and active forms of ritual, for it is natural to them to use concrete things and bodily activities to express the truths they are learning. They need processions, dramatic forms of worship (e.g. the Nativity Play), decorations (especially to express joy in the cycle of the year of Nature), festivals of many kinds. By all means let us show that these ceremonies are symbolic, but let us not starve them of the symbol and ritual through which their life becomes so much the richer. We need red-letter days of a more varied kind – a rich, new calendar of holy days appropriate to our own denomination. And let the children plan how they will celebrate the festival with appropriate ritual. Thus, whether in Sunday School or in Children's Church, we can give them ways of living out together in active worship the faith they learn. (And may I add here that I think we should consider seriously the view that the *name* Sunday School is now a hindrance and that the Children's Service or Children's Church is more satisfying to the young?).

The importance of bringing the young into real service and responsibility in Church life. Our great lack today is that of committed leaders, and we cannot expect – as we so often do – to produce these suddenly out of a hat. We must train for committed leadership by graded responsibility into which we introduce the young as soon as possible. It will be fatal if our Church leadership remains in the hands of the middle-aged and the elderly. And we must see that what the young are called to do are not just 'little things,' but things regarded as really important and significant in the life of the Church.

Above all, we must train carefully in the spiritual significance of particular services they are called to do. I wish we had more opportunities for the young to 'serve' in our worship, but let us at least instruct in the office of the choir, and the very solemn significance of taking the collection and standing with it before God as the representative of the Church that offers its life to Him.

The importance of showing the adolescent the relevance of theology to his life. Christianity is so often presented to him either in terms of practical ethics ('being kind' and so on) or in the language of classical theology which seems quite irrelevant to life (e.g., grace, justification by faith, etc.). What we have to show him is that *everyone* lives by a faith, by a belief in a 'good' which determines his choices. Theology is a burning reality: you must choose God or mammon. To do this we need to start with the adolescent *where he is*, to make a real effort of imagination in order that we may understand what are the real issues in the lives of the young. We must start with these, show them the implications of their own lives, lay bare the unconscious choices they make daily about work, money, friends, leisure, etc., and the values behind these (e.g., we can face them with the question what *do* you believe in, Luck, the Stars, Money, or what?) We have to make the Christian challenge relevant to their concrete situations and choices, to make the spiritual issues of this modern world 'come alive.' The Gospel is always the same, but we need to think strenuously as to how we can bring the young right up against it in their *real* lives. We may need to use a new technique – perhaps that of discussion rather than sermon sometimes – but our basic task here is to recover a *theology for living*, in order that we may face them with the solemn necessity of commitment, of making a long-term choice instead of wavering for ever among fleeting purposes.

In conclusion, I come back again to the clash of values in this modern world. If we thus seek to nurture the young in true societies, to hold them secure within the community of the Church, to bring them to the point of Christian commitment, we must face the fact that we sharpen the conflict between the Church and the World. I think this is inevitable (Christ said 'Not Peace but a Sword') but we must see clearly what we are doing. Conflict can only be faced in the security and the strength which God gives through the fellowship of His Church. To arm for the fight we must seek to give the young a living theology to guide and a churchmanship to hold them secure. And we must ask ourselves:

Is our local Church fellowship of the kind that really helps the young in these conflicts of values?

The Christian does not expect to eliminate conflict. (Unlike the humanist, he is a realist and knows the power of sin). But he cannot be complacent about the chaos and confusion in society, and its gross materialism. He must seek, as a citizen, to purge the general life of society, the pagan values which flourish there, and to build a truer and more coherent idea of community. He must work as a missionary among children and young people who never go near the Church, seeking to bring them into true bits of community, expressing Christian values, wherever he can contrive to create them (e.g., clubs). In the ordinary experiences of friendship, group activity, etc., he must try to bridge the gulf between life as these young people experience it and the Gospel of the Church.

From *Children of the Future*, Marjorie Reeves, The Kingsbury Press, 1943

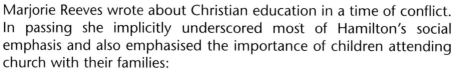

Marjorie Reeves wrote about Christian education in a time of conflict. In passing she implicitly underscored most of Hamilton's social emphasis and also emphasised the importance of children attending church with their families:

> '...the local church should be a family of families, gathered together into the society of God ... do not let us bother too much about whether the child understands adult worship. The child apprehends emotionally before he does intellectually and through joining in the activity of the Church he comes gradually into fuller understanding.'

Such emphases contributed implicitly, if not explicitly, along with studies in liturgy, to the introduction of the Parish Communion in the Church of England.

1950s
Understanding
Human Groups

In the 1950s Sunday Schools and day schools continued, in the main, to teach scripture but, ten years on, Constance M Parker and Richard J Hall reworked Hamilton's thesis that the church was – or should be – a family. Their aim, in *The Church is a Family*, was both to give the idea of Family Church more theological depth and to encourage good educational and ecclesiological practice. It is likely that the family church movement in the Free Churches and, perhaps even more significantly, the Parish Communion Movement in the Church of England, both of which became strong in the 1950s, began to turn attention away from Sunday Schools and to a consideration of the responsibility of the churches for the Christian education of children. Victor Murray also emphasised the importance of the community in the process of learning as he delineated the complementary tasks of the church and the school.

Two publications concerned with how people react to each other in groups and how groups react to each other, though not of immediate consequence in the churches, laid the foundation for fresh understanding. These were Homans' *The Study of Human Groups* and Kliens' *The Study of Groups*. Fred Milson, a Methodist Minister then teaching at Westhill College, showed the relevance of the new thinking about groups to those working with young people in his *Social Group Method and Christian Education* (1963).

We have only to watch children about the ordinary business of their day to find the answer.

They join in baking day with mother – imitation.

They investigate behind a cupboard door which has been left open – curiosity.

They turn the printed pages of a book over rapidly in order to look first at the pictures – seeing.

They spend a long time endeavouring to make a home-made motor-car go – making.

They dress and undress a doll over and over again – repetition.

They consult an encyclopaedia for a piece of information in which they are interested – finding out.

They get up their own play, including writing it, making costumes and rehearsing – doing.

They sit with their ears glued to the wireless, listening to a story – hearing.

In other words, they learn by their own activity and experience, and we must use and recognise all these ways. Isn't it true to say that generally in Sunday school we talk too much, and that we judge our success or failure by the quietness or noise of the children? We suggest that this over-emphasis on talking is another reason why we lose children. They are bursting with energy, filled with a creative urge and a desire to do, their eyes are restless for things to look at – and we seat them in chairs, or on benches, and want them to be quiet and gain information only by listening to us. We have too long made our Sunday schools of the kind which will appeal chiefly to the thoughtful type of boy and girl, and have neglected the child who 'thinks with his hands.'

Second, we must always begin with children where they are and give them somewhere to go! If we fall into the trap of teaching what we think they ought to know, our teaching and the children's interest may run parallel, but will never meet, and although the children may acquire some useful information which they may remember in future years, they will never see it as something which really concerns them. Half the Sunday-schools teachers' problems of behaviour and discipline arise from the fact that they do not begin with the child's interest. It may be an interest in pictures which starts off a course; it may be a series of questions presented in a dramatic way; it may be an interest in gangs; it may be by asking them to bring their favourite books. It is only by beginning 'here and now' that we can hope to take them with us 'then and there'! As to a goal, the children are greatly encouraged in their work and worship, as we all are, if they can see a climax to a particular course within reasonable distance. This helps to sustain interest, to encourage thought and preparation, and to give a healthy sense of achievement when reached.

These two principles for teaching, using every way and beginning with the child's interest, mean that the teacher becomes one who shares activity with the children rather than an instructor of material. This ensures not only that Christianity is seen to be something which belongs to the living present, and which continues to grow and develop, but also that the right relationship is established between teacher and children. The teacher is not just telling the children this or that story from the Bible, or giving this or that piece of information, but the two experiment together. Straightforward instruction has its place, but there are far more important purposes in Christian education – to create right Christian relationships in a setting of worship, to undertake projects of shared and creative activity, to discover Christian truth; that is, to give children a first-hand experience of the Faith in the same way as they are given a first-hand experience of the church.

From *The Church is a Family*, C M Parker and R J Hall, Independent Press, 1950

A t this point, therefore, I must make clear the nature and scope of the Christian religion as I understand it, for this will be regulative of our whole treatment.

In the full-orbed Christian faith there seem to me to be five elements. There is something to know, something to feel, something to choose, something to do and something to belong to. Knowledge, feeling, morals, action and belonging are all involved.

(i) Christianity is a historical religion. Therefore we must have recourse to history. The Old and New Testaments are the basic documents of the faith and they are historical records without which there could be no Christian faith at all. Clearly, therefore, instruction in these documents is part of Christian education.

(ii) The root of all religion is feeling, by which I mean not an emotional excitement but rather a deep sense of personal concern with the unseen world. It is something that profoundly matters and so it involves much more than historical knowledge. It brings a man into touch with the world of spirit, and whether at the primitive stage when religion is a worship of mysterious natural agents such as the sky and the thunder, or at the advanced stage in the Eucharist or in meditation upon the Scripture, there is always this sense of *otherness*. Knowledge about God is a matter of study and instruction; knowledge *of* God comes by feeling and intuition, not opposed to the intellectual process (although often assumed to be) but completing it, and informing and disciplining it. Without this, religion is mere speculation or antiquarianism.

(iii) Christianity also involves moral choice. There is a warfare in human life, and the fact of sin is inescapable. There are conflicts of ideals and of loyalties both within and without the human soul itself. If men are not aware of sin in themselves they cannot but be aware of it in the world of nations and classes. On which side, therefore, are we going to stand? The ancient prophet thundered out to his people, 'Choose ye this day whom ye will serve', and this demand with even greater insistence is at the heart of the Christian Gospel. No man can serve two masters. The choice of 'either/or' has to be made by the Christian, and to refuse to make a choice or to be blind to the existence of alternatives is more than a misunderstanding. It is a moral defect.

(iv) Then action is needed. Luther may have felt that the Epistle of James was an 'epistle of straw' because of its insistence that 'faith without works is dead', but it represents a vital part of the Gospel. For a man to be concerned only with his own personal salvation leads to a morbid interest in his own sensations and theories. If love is the characteristic of the Christian religion it must express itself in loving, that is to say, in personal relationships, in an attitude to society, in practical service to and concern for other people. The Gospel gives short shrift to those who ignore the brother for whom Christ died, or refuse to feed the hungry, clothe the naked or visit the prisoner.

Action, however, has another aspect not so commonly recognized but of great value in human experience and in education. The externalizing of an emotion helps to prevent it becoming morbid and also to recall it when it has gone. This is the psychological importance of ritual and drama and worship. They are forms of action not alternative to experience or conviction but closely associated with it. Two men who have quarrelled may come to a reconciliation through speech or correspondence, but shaking hands is almost a necessary ritual. It is more than an outward and visible sign of goodwill – it is itself a means of promoting it. It is in the truest sense of the words a 'means of grace', a sacrament.

(v) Christianity has come down to us through the agency of the Christian community. It is that community which has preserved the Scriptures and developed tradition and codified experience. Moreover, the life of that community is in intention a challenge to the world, for here the social values of the kingdom of God are cherished and embodied. The fact that the practice so far lags behind the theory does not disparage the theory; it is a witness to the truth of the New Testament view that the kingdom of God is both here now and is yet to come. In Christ we believe we have the full revelation of God, and each generation finds it to be so, but its fullness is itself in process of being revealed. 'God has yet more light and truth to break forth from his word.' And the Christian community is an essential part of the Gospel, for it is through the life and witness of the community that Christ is made known to men.

Even the man who is converted by a text owes the preservation of that text to the Christian community and must seek within the Christian community an opportunity for further light and a field of service. There is no other religion in which the believing community is itself a part of its gospel, self-critical of its own shortcomings and looking forward to a continual amplification of its message and significance. 'Belonging' is an essential part of the Christian faith.

The significance of these aspects of the faith for religious education is that they represent also different modes of Christian experience.

> There is no expeditious road
> To pack and label men for God
> And save them by the barrel load.

Religious education is clearly a far wider subject than religious instruction – which is only one of these five. It is concerned with all five and it can begin with any of them. Knowledge of the Bible, appreciation of the thrill of noble music, loyalty to the cause of Christ, helping a neighbour in difficulties, and membership of a local Christian community are each of them ways in which the Christian life can begin, although it is not, so to speak, 'full-orbed' until it is supplemented by the other modes as well. There is also a question of emphasis. Different people will emphasize different aspects of the faith according to their temperament and gifts, but it should be a matter only of emphasis and not of complete omission. The desire for the same pattern of Christian life and faith for everybody does violence not only to human nature but to the universal appeal of the Gospel itself.

Who are to be the agents of religious education in this wide sense? There are some who would restrict it entirely to the professional clergy. There are some who out of suspicion of denominationalism would leave it entirely in the hands of the teacher. The truth is that no one agency can compass the whole of it, yet neither can it be exactly apportioned to different agencies. A school is not a church – it has a limited age-range and it is concerned with many other matters besides religion. It would appear, therefore, that instruction in the Bible is the characteristic task of the school – of the Sunday school always but also, in Great Britain, of the day school; while in the United States and Canada it is the function of the churches and their Directors of Religious Education. If we say that cultivation of the emotional side of religion is the work of the Church through its worship, we cannot deny that the school assembly of a council school is often more 'worshipful' than the perfunctory type of worship which is sometimes found in a church.

Then what of the extra-Church agencies? The Boy Scouts and Girl Guides have put before young people moral and social standards in ways often far more effective than the methods of the Church, while the ritualistic side of those movements has been a training of the emotions. Where, too, does the child's home come in? In some homes all these various aspects of Christian experience are present, in some none are present. It seems, therefore, that so long as provision is made somewhere for each of these five modes of experience, it does not really matter where or at what stage any one of them comes in.

There are, however, the child's own stages of development to be considered. With him there is a time for learning by heart, a time for joining a cause, a time for quiet and reflection, a time for stimulus, a time for action, a time for doctrine, a time for taking up responsibilities of church membership. These are matters for patience, understanding and adjustment. To seek after the right thing at the wrong time turns it into the wrong thing. To expect a child to use the language of the mature Christian is to produce a race of prigs, for a prig is a person whose attitude is out of keeping with his sensibility. And priggishness is the negation of Christian excellence.

From *Education into Religion*, A Victor Murray, Nisbet & Co, 1953

This quotation from the *British Lessons Council's Primary Notes* for 1956 shows the continuity of approach in Sunday School teaching. Since there is no other attribution, it is presumed to have been written by the editor Ernest H Hayes, a layman and publisher who devoted his life to the Christian education of children in church.

For Children aged 5, 6 and 7 years.
First Year of 1956–8 Cycle.

Aims of the Course. – To help children to know and love God as Creator and Father; to begin to know Jesus as Friend, Helper and Saviour; to begin to see the continuing work of the Holy Spirit; to make an active response to God in their daily lives; to feel themselves part of God's worshipping community; to see people of all lands as members of God's family.

Principles and Methods. – To choose stories which will lead to an experience of God as Father, Son and Spirit, having regard to the child's developing interest and needs. To be led always by the child's developing interest and needs; hence, to avoid such stories as might convey false or confusing impressions to the child mind, and to keep back certain periods of Bible history in order that they may come fresh to the child at the age when they will have a special value. To show that Christian character includes such qualities as reverence for God and man, self-control, courtesy, truthfulness, helpfulness, kindness and cheerfulness. For this purpose the selection of stories includes extra-Biblical material which it is felt will help the children to understand a Scripture passage and the continuing activity of God.

1960s
Faith and Experience

Pressures adding to the momentum of change built up significantly in the 1960s. In the public sector Harold Loukes' *Teenage Religion*, based on research undertaken in schools in the Northwest of England, showed the gap between the teaching of 'scripture' and the experience of young people, and led to the development of Religious Education in secondary schools which focused on 'life issues'..Research by Violet Madge in primary schools (published in *Children in Search of Meaning*, quoted below) showed that:

> ...the religious sense is inborn. Religion begins with everyday discovery by infants, helped through spoken questions and play. We watch the slow growth of the power to communicate and to record a pattern of meaning ... on such foundations, human and healthy, a maturer faith in God can be built.

More generally, Dewey's *Democracy and Education* (1961) and Erikson's *Childhood and Society* (1963) and later Robin Pedley's *The Comprehensive School* reflected and also led public debate about education.

In 1964 and 1965 Ronald Goldman, relying heavily on the work of Jean Piaget in Switzerland, shook teachers in both Sunday and day schools with his *Religious Thinking From Childhood to Adolescence* and *Readiness for Religion*. Goldman sought principally to demonstrate the ages at which concrete and abstract ideas could be introduced to children. The implications of this for religious teaching he outlined in *Developmental Religious Education*. His work was probably the last in which an attempt was made to address Sunday and day schools through the same research project. Eventually, workers with children in the churches were able to demonstrate with equal conviction that there is a world of difference between how children think and learn in mixed-age groups and in peer groups. But the key significance of the age and experience of the learner in his or her capacity to learn had been established. *The Experiential Approach to Christian Education* by Douglas Hubery (Chester House Publications and Denholm House Press) was published in 1960. The author outlines the background to his exposition of the new approach in the introduction:

> There is growing evidence of a 'wind of change'. More teachers are recognising the frustrations within their work

and yet remain convinced of their calling to serve growing boys and girls. More are realising the failure of many existing methods of teaching and are anxious to try out new ideas. They are aware that the problems of Sunday School work cannot be solved entirely by themselves, and rightly resent being regarded as scapegoats for the existence of these problems. Yet they do want to do their best for the children in their care and make their own contribution to the answers that must be found if the problems are to be overcome.

Religious education, as Douglas Hubery argued again in *Teaching The Christian Faith Today* (National Sunday School Union, 1965), should be 'grounded in experience, and must lead through experience to new experience'. 'We can perceive only what our past experience enables us to perceive' became an accepted tenet. Then, in the introduction to *Christian Education and the Bible,* published in 1967, very largely in response to the work of Goldman, Hubery states:

If it is true that R J Goldman has opened our eyes to the limitations and possibilities of Bible teaching to the young, much more now remains to be done in a positive way to ensure the right place of the Bible in the realms of child education.

The Belgian founder of the Young Workers' Movement, Joseph Cardijn, died in 1967, leaving behind an educationally innovative movement based on the education method 'See-Judge-Act'. This method continues to be used in all the Churches as a basis for theological reflection. This reflective and participative process seemed also to be encouraged in the *Decree on the Apostolate of the Laity,* published after the Second Vatican Council of the Roman Catholic Church:

Education for the Apostolate presupposes an integral human education suited to each one's abilities and conditions ... Besides spiritual formation, solid grounding in doctrine is required; in theology, ethics and philosophy, at least, proportioned to the age, condition and abilities of each one ... Training for the apostolate cannot consist only in being taught theory; on that account there is need, right from the start of training, to learn gradually and prudently to see all things in the light of faith, to judge and act always in its light, to improve and perfect oneself by working with others, and in this way to enter actively into the service of the church. (n.29.)

In Latin and South America the sixties saw literacy education and theological developments which had a considerable social and, later, theological impact. It would be hard to overstate the importance of the work of Paulo Freire which undergirded much of this development. His method of literacy education was based on a process of conscientisation, the awakening of social and self-awareness (as he put it, 'an archaeology of consciousness'). Being able to read the Bible for themselves for the first time gave many poor people a new understanding of Jesus as a man and, moreover, as a man who had lived and suffered, as they did, at the hands of those in authority. The importance of the then newly-created theologies of liberation was not so much in the actual theology as in the process which liberated both theology and the learner and gave the world a fresh approach to Bible study. The Bible was released from Western academic captivity; people who found their own experience illuminating its pages were moved to action. The process of action, reflection, action and so on was developed and gradually in the following decades made an impact on church and theological education in Britain.

1968 was the year of student unrest and protest. Though on the face of it this seemed to have nothing to do with church life, the unrest and subsequent publications by the Youth Service led the Churches to review the role young adults could play in the Councils of the Church. That year also saw the publication of a new British Lessons Council syllabus, *Experience and Faith*. A key paragraph in the introduction reads:

> In this task [of helping children to arrive at Christian attitudes, insight and commitment] there are four major emphases: the place of the Bible, the place of the Church, the place of the Christian Calendar and the place of the pupils' own experiences and interests. To speak of Christian education as 'Bible-centred', 'Church-centred' or 'Child-centred' is to give a disproportionate emphasis to only one important aspect, and to over-simplify the whole of the work to be done. It is only as these four emphases are held together in a unity that effective teaching can be offered.

Experience and Faith was significant also because for the first time a syllabus was addressed not just to work with children but also to work with young people and adults in the churches. The publication aroused considerable interest and a reprint was needed within the year. This was followed by the first issues of *Partners in Learning,* based on this syllabus and what had become known as 'the experiential approach'. A year earlier and as significantly, the Joint Liturgical Group published its *Calendar* and *Lectionary* and, perhaps unwittingly, began the long discussion of the role of the Church's lectionary in the education programme of children. Scripture Union material, though retaining an evangelical thrust, followed a very similar approach to that followed by *Partners in Learning*.

The Infant School Years
A sense of the mysterious

Schleiermacher recognized in young children's ceaseless search for meaning the seed of religious thought and enquiry. In one of his *Discourses* he notes that

> Children search everywhere for something surpassing the accustomed phenomena and the light play of life. However many earthly objects are presented for their knowing, there still seems to be another sense unnourished. This is the first stirrings of religion. A secret, inexplicable presentiment urges them past the riches of this world.

Whether we believe that these inner stirrings prompt, or are prompted by, the twin elements of curiosity and wonder, young children's seemingly unquenchable persistence in their pursuit of meaning is very apparent...

From this elemental sense of the mysterious, moments of wonder akin to worship seem occasionally to arise. These occasions may be individual and momentary. They may well possess more of the true essence of worship than the usual adult-directed forms, in so far as the younger children are concerned: perhaps we should become more sensitive to this characteristic of child nature in our religious education? Such wonder was inherent in Alison's story of the little girl who praised the sun in six year old Margaret's response to a bowl of opening daffodil buds when she exclaimed to herself: 'How very good of God.' It was present in John's surprised tone, when coming in from a village playground he told his teacher 'I've just heard lots of silence out there'; or the silent observation of falling snow by Maurice and Jeremy through the nursery window. It was evident in Sally's puzzled amazement when she caused iron filings to move by using a magnet, and exclaimed: 'Look, they're wriggling, they're wriggling'. Seven year old Paul attempted to communicate his sense of wonder in his painting of the healing of the blind man, as Linda of the same age did when she wrote

> One morning in
> lark song I heard a lovely
> tone, The dark was
> gowing the sun was coming.

Or on another occasion

> One night very early, still light
> Two loveing Doves came flying
> To give spirit to everyone
> As they flew we saw them
> From our window

Such sensitive awareness, in which thought and feeling merge, at times touching the fringe of the mystical, may well remain unexpressed because frequently uncommunicable in the medium of words.

From *Children in Search of Meaning*, Violet Madge, SCM Press, 1965

Readiness for learning

We have long been familiar with such phrases as reading readiness, writing readiness and more recently, number readiness. These phrases mean that children have arrived at a suitable stage when they can begin to learn the particular skills of reading, writing and number. This concept of readiness for learning involves a number of inter-related assumptions which teachers implement in practice, sometimes without being consciously aware of them.

The first assumption is that there is a time in development when the maturing of a child allows skills to be learned, previously impossible, because the necessary physical co-ordination was lacking, intellectual powers were inadequate or the child was emotionally unready, in that he was uninterested and unmotivated regarding the skill to be learned. In some skills physical readiness is more important than intellectual readiness, and in others it is intellectual readiness which appears to be dominant. In all skills to be learned a child must be adequately motivated; so that some measure of readiness is necessary in all three areas of development.

Not only does this assumption mean that there is a time for each child when he is most ready to begin a certain skill, it also means a concept of readiness in continuing the skill to higher and higher levels of complexity. What we may call incremental stages in learning have to be systematised, as in reading when the spoken identification of objects in the classroom leads to labelling of the objects, which in turn leads to identification by flash-cards, which in turn leads to simple reading books, and then an incremental increase in vocabulary so that more and more complex reading material can be understood. Good reading books exploit a child's natural interests, use vocabulary natural to him and relate experiences familiar to the child.

A further assumption involved in readiness for learning is that we do not wait passively for children to grow into readiness, but we can actively assist the process of readiness by suitable preparatory learning. In developing the skill of writing, varied experiences of scribbling, drawing and painting help the child more and more to control his hand movements. The eye and hand co-ordinations necessary for a writing skill to develop may at a later stage be assisted by such exercises as those devised by Marion Richardson. Wise teachers will select and systematically introduce their children to preliminary experience relevant to the learning of the new skill.

It will be seen, therefore, that readiness for learning is not concerned merely with the specific time of the beginning of a skill, but also with what precedes it and what follows it. This concept involves the whole of the sequence of learning.

Much more evidence is needed, but there is sufficient available for us to suggest that certain religious truths may be ripe to develop at certain moments of readiness in a child's growth. The limitations I have outlined show us what kind of learning is not possible at certain stages; that is, what the children are not ready to receive. These in themselves are indicators to what is possible, and the key may lie more in the realm of emotion than intellect in the first decade of development.

Incremental stages in religious teaching should reflect the child's increasing capacity to deal with religious ideas of increasing complexity. Until now syllabuses have been largely concerned to increase the quantity of religious material with increasing age, instead of the quality. Further, it is not possible to say that at such an age a child is ready to learn the doctrine of the holy spirit or truths about the nature of the church. This is to oversimplify the whole idea. It is possible that some aspects of the holy spirit or the church may be within the reach of a child's understanding at a certain stage, principally because he has certain personal experiences which he can place alongside what is taught. Sound religious teaching will exploit a child's natural interest rather than impose upon him an artificial and irrelevant series of ideas. It will also use vocabulary natural to the child, not an adult form of words difficult for him to grasp.

Waiting passively for readiness to develop is no part of the function of the religious teacher. Many could well be less zealous and more patient, since undue and unsuitable pressures can set up negative attitudes as in other subjects. But active preparation which enriches, directs and stimulates relevant experience may be the most important function for infant school teachers in religious education. This preliminary experience is the foundation upon which the later teaching is based, but all too frequently in the past we have been so eager to get on with 'the real teaching of the gospel' that inadequate foundations have been laid. Without this valuable initial work, much of what is taught may result in a mere religious vocabulary or the crystallising of ideas too soon, which prevents a child reaching forward to higher levels of thought. Far from helping the child, we impede his religious growth. To quote only one example, the young child who, after hearing the parable of the Prodigal Son, said, 'I do think his Daddy might have gone with him!' The distortion is complete, for instead of hearing the story of a loving father, he had heard the story of a neglectful one.

We shall now explore what intellectual, emotional and physical readiness may mean for religious education.

Intellectual readiness

Powers of thought develop in a fairly predictable sequence. First, there is sensory experience of the world, through seeing, hearing, touching, smelling, tasting and total body sensations. Very soon the child begins to select from the thousands of sensations he receives and so controls their impact, choosing what is important to him. This is the process of perception, so that what is seen is not always what is perceived. The child in a moment of time will be receiving many sensations but only a few will be perceived. From the several objects and colours on his pram cover one may dominate, namely the yellow ball he enjoys handling, sucking and generally exploring. Perception is the process of recognition and leads to the naming of experience. There then follows conceptualisation, the drawing together of similar classes of experiences. A child may perceive the figure of mother, observe the things she does and also, as his horizons widen, see how other mothers behave, until a concept of mother or motherhood develops. At first the concept will be very crude and partial because of limited experience and a natural egocentric view of life, and only gradually will more objective and more sophisticated concepts of motherhood be achieved.

By the time the child begins school he will have several hundred concepts, the fruits of his perceptive experience, which act as a guide to his intellectual activity. Most of these will be concerned with home, parents, other children, his physical environment, his toys, his diet, his clothes, the sky, the sun and the moon, water, soil, sand and the myriad materials he encounters daily. Perhaps the most important concept he makes, which affects all other concepts, is the self-concept; how he regards himself and the general way he assesses his own worth. This later becomes a starting point for most of the important religious concepts he will need in order to understand the Christian faith.

Alongside these concepts, feeding them and sometimes impeding them, is the growth of the child's vocabulary. As we have seen, children may use many words for which they have no adequate conceptual thought. Words are exciting material to experiment with and they are tried out in various contexts, even though there will be no adequate meaning attached to them. They may be used simply because a child likes the sounds. It is fundamental, therefore, that children acquire a suitable conceptual basis for the words they use, namely that words should summarise for children their own generalised experience.

In the pre-school and during the early schooling years, concepts are extremely inaccurate due to the pre-operational nature of the child's thinking. This means that children arrive at mistaken conclusions because often minor details of an experience dominate the child's thinking, or the wrong associations are made. In the story of the Temptations, children frequently explain that Jesus would not turn stone into bread, because 'Jesus said he had not to eat bread alone'. This was further explained that 'by bread alone' meant 'They should have something else like cheese and something to drink'. The young child returning from tea at the vicarage and announcing that he has 'had tea with God' has a similar conceptual problem.

This is why I have called this stage of children's thinking pre-religious, in an intellectual and conceptual sense. They find it difficult to conceptualise religious truth without distorting it when faced with formal teaching, however attractive and interesting some Bible stories may be. Children at this stage are ready to receive unrelated experiences of life. Everything is a source of wonder, and 'the religious' character of everyday experience seems to be the most natural way to prepare them. This calls for a much more indirect method of religious education in which the wonder of God's world in nature, animals, the sky and all experiences which come naturally to him can be surrounded by the assumption, often unspoken by the teacher, that all this is part of the divine creation. In short, little can be taught effectively which is foreign to the child and which does not arise naturally from his experience.

Children who have achieved operational thinking at the concrete level begin to form more realistic concepts, although these are restricted to observable and concrete facts. Intellectually, therefore, they appear to be ready to absorb a great deal of data and at the same time develop the ability to relate these facts together. This is why themes based upon their own experience which will provide a related view of life and which offer a religious interpretation appear to meet the needs of junior children much more than imposing religious or biblical teachings unrelated to their real world. Immature concepts of time make systematic and chronological teaching of biblical events unsatisfactory, but juniors can and do relate all the knowledge they acquire to their life experience. I have characterised this period as the sub-religious stage intellectually, since the more spiritual truths of Christianity are frequently reduced to pre-Christian concepts. I use the term sub-religious as synonymous with pre-Christian.

Life-themes appropriate for early juniors, such as Our homes, People who help us, Shepherds and their sheep, and many others, have a threefold intellectual purpose. First of all, they include 'religious' teaching in all other areas of learning and do not seal it off as something separate and therefore irrelevant.

Secondly, religion is the frame of reference within which all other knowledge can be seen and to which it can be related. Thirdly, by using what the child knows and what he can explore for himself at first hand, religious education is being experienced at a concrete level and concepts can be formed which are not distortions. This would also seem to be an appropriate time for pupils to explore bible-lands and bible-society in the sense that they can learn some of the background facts about the way of life within which Jesus lived and taught. Much of the misunderstanding of later biblical teaching appears to stem from an unfamiliarity with the geographical and social nature of Palestine.

By the late junior years and the first year of secondary schooling, the period of pre-adolescence, our pupils are becoming less concrete minded and are becoming dissatisfied with their concrete limitations. They reveal an intermediate stage between concrete and fully adult operational thinking. They are almost ready for what I would call a fully religious conceptual teaching, but only of a fairly straightforward kind. Biblical material can now be looked at more systematically and the study of a simple life of Christ begun. Even so, such a study is a study of events and people, rather than having a significance couched in abstract terms. Historical thinking still appears to be too immature for the study of the Old Testament on a chronological basis. Alongside the beginnings of New Testament teaching, life-themes based upon the pupils' experience should continue and no opportunity should be lost in relating the experience of people in New Testament times to personal experience.

The change from concrete to abstract modes of thought appears to become possible in religious thinking about the age of thirteen years. The adolescent is now in what I would call his religious stage of development, in which he is intellectually ready to apprehend what is the Christian faith. Its concepts are now within the grasp of his intellect and experience, although he has still far to go in his religious search. But if at least by the time he enters the adult life of work he has some objective knowledge of what Christians believe, he is then able to accept or reject these beliefs at a genuinely personal level.

It is not only intellectual maturing which makes a fuller teaching possible, but also the accumulation of varied experiences which underlie the great spiritual questions raised by Christianity. As these are mainly highly charged with emotion, such as a sense of insecurity and a developing moral sensitivity, we shall look at them in more detail when we consider emotional readiness. It is enough to say that if the basic theme of religion is redemption, those to whom it must appeal should have had some first-hand experience of that from which religion claims to redeem them. In short, sin, death, frustration, enmity, lack of purpose, weakness, must have been known in some measure at first-hand if anyone is to feel the need to be saved from them. To put it in another way, we need to have lived long enough to have experienced the real problems of the human condition before we see the point of what religion offers. With childhood receding, the awakening adolescent is becoming aware of what it means to be an adult for the first time, and this creates, intellectually and emotionally, a readiness for adult religion.

Emotional readiness

Children are highly motivated in relation to religion. Although many children find long religious services a bore, loud organ music frightening and a great deal of religious language incomprehensible, they are well disposed in their early years towards religion and religious teaching. What surprises many people is that these positive attitudes slowly move towards indifference in many adolescents, if not towards more negative and hostile feelings, about Christianity. At a time when religion intellectually can mean something really relevant in the lives of young people, the willingness to think strenuously about it seems to die. There is much evidence to show that their quest for meaning, their search for answers to their problems and a spiritual hunger still continues. It is 'religion', as the official teaching of school and church, which is rejected. There are unmistakable indications that both the content and methods of religious education may aggravate, if not actually cause, this tragic situation.

Belief in God is basically a willingness to trust. It is not primarily a matter of the intellect but of the emotions. In this sense a new-born baby is ready for religion in that his entire life is dependent upon a power beyond himself. The baby does not nave to learn to trust, he does so naturally and by necessity, and the power beyond himself on whom he is dependent is initially his mother. The child feels secure with mother, and at a much later time, with father. Any disruption of the relationship with mother, the major figure in his early development, leads to insecurity which can have far-reaching and disturbing results. A mother, or a mother-substitute, someone with whom the child can have a continuous relationship, seems to supply these emotional vitamins, just as a baby requires physical vitamins, and is a condition for healthy emotional development.

From our knowledge of the young child, we know that parents are regarded in divine terms. They are endowed with the qualities of omnipotence, omniscience and even omnipresence. It is natural that parents are regarded as all-powerful by their young children and only slowly do they become aware that mother or father are not in full control. If a parent falls ill or dies, this comes as a great shock to children whose fantasies are quickly shaken. Most children cannot think of a situation when parents are not available for help, and so ideas of omnipresence are again natural. Many children, when doing what they know is forbidden, have an uneasy feeling that a parent is watching. It takes a considerable time for children to know that this is an incorrect feeling. Similarly with knowledge, children feel that the powerful people whom they trust so completely know everything there is to know about everything.

This godlike image of parents is shattered for all children, sooner or later. Bovet comments succinctly on the significance of this for religion. 'From deifying his parents, the child turns to parentalising the deity.' I do not wish to enter into a discussion here of the Freudian view that religion is merely a projection of infantile desires, but merely underline that belief in God is rooted in the parental relationship, and that children turn to God naturally as they do to a good parent. I shall return to a fuller discussion of this in a later chapter.

Vestiges of these divine qualities spread beyond parents to all the adult world, especially to such people as teachers, ministers and clergy, policemen and those seen by children to possess some visible authority. In an increasingly secular society it is surprising that so many children automatically assume that adults generally believe in God. This illusion gradually breaks down, but there is an unexpected delay, almost into adolescence, before most of our pupils become aware that not everyone is religious nor believes in God. This, in part, may explain children's eagerness to learn about religion because it seems to please the adults around them. Unconsciously, many parents, who have long since ceased to care about religion, appear to hesitate about disillusioning their children. Perhaps they themselves still yearn for the innocent and simple faith of childhood, now lost, and recaptured nostalgically through their children at times such as Christmas. This is often interpreted as deception by young adolescents, and may be part of the cynicism about adults which some young people so vigorously express.

Emotional identification with Christian beliefs, then, is the norm through British primary schools, and we must beware of exploiting this eagerness unfairly. It can so easily be misinterpreted by teachers as the time most suitable for religious teaching of an intellectual kind. What is most interesting is that in the first years of schooling children fantasise their way into religion, rather than think their way into it intellectually. Since their intellectual ideas are limited, children seem to compensate by playing, dramatising, thinking imaginatively and through creative expression. What they find difficult through words and intellect, they explore more easily through feeling and imagination. What some have called the fairy-tale stage of religion seems to extend well into the junior school and in some way religious education must use this playful way of looking at life for the benefit of their children.

In addition to all this, emotionally children in primary schools look at knowledge as all of a piece, and they find religious teachings about people of long ago in a far-off land rather artificial. It creates in their minds a dualistic world view, which becomes very evident in secondary schooling, that there is one world called 'religious' and the other called 'scientific'. The first has to do with holy things, holy people in holy clothes, dealing with holy happenings in a Holy land (why on earth do we label maps with this inappropriate title?) and on some occasions taught by a holy teacher in a holy room. In this kind of world God *was* present, moving about the physical world organising thunderstorms, interfering with battles and generally behaving unpredictably. The second is the modern world they know of, with cars, central heating and television, in which thunderstorms can be explained by natural laws, and about which they try to think logically.

The evidence, in my view, indicates this rift by the end of the junior school, and becomes more vocally expressed by the third year of secondary schooling, when some science teaching has been experienced and a more rigorous operational mode of thinking develops. The reasons are, I believe, as much emotional as intellectual. Since the content of religious syllabuses tends to be overwhelmingly in the form of bible narrative, pupils hear the same material many times. At a time when most of it could evoke a significant response and have a fresh impact when placed alongside their experience, it is received in a jaded and bored manner.

Another reason for the beginnings of negative attitudes in early adolescence is a growing critical turn of mind. Having, by their own natural disposition, distorted Bible stories into literal truths they do not convey, they now perplexingly turn round and condemn a great deal of religious education as 'childish'. To be sure, this is all part of the grand gesture of becoming more grown up, but there seems to be more to it than this. The major ingredient seems to be the way in which they have been taught to regard the Bible, almost superstitiously, as a monolithic body of unquestioned truth. By making them, often unintentionally, into premature fundamentalists, we have sown the seeds of rejection. The tragedy is that their rejection is based upon a gross misconception, before they have been exposed to what is the true nature of the Bible. It is evident therefore that we must actively teach them to exercise critical thinking about the Bible while they are within the context of belief. If we do not they will exercise critical thinking outside it and invariably will reject religion on 'childish' grounds.

A final reason for negative feelings about religion in adolescence seems to be not only the content of teaching, but the way in which it is taught. Young people seem to resent authoritarian teaching and more and more wish to explore ideas and beliefs for themselves. Good permissive relationships, allowing personal questioning and discussion, seem to be the best climate for religious education in secondary schools. In these days when adolescents are concerned about their status, we should stop thinking of them as children, and address them as young people. This would be a beginning. But a more radical change of teaching content and method is needed, if adolescents, who are searching hungrily for truth, are to turn to Christianity as a fulfilment of their emotional as well as their intellectual needs.

Emotional readiness for religion is noted by all research dealing with adolescence. Summarising these researches, Michael Argyle says, 'It is the age of religious awakening, during which time people either become converted or decide to abandon the faith of their childhood, if they had one.' Emotionally, therefore, as well as intellectually, adolescence is the age at which there is the greatest religious potential...

The place of the Bible in developmental religious education

I have called attention to both the wasteful effort of teaching the Bible too early and also the difficulties this makes for children of limited development. I would like to correct the widespread misconception that I advocate no Bible teaching before the age of twelve. I do suggest drastic reduction of Bible material in syllabuses before this age, but the difference does not lie so much in the quantity of Bible material used as the way in which we use it.

The Bible is the major source book of Christianity *for adults*. It is written by adults for adults and is plainly not a children's book. To help children become familiar with it too early is to invite boredom and confusion, and even the most enthusiastic religious educator would not wish for this result to occur. What we must try to do is to help children to encounter the experiences of which the Bible speaks at suitable stages of their development. This means a severe pruning of Bible content in the early years, for it is only later that an understanding and appreciation develops of what the Bible has to say.

A clear distinction must be made, therefore, between 'teaching the Bible' and 'teaching from the Bible'. We have been too concerned to teach the Bible as such to children, so that the whole drama of man's search for God is unfolded before them. Because much of the Bible is historical narrative it has been taught in this way, so that the sheer mass of material so often defeats both teachers and pupils.

If we teach from the Bible we recognise the linguistic, the intellectual and the experiential limitations of children in coping with it, and we select material which is suitable. The criteria for our selection would not be quantity but children's needs and experiences. In the primary school we tend to impose a series of Bible stories such as 'The Life of Moses' or 'Stories Jesus heard as a Boy' which appear to the adult to have continuity of sequence and significance. For the primary child they may have none, and, although interested and excited by them, he finds them alien and confusing. If, however, life themes are couched initially in terms of the children's experiences, biblical material can then be used to illustrate them. The Bible stories, narratives, psalms and other materials then may take on significance and meaning because they are seen by the child in a life context. Life is not used to illustrate Bible truths, but the Bible is used to illustrate life's experience. This is not a verbal, but a very drastic and far-reaching, distinction.

I would like to quote a teacher's reaction to this idea:

At first I was worried by the use of the Bible in what seemed to be an haphazard manner – for instance, in a series of lessons built round the theme 'Getting ready for Christmas,' one might find oneself using material from the Old Testament in one lesson (gifts to the tabernacle) and the New Testament the next (gifts from the wise men) both bound up with material from life (the dramatised choosing, packing and presenting of gifts). Or, on the theme of 'Hands', verses from the Psalms used with stories of the touch of Jesus' hands, together with the enjoyment of the use of our own... If one believes that the test of truth for a child is whether it is true in his experience, and that experience must provide the central theme, then this gives order and continuity. Further, this is valid teaching. It is not a case of thinking, 'Well, until a child is capable of getting down to it, this is what we must do.' It is rather a case of seeing this use of experience as a wonderful opportunity of helping children to see God in their own lives and their own lives illuminated by God.

The use of children's experience illustrated by Bible incidents is consistent with the Bible itself. For the Bible is a narrative of men's experiences in their varying relationships with God. When we teach we intend to convey the truth of which the Bible speaks. If then we use it alongside, instead of imposed upon, children's experience, both the Bible and personal experience are illuminated and gain significance. In the child's view the Bible's value is enhanced because it is no longer seen as an endless and boring book, but a mine of relevant experience which is 'true to life'. (What some teachers report after using life-themes in the way I suggest is their surprise that they use a wider variety of Bible material in this way than they do in the more conventional approach.) If this emphasis is fostered throughout the primary years, the young secondary pupil is prepared both emotionally and intellectually for the more sustained study of the Bible in sequence and chronology which awaits him.

Teaching from the Bible in this way, however, should not stop after the primary school but should continue into adolescence. Even when more mature thinking is possible, orderly bible-theme teaching may be in too much detail. Further, it is important that our pupils gain first of all a clear grasp of the New Testament ethos before they turn to a systematic examination of the Old Testament. It should be constantly reiterated that much in the Old Testament is both pre-Christian and sub-Christian.

How life-themes, children's experiences and a more child-centred use of the Bible may be applied, is explored and outlined in detail in the second part of this book.

From *Readiness For Religion*, Ronald Goldman, Routledge and Kegan Paul, 1965

In the past history of the Church preparation for life in the Church was given in a number of ways: through personal relations in family life, in attendance at and participation in the liturgy, as well as in formal instruction (often given as pre- or post-baptismal *catechisis*). In early times, in the catechumenate, the experience of worship, often including baptism and the eucharist, preceded formal instruction. In almost every age the shared worship and work of the Christian community was an important base for Christian education: Christian education is 'not only education *about* the Christian faith, but also education in the Christian faith'.

Since Christian education is one of the ways of passing on the Tradition, an understanding of the nature of the 'traditionary process' is crucial for its success. The act of passing on Tradition is a critical one since what is transmitted is *necessarily* presented and appropriated in altered terms; if the Tradition is simply repeated 'it becomes lifeless'. 'The traditions must be criticized and reformed and not simply maintained; else they become archaic or even decadent.' As persons are helped to enter into the process of criticism and the reformation of the traditions, new and richer interpretations can emerge that will have fresh meaning for our time. What enables us to hope that such inter-pretation can and will be formulated, even in the avowedly imperfect attempts we make, is our underlying conviction that it is the Holy Spirit who is the primary actor in the passing on of tradition. All our attempts at programmatic reform and revision are necessary; but even when we have wrought as well as we are able, Tradition is 'transmitted in and by the Church through the power of the Holy Spirit'.

The Challenge of our Contemporary Situation.

Since the Tradition, as a living reality, must be reinterpreted in every age and place, we need the same insight into the conditions of our age which was evidenced by the Fathers of the early Church and the Reformers. This means that we must understand 'modern man' and 'modern society' in order to know how best to communicate the Gospel to our contemporaries.

While there is not such a person as *the* 'modern man', there are certain characteristics of society which are increasingly common in every part of the world. Society is, or is becoming, industrial, technological, secularized, differentiated, urban and mobile. There are large differences from one society, country, continent, family and individual to another. But these charac-teristics have affected the actual situation of most people and the hopes of all. Because of these developments 'modern man' experiences an increasing control over his own material destiny – or he knows that this is possible. This leads him to place more and more reliance upon himself and society.

But, modern man hopefully mastering his environment is by no means the total picture. While many find prosperity and hope, others are deprived of both; or they may be offered material benefits only at the price of humiliation, loss of freedom or dignity. These people, for whom the ladder of education leads downwards – because of lack of skill or motivation – form the army of the under-privileged in modern society. Even at the upper end of the scale one can find men and women who succeed at one role – particular work – at the price of all others. Many, sensing this is so, revolt against the educational process by which society exacts its due from those of outstanding natural gifts.

This situation should have an impact upon education. First, modern man does not live in one particular social pattern but rather plays an increasing number of different social roles. His personal existence is made up by these roles: work, leisure, family, community, etc. He finds his 'self' in these roles. Secondly, his education is more or less proficient in preparing him for life in such a society. He learns basic skills – and perhaps some highly specialized ones as well. *But* more and more it is obvious that one main aim of schooling ought to be to teach men *how to learn* as well as helping them to accumulate knowledge. The most basic skill in a rapidly changing world is that of knowing how to learn continually in order to stay abreast of developments. This involves a willingness continually to question old ways and a readiness to drop them as soon as they no longer work.

The impact of such an attitude is most strongly felt in matters of faith and ethics. Conscience and traditions are not exempt from the willingness to question and adapt. This can lead to a tendency to become 'other-directed' in ethics as continual reflexion and conversation with others play a larger role in one's life. But this can also lead to a strengthening of ethical conviction and action, as issues such as racial equality, social and economic justice and peace are explored more deeply.

Moreover, the claims of traditional religion seem to have less and less to say to modern man. The argument that something has upheld many generations before him is not in itself a strong recommendation. This loosening of traditional ties has produced feelings of insecurity in modern men, both in younger and older countries.

In the younger countries, for instance, religion may have been a strong motivating force while one was still living in the village, small town or tribe, and yet be unassimilable to one's life in the city. Nevertheless, it may haunt a man as a fear when he discovers he can no longer live by it.

In the older countries, where religion has long been part of the society in which he lives, modern man has increasingly turned away from it – no longer seeing it as a vital part of his life. To be sure, modern man, not wishing to lose the possible value of an ancient tradition may make certain ceremonial gestures toward his religion, such as baptism, marriage and burial, but these are made merely with religiosity and not faith.

Religion may, however, function effectively in various ways for modern man: it may offer him a community, or a way to educate the children, or a support for his style of life (whatever we may think about the rightness of these reasons). It can also, of course, be that in spite of all his objections the content of religion simply captivates him and involves him in an adventure of faith. The fact still remains, however, that the ancient sanctions are no longer binding. He wants to try it out for himself, and only if religion has a real function in his life will he commit himself.

The tendency to continual reflection on the part of many people, the loosening of traditional ties, and the increasingly pragmatic orientation of men point to the need for helping them 'learn how to learn'. In the context of our discussion this means not an empty adaptability but an ability to see how to relate the two 'givens' of which we have spoken: the Christian tradition and the constantly changing contemporary situation. It is the constant change of this latter which makes necessary learning continually how to relate the Gospel to the world, whether this involves the support or the resistance of elements in that world. Such learning and constant adaptation is not for the sake of conformity but to the end that men are able in all times and places to receive guidance and power from the Gospel of Jesus Christ.

Our modern situation poses challenges to *all* Christian traditions. The challenges may vary in detail from place to place, but it is obvious that merely presenting the Tradition as a deposit of formulae and propositions is insufficient to catch the imagination of modern man. Furthermore, such education is not able to aid him in his continually changing situation. But, if it is true that tradition is primarily a 'stream of life', we have a resource with which to meet some of the needs of contemporary man. As a stream of life, 'tradition is continually renewed from its original source – *in* its new context – it quickly sags toward obsolescence and caricature' if this is not so. Thus it has always been true that the Church has adapted itself in order continually to place the claims of the Gospel squarely and relevantly before its society. But the speed of such adaptation must increase; again, we must realize that such continual adaptation must become a way of life rather than looking merely for an occasional updating made necessary by accumulated pressures.

The most positive potential in this situation is that an increasing willingness to question traditional positions and attitudes can make men more able to enter into ecumenical experiences which will enlarge their vision of the Church and its mission through contact with diverse Christian traditions and with the secular world. In this context they should be more able to search for the Tradition by re-examining sincerely their own particular tradition...

Common Features.

There are three features which seem to be evidenced in all ages of Christian education, and which can still provide guidance. First of all, and perhaps most important, is the understanding in all ages that direct experience of the Christian life is primary in preparation for living that life oneself. One example is the case of Eastern Orthodoxy where the child of Christian parents receives baptism, confirmation and first communion as an infant – in other words he becomes a 'fully ordained Christian'. In this case catechesis or instruction is to guide the individual in understanding the meaning of being a full member of the church and to explain to him the consequences of such a status. Another of the classic examples of an insistence upon direct experience is pietism. Here, as a matter of fact, personal conversion and 'experience' of faith is made central and all preaching and instruction is made subservient to this end. Even though there is a pervasive individualistic emphasis in pietism (as contrasted, for instance, to Eastern Orthodoxy) the role of the community cannot be overlooked. It is in the context of the pietist conventicle that a person obtains his initial experience of what life together as Christians is like.

Even in the examples from the early church and the Reformation a similar basis in experience is evident. In the catechumenate the experience of worship, of Christian discipline, and living in community goes hand in hand with instruction; in Reformation times the presupposition of catechetical instruction was life in a Christian family, town, church and school. In all ages, then, preparation for the life of faith seeks a full response from the individual on the basis of his experience. It seeks not only assent by the mind but also willing and joyful acceptance by the entire man. And to remember this helps correct that intellectualism which can characterize teaching conducted on the basis of written material of all kinds, including catechisms and confessions.

Secondly, we discover that there are two dimensions of education that are stressed throughout the history of the church: *its focal and its continuous character.* In different times and traditions education has been focussed on Baptism; sometimes the focal point has been Confirmation and First Communion; and again in other traditions personal profession or conversion is the point to which Christian education is directed. But it is also true that Christian education is a continuous process in the life of a Christian. Neither the *focal* nor the *continuous* character of Christian education is sufficient by itself: both elements have to be conserved and related to each other. Christian education is, in the last analysis, a continuous activity in the life-long equipping of persons for engaging in the worship, mission and service of the Church in the world. But this activity also includes certain high moments, such as those named above, when the learner can be given the invitation and opportunity to engage in a more intense encounter with the living tradition of the Holy Catholic Church.

Thirdly, Christian education is carried out *in the context of the Church.* Teacher and pupil are held together in a relationship that is personal; and both are seen to stand within the fellowship of the Church. The teacher passes on not a possession of his own but rather what has been committed to the Church; in apprehending what is taught the learner comes to share in the living heritage of the Church. To remember this is a defense against too great individualism. Naturally, the response of the pupil is personal and must be individually made; but it is not made in isolation. Teacher and student are both within a community of faith – a community which extends outward not only in space but in time as well. This context of Christian education means that both teacher and student are dealing with the givenness of Christian life and doctrine and are together seeking to understand and appropriate them more fully...

'Ecumenical Education'

When we use the phrase 'ecumenical education' we are not thinking of a new type of Christian education which is 'ecumenical' in opposition to education which is carried out in our various churches. The churches still provide the primary context in which most Christian education is received. Rather we seek to point to the obligation of our churches to educate for life in the oikumene – for life in the world and in the ecumenical situation which is a part of the life of all our churches today.

In a sense one can say that our reflections on this arose from the very situation of our consultation. We began from the situation in which we found ourselves. Rejoicing in our being together in such a time and place, open to each other and to the pressures of the contemporary world, we asked how it was possible for us to come together in this rather uncharted relation. In part our reasons were individual – a sense of inadequacy and frustration engendered by our divisions; the calling of a new vision of the Church in the world. But, when we probed our experiences, we all found some Christian communities in which we have shared: we have experienced Christian fellowship not only within our own churches, but across confessional dividing lines. This certainly includes our experience in this consultation, but we have all shared in other such communities – whether in official meetings, as members of staff of ecumenical institutions, or in such places as work camps, ecumenical study commissions, and the like.

These experiences gave us new attitudes:

1. *to the traditions in which we grew.* We saw them as life and wisdom which have not merely to be received, but also to be transformed by an ecumenical spirit. Just as history is truly known when it is discovered to be the living past in the present, so our own 'histories' yield new meaning and power as they come alive in our ecumenical situation.

2. *to the secular world.* We recognized 'secular man' within ourselves as well as outside us. We became more ready to see the world as the continuous sphere of the operation of Him who is also at the heart of our own histories, our traditions.

The fruit of the ecumenical experience is a growing openness to Jesus Christ, who is both the heart of Tradition and the Lord of the world. Such an experience is possible when one is drawn into a community which has this dual relationship to Christ as the systole and diastole of its being. Such a community has a deep commitment to Christ which is both a necessary discipline and an unbelievable liberation.

What we call 'ecumenical education', then, is the series of events by which people of all ages are drawn into the authentic life of such a community. This kind of education is not an 'it': to be added to or expressed in a curriculum or a programme of action, nor even in a conscious studying of one another's traditions. These may be ways of exploring commitment in such a community. But finally study is barren apart from actual experience of the life and worship of the community.

Priority of Experience.

An affirmation of the priority of experience is in line with the lessons we learn from a study of the history of Christian education. If such an understanding of Christian education is to be communicated to teachers – in theological colleges, or Christian education seminars, or in weekday and Sunday school classrooms – it can only happen within an experience such as we shared together. Only as shared experience – not as idea, programme or explanation – can this be communicated.

For this reason we wonder whether the whole self-conscious structure and apparatus of 'Christian education' may unwittingly stand in the way. Certainly it will until and unless it sees the beginning and end of its task in terms of relations with a *community* committed to the Person at the heart of Tradition and to persons in their whole life in the world. This is the invariable and essential condition under which any of the Church's educational tasks may be discharged – from the training of its clergy to the preparation of its catechumens.

In all areas of education what is needed first is not the teaching of 'right answers', but the bringing of students repeatedly to the point where their questions need such answers. Experience needs formulation. The more a person continues to grow in the Christian community, the more his experience includes encounter in work and thought with Christians of other traditions, the more likely he will be to ask questions which can lead him to an understanding of the ecumenical nature of Christ's Church.

From the *Report of a Consultation on Christian Education and Ecumenical Commitment*, published in the 'Risk' series, World Council of Churches, 1966

We are now entering a new era of methodological concern. This is in no sense a return to the questions raised in an earlier phase of catechetics; it is a pushing ahead to a synthesis never before possible. Writers in the catechetical field usually refer to the first third of this century as the period of *method*. The teaching of religion was improved by the adoption of some rather obvious principles of educational psychology. It is usually said that the past third of a century has been characterized by the improvement of the *content* of religion teaching. Few people would deny that what is found in the average religion textbook today is a decided improvement over the contents of these books a few decades ago. Nevertheless, it may have been premature to suppose that this improvement of the content is the essence of the problem.

I suggest that the last third of the century will be concentrated upon questions that are neither of content nor of method. There is no single word to describe what is at issue. I used above the phrase 'sophisticated methodological questions.' If the word 'methodology' were used here, it would have to carry the sense of a style of thinking and a way of communicating. This is miles removed from the earlier kind of questions on method but even further removed from the insertion of a new content. Much of the discussion on method has been useless because the pre-conditions of a teaching situation were inadequate or non-existent. The teacher's question of how to get his material across to students is part of a much larger problem that must be tackled if teachers are to have a fighting chance. But concentration upon content is also an inadequate approach. It is based upon the misconception that there is a content to Christianity which is separable from a way of living and communicating with others.

The question for the future, therefore, cannot be method or content. The question is the inner relationship of these two, both in human life and in Christian faith. In the whole field of educational theory there will be more concern for how a person thinks than what is held before the mind. Does the thinking originate creatively and is it moving toward more fruitful insights? Education will be concerned with helping a person to think in a manner that will enable him to find his own answers at a later time. Schools cannot provide answers to questions yet to be asked. Schools could provide a way to approach questions that will set a person in the direction of truth.

This educational principle is certainly applicable to religious education. In fact, I would claim that it is especially important here. A religion that includes belief in creation and incarnation is concerned with how man thinks about this world and how he goes about living and communicating with others. Christian faith is not a certain content but the way a people look toward God. This is not to deny the value of doctrinal elaborations in Christianity. But the worst enemy of orthodoxy is the short-circuiting of the process that leads there. We need a life-long methodology for moving in the direction of orthodox formulations.

From *Vision and Tactics – Towards an Adult Church*, Gabriel Moran FSC, Burns and Oates, 1968

1970s
Drawing Insights Together

The twentieth century shows how slow the Churches were, in spite of rapid social change and the lessening numbers of children and young people attending churches, to appropriate the insights of Christian educationalists. Writing in 1971, J Kenneth Meir could still claim:

> Ultimately our movement's strength (i.e. of Sunday Schools) depends on those who teach. Our glory is that the over-whelming majority of Sunday School teachers have regarded their task as a labour of love... It is the teachers in church and school who may decide whether tomorrow's citizens will be pagan or Christians.

From *Labour of Love*, Methodist Youth Department

Yet also in 1971, a report published jointly by the Congregational and Presbyterian Churches began with the warning:

> Fewer and fewer young people are today actively engaged in the life and work of the church, and show little interest either in its worship or assuming the responsibilities of membership.

In the same year the World Council of Christian Education united with the World Council of Churches. Whatever pragmatic reasons led to this union, it symbolised the awareness, which was one of the themes of the century, that the Christian education of children was central to the church's task. This was a major theme of a European Conference organised by the World Council of Churches and the Lutheran World Federation in 1973, to 'evaluate the Sunday School contribution to Church education in Europe today'. Significantly the report of the conference, reflecting the contributions of speakers and of discussion, was entitled *Learning Community*. Perhaps for the first time many of those attending the conference spoke openly of the theological task of the Church in nurturing and teaching children in terms which implied the end of the separate institution, the Sunday School. The break between faith teaching in the church and Religious Education in day schools in Britain was more or less complete. At the beginning of the decade, in circles concerned with Religious Education in schools, a debate raged about the dangers of nurture and indoctrination but soon, in response to the growing numbers of children in schools from immigrant backgrounds, the emphasis was turned to the teaching of the phenomena of religions. Later a more balanced approach evolved which drew together learning about religions and learning from religions, though the latter was often more recognised in the theory than in the practice.

A new *General Catechetical Directory* of the Roman Catholic Church was published on Easter Day 1971, which radically challenged the use of catechisms for the teaching of the faith. The Sacred Congregation for the Doctrine of Faith agreed the text of the new Directory, which reflected thinking developed and shared in a number of international conferences. The introduction states:

> The purpose of this Directory is to present the fundamental theological-pastoral principles, taken from the magisterium of the Church and especially the Second Vatican Council, for the guidance and better co-ordination of the ministry of the word. Hence the emphasis on theory, though the practical aspect is not neglected.

Aspects of the practical task were made clear:

> It must be borne in mind that if the Christian faith is to take root in successive cultures it must needs develop and find new forms of expression. Today's believer is not in all respects like the believers of yesterday. Hence the need to ensure the continuity of the faith and at the same time proclaim the message of salvation in a new way.'

At last, information about the liberation occurring in Latin and South America became readily available in Britain through, for instance, the translations of Freire's *Cultural Action for Freedom* and *Pedagogy of the Oppressed* (Penguin), *Theology of Liberation* by Gutierrez and *Jesus Christ Liberator* by Boff (both published by SCM Press), all published in 1972.

In 1976, with the publication of *Will Our Children Have Faith?*, the work of the United States scholar John Westerhoff began to be influential in Britain and continued to be so during the next decades. Westerhoff's delineation of how an understanding faith is developed was later compared with the findings of James Fowler (see the next section). Also in 1976 the Consultative Group on Ministry among Children of the British Council of Churches published *The Child in the Church*. The emphasis was on the place of the child in the church and on the nurture of children, but perhaps of equal importance the publication was a symbol of renewed self-confidence of those concerned with in-church education. They were dealing with a subject that was discrete and had standing in its own right; at times they looked enviously at the funding and academic standing of Christian (Church) Education in the United States of America. Eventually a further dimension of understanding would be added through the churches' social experience. *The Principles and Practice of Community Work in a British Town* was seminal and led to various forms of church-related community work. Liturgical studies continued to enrich church life; *The Study of the Liturgy* (edited by C Jones, G Wainright and E Yarnold, SPCK) was published in 1978. The generally more formal approach to worship represented by liturgical studies was balanced by the growing phenomena of the informal worship of charismatic and Pentecostal churches. 1979 was designated by the United Nations as the International Year of the Child. It spawned many conferences, and the writing of Hans-Ruedi Weber led many people to a new awareness of how 'Jesus transcended prevailing traditions about the position and education of children.'

A discussion of conscientization calls for a number of preliminary remarks, and I would like to begin today by telling where that great mouthful of a word 'conscientization' came from.

Many people, especially in Latin America and the United States, insist that I invented that strange word, because it is a central idea in my thoughts on education. But I didn't. The word was born during a series of round table meetings of professors at the Brazilian Institute of Higher Studies (ISEB), which was created after the 'liberating' revolution of 1964, under the wing of the Ministry of Education.

The word was excogitated by some one of the professors there, but I really can't remember who. Anyway, it came out of our group reflections. I recall, among others who met there with us, Prof Alvaro Pinto, a great philosopher who wrote a book, *Science and National Reality*, and a more recent one entitled *Science, Awareness and Existence*. There was also a sociologist, Professor Guerreiro, who is presently at the University of California.

I used to compare notes regularly with all of them, and it was there at the ISEB that for the first time I heard the word 'conscientization.' As soon as I heard it, I realized the profundity of its meaning, since I was fully convinced that education, as an exercise in freedom, is an act of knowing, a critical approach to reality. It was inevitable, then, that the word became a part of the terminology I used thereafter to express my pedagogical views, and it easily came to be thought of as something I had created.

Helder Camara was the one who popularized the term and gave it currency in English. Thus, thanks to him rather than to me, the word caught on in Europe and in the United States.

In 1965 I wrote an article for the review *Civilisation et Développement* entitled 'Education and Conscientization.' But it was Helder Camara who, as I have said, in his wanderings about the world, popularized the word so that it is a commonplace today in the United States, where a great number of articles are being written about conscientization. Nonetheless, I am more and more convinced that the word should really be used in its Brazilian form, *conscientização*, and spelled that way. That is why I entitled an article I recently wrote in English 'The Conscientização Progress,' not 'The Conscientization Process.'

What is *conscientization*? I have noticed that conscientization is frequently taken to be synonymous with the French expression *prise de conscience*, yet the two must be carefully distinguished. To show why, let me define the scope of each of them. As a matter of fact, conscientization is possible only because a *prise de conscience* is possible. If human beings were not able to *become aware*, there wouldn't be any conscientization.

Well then, what is this conscientization?

One of the distinguishing traits of humankind is that only it can stand off from the world and the reality of things around it. Only humankind can stand at a distance from a thing and admire it.

As they objectivize or admire a thing (admire is taken here in the philosophical sense of ad-miring, looking at), humans are able to consciously act on the objectivized reality. That, precisely, is the human praxis, the action-reflection on the world, on reality. And yet, in their approach to the world, humans have a preliminary moment in which the world, the objective reality, doesn't yet come to them as a knowable object of their critical consciousness. In other words, in their spontaneous approach to the world, the normal, basic human attitude is not a critical, but an ingenuous one.

Not that there is no knowledge of reality at this spontaneous stage: but what we don't have yet is a critical attitude. There is one kind of perception of reality that gives us a real, if limited, knowledge of it: the Greeks called it *doxa* (mere opinion, or belief). Knowledge that stays at the level of mere *doxa* and goes no further to the level of a task (the reality's reason for being, as Mao Tse-tung would say) never becomes full knowledge, it is not a *logos* of reality.

To become aware, then, all it takes is to be a human being. All it takes is to be human to seize reality in the dialectical relations that flow between humankind and the world, the world and humankind; those relations are so intimate that we really shouldn't talk about humankind and *world*, but just about humankind, or perhaps world-human. This first level of apprehension of reality is what the French mean by *prise de conscience*. The taking awareness of reality exists precisely because as situated beings – closed beings, in Gabriel Marcel's words – human beings are with and in the world, gazing at it.

This *prise de conscience* is not yet conscientization, however. Conscientization is a *prise de conscience* that goes deeper; it is the critical development of a *prise de conscience*. Hence, conscientization implies going beyond the spontaneous phase of apprehension of reality to a critical phase, where reality becomes a knowable object, where the human takes an epistemological stance and tries to know. Thus, conscientization is a probing of the ambience, of reality. The more persons conscientize themselves the more they unveil reality and get at the phenomenic essence of the object they stand in front of, to analyze it. For that same reason, conscientization without a praxis, i.e., without action-reflection as two paired, dialecticized elements permanently constituting that special way of being in the world (or transforming it), is peculiar to human beings.

Conscientization implies a historical commitment. Conscientization, then, is a commitment in time. In fact, there is no conscientization without historical commitment. So that conscientization is also a historical awareness. It is a critical insertion into history. It means that humans take on a role as subjects making the world, remaking the world; it asks humans to fashion their existence out of the material that life offers them. The more they are conscientized, the more they exist.

The mere fact of finding oneself oppressed will move a step ahead and become a process of liberation only if this discovery leads to a historical commitment that means involvement. For involvement is more than commitment: it is a critical insertion into history in order to create it, to mold it. And so, when oppressed individuals see they are oppressed, if they do not set out to do something to transform the concrete oppressing reality, they are not historically committed, and they thus are not really conscientized.

Conscientization implies, then, that when I realize that I am oppressed, I also know I can liberate myself if I transform the concrete situation where I find myself oppressed. Obviously, I can't transform it in my head: that would be to fall into the philosophical error of thinking that awareness 'creates' reality, I would be decreeing that I am free by my mind. And yet, the structures would continue to be the same as ever – so that I wouldn't be free. No, conscientization implies a critical insertion into a process, it implies a historical commitment to make changes. That is why conscientization bids us to adopt a utopian attitude toward the world, an attitude that turns the one conscientized into a utopian agent. Before going any further, let me explain what I mean by that word 'utopian.'

The acts of denouncing and announcing. For me, utopian does not mean something unrealizable, nor is it idealism. Utopia is the dialectization in the acts of denouncing and announcing – denouncing the dehumanizing structure and announcing the structure that will humanize. Hence it is also a historical commitment. A utopia supposes that we know critically. It is an act of knowledge. For I cannot denounce the dehumanizing structure unless I get at it and know it. Nor can I announce, either, unless I know. But – this is important – between the moment of an announcement and the accomplishment of it there is a great difference: the announcement is not the announcement of a project, but of an ante-project. Because the ante-project becomes a project only through a historical praxis. Besides, between the ante-project and the moment of accomplishing or concretizing the project, a period intervenes that we call historical commitment. For this reason, only utopians – and revolutionaries too, to the extent that they are utopians (what was Marx but a utopian? what was Che Guevara if not a utopian?) – can be prophetic and hopeful.

Only those who announce and denounce, who are permanently committed to a radical process of transforming the world so that human beings can be more, only they can be prophetic. Reactionaries, oppressors, cannot be utopian, they cannot be prophetic, and because they cannot be prophetic, they cannot have hope.

What future have oppressors but to preserve their present status as oppressors? What scope for denouncing can oppressors have, other than the denunciation of those who denounce them? What scope for announcing do oppressors have, other than the announcement of their myths? And what can be the hope of those who have no future?

I see a great possibility here for a theology, the utopian theology of hope. The utopian posture of the denouncing, announcing, historically committed Christians who are convinced that the historical vocation of humankind is not to adapt, not to bend to pressures, not to spend 90 percent of their time making concessions in order to salvage what we call the historical vocation of the church. We humans have an unbelievable historical vocation, and we cannot jeopardize it for any one fact, nor can we compromise it for any single, isolated problem, because the church has the whole world. Why, then, risk one's entire historical task over any single fact? That would be, not to be utopian, but to be, literally, Machiavellian, horribly Machiavellian. It would be to concede, and to forfeit one's soul in the concession.

Conscientization reshapes reality

Conscientization clearly has to do with utopia. The more we are conscientized, the more we become, by the commitment that we assume to change things, announcers and denouncers. This commitment ought to be permanent, though, because if after denouncing a dehumanizing structure and announcing a more human one, after committing ourselves with reality (after all, the project is going to be accomplished only if we work at it), after understanding the project and being convinced of its importance (being conscientized about it), if we were then to stop being utopian, we would simply bureaucratize ourselves. This is the danger inherent in any revolution, once it ceases to be permanent. One masterly way to avoid that danger is by a cultural revolution, that dialecticalization which has no yesterday, today, or tomorrow, and which avoids becoming static because it is an ongoing effort for change.

That's what conscientization is: a seizing of reality; and for that very reason, for the very utopian strain that permeates it, we can call it a reshaping of reality. Conscientization demythologizes. Obvious and impressive as the fact may be, an oppressor can never conscientize for liberation. (How would I possibly demythologize if I am an oppressor?) A humanizing endeavor can only be an endeavor to demythify. Conscientization, then, is the most critical approach conceivable to reality, stripping it down so as to get to know it and know the myths that deceive and perpetuate the dominating structure.

One might protest: 'But how can we ever find the process, the how of conscientization?'

The how of it brings up an important point, one that seems to me to be the essential difference between education as a means of domination and education as a means of liberation.

An education that is used to domesticate merely transfers knowledge, as the educator passes on his thirst for knowing to his pupils, who, passively, receive that knowledge. In that sort of relationship, conscientization is impossible. We can see a certain incipient conscientization in it, though, despite that education, in the way the students react, because the natural intentionality of human awareness cannot be thwarted by any educator's domesticating purpose.

A conscientizing – and therefore liberating – education is not that transfer of neatly wrapped knowledge in which there certainly is no knowledge; it is a true act of knowing. Through it, both teacher and pupils simultaneously become knowing subjects, brought together by the object they are knowing. There is no longer one who thinks, who knows, standing in front of others who admit they don't know, that they have to be taught. Rather, all of them are inquisitive learners, avid to learn.

Education for freedom

Those who propagate the superstructure's myths are, equivalently, bringing the superstructure itself right into the infrastructure – and thereby conditioning the infrastructure, too. In any serious changeover, such as a revolution, the myths from the previous structure will carry over and continue to influence the new governmental structure. Unless we critically grasp this fact, we will never understand how, even after an infrastructure has been changed, people will continue to think as they did before.

An understanding of this dialectic and this sort of subdetermination (which Marx certainly had) will persuade us that a mechanistic view of social changes is no good. Someone with a mechanistic approach would expect that if the infrastructure were changed, the superstructure would automatically be changed too – but that is not what happens. That was the problem that baffled Lenin, after the Soviet Revolution; Stalin wrestled with it – and solved it finally by shooting down the peasants. It is the dilemma facing Fidel Castro today with his peasants, though it is not so crucial for him. It is also the problem that Mao Tse-tung had and has, but he came up with the most genial solution of the century: China's cultural revolution.

What is cultural action? What is a cultural revolution? In generic terms, but in the good sense of the phrase, it is the way we culturally attack culture. It means to see culture always as a problem and not to let it become static, becoming a myth and mystifying us.

Whereas education, in practice, too often merely inverts the praxis and domesticates students by pumping myths into them, education for freedom, on the other hand, strives to expose that inversion of praxis at the moment it occurs, so that it will not take place. A noble objective, indeed. But how to do it? As we turn our attention to see our misdirected praxis, we fix our eyes on, as the object of our knowledge, that domesticating capability of an inversion of praxis, the very prostituting of our transforming action. At that moment our act of knowing illuminates the action that is the source of our knowing. And right there we have the permanent, constant dynamic of our attitude toward culture itself.

Otherwise we risk falling into an elitist position, hence one that is neither liberating, nor human, nor humanizing. But even supposing that we avoid that pitfall, how are we to undertake a program of cultural action, or of education for freedom, when we know that people are all the while being dominated through the so-called mass media – which are really means for sending messages rather than for communicating, for propagandizing and domesticating rather than for liberating. We must save that word from the distortion being done to it. The term communications media is being made to cover a wholesale invasion by slogans. But communications is not sloganizing: it is something completely different. As all of us recognize, cultural action for freedom is ultimately a kind of action.

Let's turn, for a moment, to the desperate situation of the peasants in northeast Brazil. Their awareness of what is going on is so primitive that they are wholly unable to get a structural view of reality. They are incapable of envisaging their plight as a result, in the world they live in. Yet even a peasant is a man, and any man wants to explain the reality around him. How can he? one might ask. What reasons can he find? How does his dulled brain conceive his wretched lot?

Normally, he will try to size up his situation. He will look for causes, the reasons for his condition, in things higher and more powerful than man. One such thing is God, whom he sees as the maker, the cause of his condition. Ah, but if God is responsible, man can do nothing. Many Christians today, thanks be to God, are vigorously reacting against that attitude, especially in Brazil. But as a child, I knew many priests who went out to the peasants saying: 'Be patient. This is God's will. And anyway, it will earn heaven for you.' Yet the truth of the matter is that we have to earn our heaven here and now, we ourselves. We have to build our heaven, to fashion it during our lifetime, right now. Salvation is something to achieve, not just to hope for. This latter sort of theology is a very passive one that I cannot stomach.

How could we make God responsible for this calamity? As if Absolute Love could abandon man to constant victimization and total destitution. That would be a God such as Marx described.

The impotence of the oppressed

Whenever men make God responsible for intolerable situations, for oppression, then the dominating structures help to popularize that myth. If God is not the cause, they whisper, then destiny must be. Human reason at this level easily becomes fatalistic; it sits back and sighs: 'Nothing can be done about it.'

Sometimes another scapegoat is found, and it too is a myth spread by the dominating structure: the helplessness of the oppressed. The dominated mind looks inward and decides that it is totally unable to cope with its misery: it concludes that it is impotent. A Presbyterian clergyman from the United States once told me that the whites in his country say God made the blacks inferior. It was a fine example of what the author of the book *Picture of the Colonized Contrasted with the Picture of the Colonizer* meant when he wrote: 'The oppressor always draws a picture of the oppressed.' For the oppressed mind in its desperate plight, I repeat, there seems to be nothing that can be done.

For the critical mind, though, for the mind that conscientizes itself, beyond this situation there is the future, what we must do, the thing we must create, the historical futurity we have to bring into being; and to do that, we must change whatever it is that prevents the humanization of our fellow humans.

As we examine the structures and the reasons why they are so intolerable, as we expose the oppressive situation, we are forced to a decision: we either commit ourselves or we don't – but we will have to answer to our consciences for our choice. The process of conscientization leaves no one with his arms folded. It makes some unfold their arms. It leaves others with a guilty feeling, because conscientization shows us that God wants us to act.

As I conscientize myself, I realize that my brothers who don't eat, who don't laugh, who don't sing, who don't love, who live oppressed, crushed and despised, who *are* less each day, are suffering all this because of some reality that is causing it. And at that point I join in the action historically by genuinely loving, by having the courage to commit myself (the term is used here in its psychological sense). A North American theologian has called those rationalizations 'fake generosities,' because to escape my guilt feelings I go in for philanthropy, I seek compensation by almsgiving, I send a check to build a church, I make contributions: land for a chapel or a monastery for nuns, hoping in that way to buy my peace. But peace cannot be purchased, it is not for sale; peace has to be lived. And I can't live my peace without commitment to humans, and my commitment to them can't exist without their liberation, and their liberation can't exist without the final transformation of the structures that are dehumanizing them. There is only one way for me to find peace: to work for it, shoulder to shoulder with my fellow human beings.

Fear of freedom

It is very interesting to observe how in the seminars I have given in various countries, two attitudes are produced. Often I am violently attacked because many people, when they hear me, start to despoil themselves – and their almost immediate second reaction is to strike back at whoever made them do that. Observing this process can be extremely interesting.

A similar process takes place with very simple persons, too. Many of them run away from freedom. Oppression is so potent a thing that it produces fear of freedom. That fear crops up whenever any discussion or even mention of freedom makes them already feel it as a threat. But freedom isn't something that is given. It is something very arduous, because nobody gives freedom to anyone else, no one frees another, nobody can even free himself all alone; humans free themselves only in concert, in communion, collaborating on something wrong that they want to correct. There is an interesting theological parallel to this: no one saves another, no one saves himself all alone, because only in communion can we save ourselves – or not save ourselves. You don't save me, because my soul, my being, my conscious body is not something that A or B can save. We work out our salvation in communion. Each one of us must set out in quest of his salvation, we must do it ourselves. I don't mean that God hasn't saved us by the divine presence in history: I'm talking now on the human level.

Conscientization: a painful birth

Bringing together all the things I have said, we see that conscientization is a painful birth. There is no palliative for it like those exercises that women use to avoid birth pangs. Conscientization also involves an excruciating moment, a tremendously upsetting one, in those who begin to conscientize themselves, the moment they start to be reborn. Because conscientization demands an Easter. That is, it demands that we die to be reborn again. Christians must live their Easter, and that too is a utopia. Those who don't make their Easter, in the sense of dying in order to be reborn, are not real Christians. That is why Christianity is, for me, such a marvelous doctrine. People have accused me of being a communist, but no communist could say what I have just said. I never had any temptation to cease being, to stop existing. The reason is that I am not yet completely a Catholic; I just keep on trying to be one more completely, day after day. The condition of being is to go on being. I have never yet felt that I had to leave the church, or set aside my Christian convictions, in order to say what I have to say, or go to jail – or even refuse to. I just feel passionately, corporately, physically, with all my being, that my stance is a Christian one because it is 100 percent revolutionary and human and liberating, and hence committed and utopian. And that, as I see it, must be our position, the position of a church that must not forget it is called by its origins to die shivering in the cold. This is a utopia; it is a denunciation and an announcement with a historical commitment that adds up to heroism in love.

Each of us has to give witness, and conscientization is a summons to do that: to be new each day. Hence it is peace, and it enables us to understand others.

Conscientization could never be an imposition on others or a manipulation of them. I cannot impose my opinions on someone else; I can only invite others to share, to discuss. To impose on others my way of not being would be a real contradiction. For loving is not only a free act, it is an act for freedom. And love that cannot produce more freedom is not love.

'Conscientizing as a Way of Liberating' from a taped version of a talk given by Freire in Rome in 1970, published in the March 1974 issue of the Mexican quarterly *Contacto*. It was included in *Liberation Theology: a documentary history* (Orbis, 1990).

Fundamentally, there is widespread disillusion with an organisation that seems to have narrow horizons and wrong priorities. As the church functions at present, it seems not to present Jesus Christ. Too often the image is of the jumble sale or sewing circle rather than involvement in the community. The church does, of course, do far more than many of its critics, young and old, think, but the gap of communication is so great that the facts are not always known. It gives every indication of having its back against the wall and 'young life instinctively knows that you can't build life out of negativities and defensive manoeuvres' (Ross Snyder, writing in *The New Creation and the New Generation*, A H van den Heuvel (ed), Friendship Press) ...

... Thus the church is challenged to creative attitudes in social partnership. Dr. Milson puts it this way – 'In a civilised community, the most frequent message flashed across the generations from older to younger people would be "Come over and help us". The young are best seen as social partners with the old, called to share a destiny in the last decades of the twentieth century, but a destiny which is not yet clear. So the young are invited on equal terms to define the task, as well as to share its labours: we need their ideas as well as their muscles or their willingness to put circulars in envelopes; they should be active, not sleeping partners. There is ample evidence that this approach finds an encouraging response from a significant number of young people and often in unexpected quarters. There is nothing so encouraging as a cry for help; and the failure of many of our institutions – for example, churches, trade unions and political parties – to flash this message has more to do than we think with the "youth problem".' (F Milson, *Youth Work in the 1970s*)

From *The Church and Young People,* a joint working party report of the Congregational Church in England and Wales and the Presbyterian Church of England, 1971

Taking education seriously

In conversation about how people learn the assumption is sometimes made that we know how children learn but that adults are in some ways different. Ministers and clergy defend traditional liturgical practices and ways of conducting meetings by hinting that this is the rational way to do things. Walter Persson said, 'I do not like the phrase "impact on children". Impact should be as much on child, teacher and church. Freire says, "We start by acting not by thinking. It is not a creed but a deed which helps children to grasp the Gospel. If we teach in a theoretical and objective way we are lost; actions are more understandable. Jesus practised the method of acting to teach the disciples; he sent out the disciples and then explained. Children need a less authorised and more living version of the Christian life."'

In the education of children, action is important; we know also of the importance of physical context, varied stimulation, colour, sound, games, conversation, the use of imaginative resources – books and visual material. We know it is important to give the child opportunity to discover new information or a new insight or idea for himself in a context which directly relates what he is discovering to his own life. Above all, we know that experience is decisive and because this is so, that what each person perceives is unique to himself. 'Now it comes about that whatever we tell the learner, he will make something that is all his own out of it, and it will be different from what we held so dear and attempted to "transmit". He will build it into his own scheme of things, and relate it uniquely to what he already uniquely holds as experience. Thus he builds a world all his own, and what is really important is what he makes of what we tell him, not what we intended.' (Postman, N and Weingarten, C, Teaching as a Subversive Activity, Penguin)

It has yet to be demonstrated that adults learn and perceive in ways which are decisively different from those in which children learn. Everything that is important in the learning situation and process for the child is important for the adult. The generalisation that a person notices twenty per cent of what he hears, thirty per cent of what he sees, fifty per cent of what he both hears and sees, seventy per cent of what he himself says and ninety per cent of what he himself does is true, irrespective of the age of the person...

The challenge to the church is that in its dealing with adults it will have to find the courage to move away – in the main, if not wholly – from an educational approach derived from ancient Greece and to develop the use of an experiential approach which has validity for both children and adults. Or, to use the words of *Seeing Education Whole*, '... present authoritarian practices, which heighten the difference between the educator and the educatee, and build upon the distinction between school learning and life, must be replaced by those that bind educator and educatee together in a common activity of learning and of transforming the reality with which they are faced.' *(Seeing Education Whole, WCC, 1971)* ...

The involvement of children in the total community life of the church might cause church leaders to take seriously how people of all ages learn and are influenced and express themselves spontaneously. This could set in motion profound changes in church life.

From *Learning Community*, J M Sutcliffe, NCEC, 1974

Liturgy and Christian formation

The documents of liturgical renewal have had little enough to say about children. It is arguable that by that omission seeds of potential disaster have been only too effectively sown. To juxtapose 'The child' and 'Worship' is to produce a combination of emphases that falls unexpectedly on too many ears. For this is not a natural connection for the modern Church to make.

It is important to seek the reason for this situation. Doubtless there are many. Yet the most significant of them is surely that, within the general Christian community, inherited memories of dealing with children are bound up primarily with the institution traditionally known as the Sunday school. If this diagnosis is in any way sound, the implications of it must bear scrutiny.

The Sunday schools of the nineteenth century were quite clear and realistic about their task. They engaged themselves in teaching children to read and write, and then – when an age of wider literacy dawned – in passing on the elements of the Christian Faith to children who lacked the privilege of a Christian home. They knew themselves to be inadequate substitutes for the Christian family. Their emphasis, accordingly, was a modest one. It was upon instruction. It is this concern that has heavily governed the thinking of the Church in connection with children ever since. The difference now is that we do not call it instruction. We call it education.

The distinction at this point should be neither unfairly exaggerated nor improperly minimized. The shift from instruction to education is the indicator that reflects the new thinking about children, their growth, and their learning process, that has gone on over recent decades. Instruction tended to work with the model of the child as a receptacle into which slices of knowledge were to be inserted. Education speaks of a process of leading and discovery whereby the child, his interest aroused, is put in the way of learning, and is encouraged to deeper understanding through widening experience. The difference is real. Equally obvious, however, is the fact that whether the emphasis be on instruction or on education it is basically on learning. The overriding concern is not the child and worship. It is the child and learning.

That this is so becomes more than usually apparent when atten tion is paid to contemporary disputes about the use of the Bible with children. On the one side it is argued that the Bible is not a children's book, that the unreflecting teaching of biblical mate- rial implants in the child's mind all kinds of misunderstandings and misconceptions about the Christian Faith which block the road to mature faith and positively encourage rejection of Christianity when adolescence is reached. So the concern is all for ordinary, everyday experience.

Scripture is sparingly and cautiously used. It is introduced to illustrate human situations and issues of common life. On the other hand, the opponents of this view will argue that the Bible is being sold short, and that children are being left in ignorance of its riches. The cry is for a return to straight scriptural teaching that starts with the Bible, ends with the Bible, and keeps the Bible central.

It sounds like a specific and particularly important instance of the familiar battle between education and instruction. In a way it is. Yet it has more fearful dimensions. For the supremely signif- icant thing revealed by it is that, in the end, both parties operate with the same ground rules. Learning is the preoccupation, not worship. And not infrequently both parties, logically enough, tend to have imperialistic designs upon the 'adult' service of worship, and are eager to tilt the liturgy dramatically in the direction of their own particular learning model. The 'educa- tionists' complain bitterly of the medieval nature of worship where people sit and listen to a Word addressed to them, and object that the whole process is educationally nonsensical. The 'instructionists' increasingly extol the virtues of the all-age Sunday school, and are sometimes prepared to urge the curtail- ment of worship, if necessary, in order to subject the adults to the instruction given, at simplified level, to the children. From both directions a take-over bid is made. Whatever the shape of the palace, learning is king.

All this is not the assumption of the few – those perhaps who deal with children in the church context. Rather is this the assumption of the many. The uncovering of what is at stake may perhaps be more clearly achieved by the posing of some key questions. Does what is done with the children on Sunday mornings really prepare them over the years for real participation in the worshipping assembly of the People of God? Is the transition in the early 'teens from Sunday school or Junior Church to Service of Worship a smooth one because taken by prepared people who are simply advancing a further step along the same track? Or does it seem to them like a sudden unconnected jerk from one kind of activity to another?

That such questions are real and searching is indicated by two significant and common attitudes. A generation that has passed through the traditional Sunday school tends to find it particularly difficult to understand the true nature of worship. Almost inevitably the assessment of it is likely to be made in instructional terms. Too easily worship may be viewed as essentially a form of adult instruction. Where this happens the emphasis is laid upon the sermon, for which hymns, prayers, and the like constitute a kind of preparation. And the function of the sermon is seen to be instructional. 'What have I learned today?' becomes the question. 'Was it clear and understandable?' becomes the criterion. The underlying assumption is that what the children get on *their* level the adult should be getting on *his*.

The other common attitude is equally interesting. It is likely to be found among the generation which has passed through some variations of the more modern 'Family Church' system, most widely practised in the Free Churches. Equally there is likely to be a problem of understanding the real nature of worship. Equally liturgy may be viewed as basically a form of adult education. The difference is that now the 'adult' service is likely to be criticized on the ground that it is educationally out of date. Children are being dealt with on sound educational principles. Informality is encouraged. Discussion takes place. Activity is all. And then – the teenager is suddenly thrown back into the dark ages and made to sit still on a chair, keep quiet for much of the time, and listen.

Here then are two different attitudes, widely represented within the Christian community. The space between them is vast. Yet it is not the distinction that finally impresses. For underlying both is the one familiar and crucial assumption already identified. Whether for the child or for the adult, education, instruction, learning, is the name of the game.

But is it? Or is the name of the game really worship? It may assist towards the reaching of firm conclusions to inquire what is our goal for the child. Surely the concern is that the children shall, in years of understanding, respond to the call and claim of God and commit their lives to him. Clearly – and fortunately – such a commitment cannot be stage-managed or coerced. It can, however, be prepared for so that in due time a conscious and understanding confrontation with God becomes possible. How is such preparation to be made?

Certainly the presence, challenge, and claim of God can be known and experienced in all sorts of strange places. Commitment to God can be made in the most unlikely circumstances. All this is finally – and fortunately – beyond human control. Yet none of this alters the fact that what might fairly be called the 'familiar' point of confrontation with God is the corporate worship of the Church. There is nothing surprising or accidental about that. For this is precisely the thing with which the Liturgy is concerned.

Such a confrontation with God in corporate worship is, of course, an indirect one. What else could it be? God is not a visiting preacher who could be ushered in, pointed out, introduced, and invited to 'say a few words'. No one has 'seen' God. Any confrontation has to take place *through* something or someone else. In the Liturgy, that 'something else' is focally and centrally the biblical tradition. The Word is proclaimed in Scripture and in sermon in order that a highway be opened that may become 'the way of the Lord'.

Nor is this the whole. In praise and prayer it is the presence of God which is being sought and celebrated. In the Eucharist it is the presence of God in Christ which is being expected, anticipated, and received. From first to last corporate worship is concerned with an encounter with God which offers life and claims commitment.

It is *all this* for which the child is being prepared. At this point the Christian community has discharged its task faithfully when through the years it has made a child 'ready' for a conscious confrontation with God in corporate worship. Yet if this is the goal and the concern, there seems something more than a little odd about the desperate eagerness in too many places to remove the children from that worship. To keep them strangers to the Liturgy for as many years as possible would appear to be a curious kind of 'preparation'.

In not a few quarters even to raise this issue is to unleash a barrage of outraged argument. The 'adult' service is no place for the children – at least, not for more than fifteen minutes. They will be bored. They will be fidgety. They will be unhappy. They will revolt. They will come to loathe the whole enterprise. Are we still in the nineteenth century? Have we learned nothing from the educationists? The attack seems overwhelming. Where infants are concerned, part of it may well have proper force. Yet it may be worth while to probe deeper and attempt to disentangle the issues. For it seems likely that a wide range of presuppositions are being paraded.

Certainly it is true that were the aim instruction we should be criminally foolish to encourage children to be present at the Liturgy. We have, however, already argued that worship is not a form of adult education. 'What have I learned today?' is quite the wrong question for any worshipper to ask as he stumbles out after the Blessing. The central concern of corporate worship is the presence, coming, challenge, and claim of God. It is not immediately apparent that this is necessarily irrelevant to everybody under the age of fourteen.

Other hesitations seem to be bound up with a curious preoccupation with intelligibility. Taken to its extreme this would result in the conclusion that children should not be confronted with things they do not understand. Yet few positions can be more outdated than that. Any educationist could drive a coach and horses through it with one hand tied behind his back. In reality all sensible parents know that the child develops precisely because in the family he is not insulated from everything beyond his own level of experience and understanding. It would be odd if the Church at the heart of its life were to stand inflexibly for a diametrically opposite position.

There is, of course, no virtue in deliberate and sustained unintelligibility. If corporate worship were (or is) a matter of sitting still for an hour and listening to an intellectual address, then woe betide the child (and the adult as well). But if the Liturgy is a mixture of activities all of which are designed to act as a highway along which God meets his children, then we dare not too quickly or lightly exclude the child.

It might seem attractive at this point to follow relentlessly the apparent logic of the argument and claim that all children of all ages should be present for the total act of corporate worship

Sunday by Sunday. To make such a leap would, however, be to move too slickly and easily. In any event the primary aim must be to uncover relevant governing principles. For reasons that will emerge diversity of practical application is likely to prove necessary and inevitable.

What is this corporate worship to which we seek to introduce our children? It is that central Liturgy of the Church which is built round the twin poles of Word and Supper. Should the children be present at the celebration of the Supper? Certainly experience at many a Parish Communion would prompt an affirmative answer. To bring the child from earliest years into intimate touch with the beating heart of Christian worship may be to offer him a gift of incalculable worth.

Nevertheless, no unqualified plea in this direction can or should be made. A divided Church manifests divergent eucharistic theologies which themselves contribute to differences of eucharistic practice. All this is not simply to be ignored when the matter of the presence of children at the Supper and their participation in it is an issue. Some eucharistic understandings may allow the child to 'communicate' equally with the adult. Others may confine the sharing of the Supper to the 'committed' membership and radically call into question any non-communicating attendance. At these extremes the implications for the child are at least clear-cut.

The most difficult decisions are likely to arise in the area in-between, in those church situations where theology on the one hand debars the full participation of the child, yet on the other hand combines with a strong sense of the 'family' character of the Church to encourage his presence. Two possibilities then emerge. Either the bread and wine are simply withheld from the child or he is offered what is felt to be some fitting 'substitute'. Both practices demand scrutiny.

The Eucharist reaches its fullness and fulfilment in 'Communion'. There is accordingly always a sense in which non-communicating attendance fundamentally denies the focal intent of the celebration. To take this fact seriously is not to rule out all such attendances on all occasions. It is to put a serious question mark against the deliberate institution and regular encouragement of such attendance on the part of one group within the Christian community. Certainly it may be argued that what is being offered is a form of 'spiritual' communion. Yet it has then to be asked why a group that is adjudged capable of and apt for this somewhat hazy reality must be debarred from the more regular form of *communio in sacris*.

A more powerful case is likely to be made along the lines of the enormous significance of setting the child in the context of the full eucharistic celebration. Will not the riches of corporate worship make their impact upon him here with unexampled force? Will he not be exposed in this way to influences the range and force of which cannot finally be measured? Will he not by this means be brought to look after and long for the eventual fullness of what he is enabled dimly and partially to experience?

The argument is a powerful one. It catches completely the insight that worship does not operate wholly at the conscious level. It gives proper recognition to the truth that familiarity with the Eucharist over the years can potently assist in preparation for the eventual and meaningful participation in it. Yet still questions must be pressed. On the one hand, theological objections to the proposed practice, in so far as it is regular rather than occasional, must be seriously weighed. On the other hand, the extent to which spurious sentimentality may be replacing sober judgement must be realistically envisaged. The understanding of the Church in terms of the image of the modern family has been far too slickly provided with a New Testament imprimatur, and the liturgical corollaries drawn from that image demand relentless questioning. It may well be that the case for non-communicating attendance of children at the Eucharist can be made. It is not, however, clear that it has yet been made.

The other possibility remains. It is that the child from whom the bread and wine are withheld should be present at the Eucharist and, at the point of 'communion', be offered some appropriate substitute. Here once more the reservations crowd in. What is a Christian community in fact saying to itself and to its children in such a situation? Powerful and convincing reasons can be given for the attempt to draw the children into the worshipping assembly and to set them at the heart of the liturgical action. Yet the problem and the peril of offering them at the climactic moment 'a pat and a blessing' and thereby something *other than* the corporate worship of the People of God should surely be plain. And if such a distinction is made solely in the case of *children*, the danger is compounded. As always, it is fatally easy to embrace apparently attractive practices in harmony with modern sentiment before the theological, liturgical, and psychological realities have been searchingly weighed.

We have affirmed that the Liturgy is built round the twin poles of Word and Supper. We have glimpsed the problems and possibilities bound up with the presence of children at the Supper. How does it stand with them in relationship to the Word?

To answer that question convincingly will require a closer and keener examination of what the Church should be seeking to do for and with its children. If the concern is the preparation of the child for response and commitment to the call and claim of God, then the goal is Christian 'formation', and the road is Christian 'nurture'. There is a 'Tradition' into which the child is to enter, so that in and through it the encounter with God in Jesus Christ may take place. When the life of the Church is healthy and strong, it is the place where the Tradition of the People of God is effectively handed on in such manner as to illumine, disturb, and transfigure developing experience and elicit appropriate responses and commitments.

It should be emphasized that this handing on of the Tradition is not the transfer of a packaged body of knowledge. The Tradition is a living thing, though not formless or lacking in content. No passive, uncritical reception is involved but rather an engagement which leaves neither partner untouched. The Tradition has form but is constantly being re-formed. To receive it is to enter into it, to experience Christian 'formation' by being progressively initiated into the ethos and mores of the People of God. It is not to achieve mastery of a corpus of belief so much as to obtain the freedom of a city. It is to find a standing ground and gain a perspective and explore a new world which promises to become home.

Clearly every aspect of the corporate life of the Church should assist the process of Christian formation. Equally clearly the liturgical assembly is a supreme vehicle of that formation. In the Liturgy the Tradition is being crucially and centrally handled and unleashed; for Scripture permeates the Liturgy, and Scripture is the normative focus of the Tradition. As the Word is proclaimed in Scripture and sermon, the Tradition moves massively into the centre of the arena. For the Bible is not essentially a deposit of truth to be conveyed, but the witness to a constant reinterpretation of the Tradition as in each fresh critical situation God grapples with his People.

So it is that when the Word is truly proclaimed in the Liturgy the Tradition is set in motion and becomes a living thing. A search-light plays upon human horizons. Present experience is grasped by the future of God. A new world supervenes upon an old. Such at least is the intention, the hope, and the prayer. Certainly it is the whole man including mind and imagination that is confronted. Yet the essential thrust is upon the will. Only inci-dentally and peripherally can the response be: Now I understand! Now I know! Centrally and substantially it is to be: This is where I belong – and, this being how things are, now I must choose.

It is against such a background of understanding that the place of the child is to be assessed. Three key terms demand constant attention and proper interrelatedness – exposure, readiness, and preparation. As the Church deals with its children, it must never lose sight of its primary responsibility to 'prepare' them for response and commitment to the call and claim of God. Such preparation involves continuing 'exposure' to the living Tradition from earliest years. Yet while the Tradition can and should make a profound impact below the conscious level, it is not simply an indefinable atmosphere. It also has content. So it is that the 'readiness' of the child for engagement with it becomes significant at every stage of the journey. Too easily that readiness can be lacking, or worse still can suffer distortion.

This is why the 'movement' of Christian formation must be care-fully and sensitively observed. It is the movement *from* exposure to the Tradition *to* conscious confrontation with the Tradition. How is that movement to be made?

Where the parents are Christians, it is in the Christian family that exposure to the Tradition will and should begin. Equally, it is there that the readiness of the child for a conscious confronta-tion with the Tradition will take initial shape or suffer initial distortion. The stakes are high. The demands, however, are not impossible. What is required of the Christian family is not a highly articulated understanding of the Faith or a sophisticated domestic practice of its disciplines, however praiseworthy and desirable these things may be. Rather is the family required to be the place where the Tradition and the twentieth century meet in fruitful interplay to create a quality of being and a style of living which may mediate and bring near to the child that world which the Tradition bears.

Within the Church context, such exposure to the Tradition must continue. This at least means that from earliest years the child may find a place within the liturgical assembly and be present at part of its activity. For worship is not only the proclamation of the Word. Rather is it a totality of action every part of which is controlled and coloured by the Tradition since it is the Tradition that provides the script for the liturgical drama. From first to last in corporate worship a drama is being enacted, a Presence is being realized, a story is being told. To be part of the worshipping community at prayer and praise is to deepen that exposure to the pressures of the presence of God already experienced within the family circle. It is to continue an exposure which may prepare the way for a conscious confrontation in later years at the point of the proclamation of the Word.

But there are other requirements. Facility with the grammar and syntax of the Tradition must be gained. Within the Christian community the Tradition is borne crucially and most explicitly by the proclamation of the Word. It means the introduction of a language world in which the child must one day move with comparative freedom. Only if this is accomplished can the confrontation be expected to take place with power. How is this basic literacy to be achieved? In the last resort it may be gained by participation in the Liturgy itself. The child learns to speak and handle the language as he lives within a family that communicates in his native tongue. In this way Christian literacy *may* be achieved. It cannot, however, be concluded that it *will* be achieved. One hour a week within the worshipping community, many of whose members themselves still stumble over the grammar and syntax, offers but limited opportunity. Some more deliberate provision may be judged necessary.

Even beyond this the contours of the Tradition must impose themselves and become familiar. To gain a purchase on a new language world is not enough. The landmarks of that world need to be known and identified. Again, this *may* in the last resort be accomplished through participation in the Liturgy itself. But again, it cannot be assumed that it will thus be accomplished. It is the old problem of the wood and the trees; and in that Scripture is the normative witness to the Tradition, it is a problem that is focused in the encounter with the Bible.

Scripture lessons may be read and expounded. Yet too often they are heard by those who lack familiarity with the total context which gives them life. They descend on waiting ears like strange visitants lacking both ancestry and progeny. Where the proper overview of the Tradition is lacking, its impact is likely to be disastrously blunted. It is when the shape of the Tradition is known that a satisfactory conscious confrontation with it becomes more than an outside possibility. To provide the child with a picture of the biblical landscape is to assist his initiation into the world the Tradition bears.

To take such considerations seriously is to be pressed towards responsible and delicate decisions as to the age at which a child should be encouraged to be present at the Liturgy for Scripture readings and sermon. The issue has only been by-passed, not met, where for other reasons the true proclamation of the Word has been replaced by a 'brief address' which children may reasonably be expected to 'sit through'. More profound realities are at stake than this. Within the Liturgy the child may find his exposure to the Tradition clarified and heightened. He may also begin to assimilate the Tradition's grammar and syntax and find its total shape bodied forth before him, so that in due time a conscious confrontation with the Tradition may take place in meaningful fashion.

Yet preparedness for a grappling with the Tradition is bound up with a literacy and an overview which are only gradually to be obtained and which many adults in the worshipping community itself may only falteringly and partially possess. A tension is revealed of which the child is the most obvious focus. He needs constant experience of the liturgical assembly that he may be continually exposed to the Tradition. Yet he may need withdrawal from the proclamation of the Word in order that he may be deliberately prepared and made ready for that critical confrontation with the Tradition that is concentrated there.

To lose sight of that tension and the precise nature of it is the short road to disaster in the making of any alternative provision for the children at the time of the liturgical assembly on the Lord's Day. If the child is to be withdrawn from the Liturgy at any point, then what is done for him and with him must at all costs be conformed to the nature and thrust of the liturgical activity itself. The learning model must never be allowed to infiltrate and control. Scripture must be seen and used not as a quarry of ideas or beliefs or directives but as the normative witness to the living Tradition into which the child is being initiated. It must be used in such a manner that it speaks of that living Tradition and points to the Lord of that Tradition and the community which is its bearer.

To approach the child in his temporary separation from the Liturgy from such a perspective is to glimpse the lineaments of that response which is required of him. Hitherto the thrust of the argument might have encouraged the conclusion that the child was to be viewed simply as an adult in the making, doomed to suffer his exposure, learn his grammar and syntax, and obtain his overview solely in order that one day he might emerge from the process into a totally new situation of challenge and response. Nothing could be further from the truth. Each step of the way has its own significance. At every stage of the pilgrimage a claim is to be made and a response invited. Here once more the pattern of the Liturgy casts its shadow before it. The commitments to be made may be infinitely varied, provided only that they do not violate the integrity of the growing child. Yet to use Scripture liturgically and faithfully is to be given guidelines which indicate the shape of the goal towards which the Tradition presses. As the Bible engages the growing experience of the child, the crucial response that it seeks is not: 'This I have learned today', but something much more like: 'This is my life. These are my People'.

In the end what emerges is not a uniform programme or solution, but rather an attitude, a signpost, an understanding, a goal. The aim of the Church in the coming days must be to maximize the child's involvement in the Liturgy not minimize it. His withdrawal at points in the Liturgy may be adjudged necessary. Yet if and where such a decision is made, alternative provision must sensibly conform to the liturgical reality and not be shaped by other models or criteria.

Nor, when the child is present within the liturgical assembly, may the Church quickly and lightly offer him something different, go juvenile for ten minutes, or substitute for worship a few spoonfuls of elementary instruction. True worship speaks of mystery, with heights and depths that none of us can fathom. We are being exposed to realities which hit us and meet us at levels below the conscious mind. To expose the child to all that may be a dangerous business, but dangerous probably for reasons quite other than we usually imagine.

If we are honest we may have to confess that some of our hesitations are sheerly practical, though none the less real for that. Our peace may be disturbed. We shall be distracted by the constant effort of ensuring that the child observes 'proper behaviour'. Being a child he is unpredictable. He may wriggle. He may move. He may break the solemnity. And should not worship be solemn?

Yet there may be a more profound obstacle. Deep down in our hearts we surely know two things. One is that if God is to break through in worship to the child it is likely to be through *us*. The other is that our children always know when we are involved in something that really is of life and death significance to us. They may not understand it. It may remain largely a mystery to them. But it is a mystery shot through with its own queer meaning, because it matters to us and matters desperately.

This is the frightening dilemma. Will they be bored because basically we are too? If so, then to keep them in corporate worship might be disastrous, though for reasons quite other than the ones traditionally advanced. What if the only worship we have to offer to our children is so intellectualized that it cannot ring bells with them! What if we cannot guarantee to them a worshipping congregation so fully and desperately involved in playing out the Liturgy that it would communicate to them a sense of the wonder, the joy, and the mystery of God!

The problems remain. Yet two things may be tolerably clear. Whatever we do with the child when and if he withdraws from the Liturgy, we must seek to make room for God to engage his growing experience and elicit his limited response, and we must strive to make him ready for that conscious confrontation with God which corporate worship may one day bring. And when he is present in ˙the sanctuary, we must offer him authentic worship, not some distortion or juvenile corruption of it. So that when at least he comes to take his place as a full participant in the total liturgical action, he may come not as a stranger but as a traveller corning home.

By Neville Clark, from *Worship and the Child*, a collection of essays by members of the Joint Liturgical Group, E C D Jasper (ed), SPCK, 1975

Towards a theology of education

What is education? This is a difficult question, but somewhat easier than the question, 'What is theology?' As I needn't tell classicists here, and it would be highly impertinent of a one-time scientist to try to do that in any case, the word 'education' derives from the Latin verb *educare*, which I understand is an intensive form of *educere*. Its context is that of, for instance, leading ships out of harbour, leading an army out of camp, leading water down from a reservoir or a storage tank. I think at once we see the point. Ships do not fulfil their purpose in a harbour, armies do not fulfil their purpose when they are confined to barracks, and water does not fulfil its purpose of refreshment if it stays up there in the reservoir or the storage tank. In other words, the context for the word education is that of helping someone or something to fulfil its true purpose – ships on the high seas, an army keeping order, water refreshing people. Therefore whatever we think about education ought to reflect and match our ideas about humanity and human fulfilment. Education and ideas of humanity go hand in hand. If we have a religious estimate of man we shall then have a religious view of education.

Perhaps I could just develop this point of view by explicit reference to a book which I don't carry about as the Bible, but which gets a good deal of quotation, *The Fourth R*. Approaching the topic in very general terms we say in it that 'one of the basic educational questions is plainly what kind of a being is this whom we seek to educate? Are human beings no more, though no less, than a combined topic of the natural and behavioural sciences? Do we differ, as socially acceptable citizens, at all significantly from house-trained dogs? Or are human beings anything more than extremely elaborate computers whose major distinction is they are comparatively cheap to come by?' Now if this is one's view of the nature of man the educational process need plainly be no more than a process, highly complex of course, highly professional, of individual and social conditioning. What is quite clear is that what we do in education depends quite basically on our understanding of what it is to be human. And against this background, we remark in *The Fourth R* that 'much contemporary educational thought gives the appearance of being dominated by a standpoint which sees human life and existence wholly within a framework supplied by the concepts and beliefs of the natural and behavioural sciences, and by the assumption that honest doubt is somehow more honest than honest faith. It is often a presupposition in educational thinking that the contemporary intellectual debate, so far as religious belief is concerned, has been settled once and for all in a secularist way. Against such a restricted view of human existence a religious education, faithful to the theological perspectives which lie behind it, will be constantly endeavouring to do justice to a wider perspective on human nature, a broader and less restrictive humanism.'

The purpose of education, then, is to educate children or adults that they fulfil their true purpose as persons with a faith dimension, with a transcendence, with a life not restricted to spatial-temporal behaviour. In short, that they will be helped to fulfil their true purpose as religious people.

The nature of religion

But now you might say what is religion in this regard? I do not propose to add to those twenty-five or thirty definitions of religion you used to find in traditional books on the philosophy of religion. Suffice it for our purpose very briefly to give an answer from three directions. It will be clear why presently. First, we may recall that well-known remark of another philosopher-educator, A N Whitehead. 'Religion', he said, 'is the vision of something which stands beyond, behind and within the passing flux of immediate things.' Those prepositions, 'beyond, behind, and within', are chosen as a set of mutually balancing qualifiers, each correcting the emphasis the other might suggest. All are saying, 'do something or other with the passing flux of immediate things beyond, behind, within, until the faith dimension breaks in on you.'

Second, we may recall Rudolph Otto. Religion is a sense of the numinous, a sense of mystery, *tremendum et fascinans*, awesome and inspiring. The feeling of it, says Otto, may at times 'come sweeping like a gentle tide, pervading the mind with a tranquil mood of deepest worship. It may pass over into a more set and lasting attitude of the soul, continuing, as it were, thrillingly vibrant and resonant, until at last it dies away and the soul resumes its 'profane', non-religious mood of everyday experience. It may burst in sudden eruption up from the depths of the soul with spasms and convulsions, or lead to the strangest excitements, to intoxicated frenzy, to transport, to ecstasy. It has its crude, barbaric antecedents and early manifestations, and again it may be developed into something beautiful and pure and glorious. It may become the hushed, trembling, and speechless humility of the creature in the presence of – whom or what? In the presence of that which is a Mystery, inexpressible and above all creatures.'

In this context Otto has something to say of relevance and importance for education. There is only one way, he says, to help another to an understanding of this experience. 'He must be guided and led on by consideration and discussion of the matter through the ways of his own mind, until he reaches the point "the numinous" in him perforce begins to stir, to start into life and consciousness. We can co-operate in this process by bringing before his notice all that can be found in other regions of the mind, already known and familiar, to resemble, or again to afford some special contrast to, the particular experience we wish to elucidate. And then we must add: "this X of ours is not precisely this experience, but akin to this one and the opposite of that other. Cannot you now realize for yourself what it is?" And then the concluding sentence. "In other words our X (God, mystery, whatever you want to put in) – cannot, strictly, be taught. It can only be evoked, awakened in the mind; as every-thing that comes 'of the spirit' has to be awakened."'

In a way my own approach tries to unite these two. (Though as an aside I could say, with many others, I would be quite critical of the developments in Otto here and there.) Hence, broadly speaking, I would say that to talk of religion is to talk of situations not restricted to what is seen, heard, touched, tasted and smelt – not restricted to 'the passing flux of things', not restricted to states of affairs, facts and circumstances immedi-ately obvious. It is an occasion where the passing flux of immediate things comes alive with a feeling of the numinous – the William James phrase 'a sense of presence'. It is a vision of the eternal disclosed through the temporal. It relates to what is seen, and more. Now how do we gain access to this 'more', this dimension which a religious faith would supply to our under-standing of humanity and the universe? By peering into another realm? By essaying some descriptions of another world? No. If positivists taught us one thing it is that both those answers are unintelligible. We only know this 'more' by being awakened to it, in Otto's phrase, by coming to see, by responding to what is disclosed around things temporal in a moment of vision. Only then do we come to ourselves, do we find fulfilment and freedom...

A note on 'disclosures' and 'models'

One last comment to round off this introduction. It is clear that I set high store on the situation which I call the 'disclosure' – that which is evoked, that which is stirred within us, to use Otto's phrase. And in this way I accept what I think the Bloxham report would say about an existentialist approach to education. I think the theological revolution, of which I see myself as part, can be expressed like this. In the Bloxham report it is said that this existentialist approach sees religion, all religion, as man-made construction, a symbol system, rather than a God-sent revelation. Now certainly the symbols do not themselves have the authority of God Himself. That is a lesson we are only just learning, and learning by a very hard way. Yet I would not say that the symbols were then man-made. For in any situation of the kind I have called 'the moment of vision', 'the disclosure', I believe there do emerge some focal images, some symbols, given in the sense that they are part of the situation. They are not God-given by having the labels on the bottle, so to say, but they are given in the sense of being there, part of the situation. It is in terms of these focal images that we shall be articulate about the situation. Here are models, each of which licenses a particular brand of discourse. In other words, what I am saying is that our theology, our symbol system, is not man-made in the sense that having had some overpowering disclosure we then go to the deckchair in the garden, and wonder how to talk about it. My suggestion rather is that given in the situation itself there is some focal image. There is some reason why we should talk about the situation in certain particular terms rather than in some other. In this sense the disclosure situation has a given model, a given image, about which we can then reasonably begin to be articulate.

Let me just develop this view of models, to show its relevance to the school situation. We may suppose that the Hebrew shepherd on the hillside with his sheep often had moments of vision when, around the man's work of shepherding, God disclosed

Himself. In such a situation, the relationship between God and the shepherd would be of the same form as that between the shepherd and his sheep. When the shepherd was aware of the situation coming alive around his sheep, then – the form being repeated, the situations being isomorphous – he could speak of God in terms he would use of his sheep – 'leading them by the still waters and feeding them in the green pastures'. God could be talked about in terms of those words, supplied from an isomorphous situation. *Psalm* 23 could be articulated. And it is in this kind of way, I think, that 'shepherd' became a model for God, and licensed the extended kind of discourse we find for instance in *Ezekiel* 34. But that is not the end of the story. The pattern of Hebrew social and political life often mirrored the pattern of the sheep and shepherd. And when that happened, we may presume there was what I have elsewhere called a 'cosmic disclosure', embracing both. God talked of in terms of shepherd was linked with the social and political problems, and the hopes, of the Hebrew people. In this way 'shepherd' did provide an extremely fertile model which, based in one partic-ular situation, was used to articulate others, for it could so easily fit the social needs and political hopes of the Hebrew people.

More generally, I see theology as what could be called a multi-model discourse, made up from an inter-weaving of the various strands of discourse which develop from the various models, each of which enables us to be articulate in its own way about a vision of God, God disclosed around particular situations. But notice that here is language never final, never sacrosanct. In large measure it is, yes, a man-made construction. But it is always originating in, and licensed by, a model which is given in the situation of disclosure or revelation.

So far, then, I have tried to outline a view of theology which sees it as the constant exploration of a disclosure situation in terms of the models which those situations provide. What happens when we bring this view of theology alongside the theory and practice of education, and the context of the boarding school in particular?

I need hardly say I speak here as a spectator. I do not have the involvement that all of you here have … The intention is to bring pupils to maturity, a maturity which for the most part is seen in terms of Christian fulfilment. Now once upon a time, so to say, those aims could be translated into a clear and clearly recognizable pattern of existence, in which a boy or girl found his or her place, a place providing for development and security. Against the understanding of education I mentioned earlier, the school community spelt out a pattern of living which was, by and large, deduced from a particular theological understanding of the gospel...

I think we are moving culturally and sociologically into an era as different from the late nineteenth century and the thirties of this century as these were from pre-Renaissance times and as those were from the fourth century or ancient Rome. We have got to see our tasks and our problems today against that kind of background, against that kind of measure.

Theology, it seems to me, was from the beginning bound to be mistaken. It was never restless enough. It was not always restlessly trying to translate into human finite words and images the inspiration and mystery of an infinite vision. We have learnt slowly that what is wanted of the theologian is the labour of the pioneer, struggling with difficulties, and the devotion of the lover. Theology is the pioneering of a vision, and in so far as we give any meaning to a phrase like 'theology of education' then the structure of the school community – staff/pupil relations, character of the teaching – must reflect a common exploration. It must reflect the ideas of the pioneer and the lover, rather than be made up of communities where one person retails to many what he considers to be universal truths. It seems to me that we shall not get any satisfaction about worship until we have restructured the schools. And we shall not get better ideas of God until we have restructured the schools. This means that with problems on both sides, like the communities around them, schools are faced with radical tasks of the highest complexity. The restructuring of society, the re-ordering of worship, the restyling of theology: we have to do all these, in the boarding school and in society, at the same time. Our only hope is to move, if we can, towards creative decisions where God can once more, and will once more, reveal Himself, and lead us on in faith, as both pioneers and lovers.

By Ian T Ramsey, Bishop of Durham, from *Learning for Living* Volume 15/4, summer 1976

Faith and its expansion

Faith, as I have used the word, is a verb. Faith is a way of behaving which involves knowing, being, and willing. The content of faith is best described in terms of our worldview and value system, but faith itself is something we do. Faith is an action. It results from our actions with others, it changes and expands through our actions with others, and it expresses itself daily in our actions with others.

After reflection on my own and others' faith pilgrimages, I have been able to describe four distinctive styles of faith. This conceptualization is not original, and I was first influenced to think about a stage theory for the development of faith through the important research of my friend James Fowler. Since we began communicating, however, I have proceeded in directions for which only I can be held responsible. Nevertheless, I do need and want to acknowledge my early debt, and to suggest that Fowler's research may necessitate significant changes in my own ideas.

At this point, I am prepared to suggest that faith (understood as a way of behaving) can, if provided with the proper interactive experiences, expand through four distinctive *styles* of faith. Each style of faith to be described is a generalization, and none are meant to be boxes into which persons are placed; neither are they to be used as judgments upon ourselves or others. I have named the first style of faith, *experienced faith*; the second, *affiliative faith*; the third, *searching faith*; and the fourth, *owned faith*. I have tried many ways to describe the relationship between these styles of faith and the best I've found, though still inadequate, is drawn from the analogy of a tree.

First, a tree with one ring is as much a tree as a tree with four rings. A tree in its first year is a complete and whole tree, and a tree with three rings is not a better tree but only an expanded tree. In a similar way, one style of faith is not a better or greater faith than another. Experienced faith, the first identifiable style, is complete and whole faith. One seeks to act with other faithing selves in community and hence to expand into new styles of faith, not so as to possess better or greater faith, but only to fulfill one's faith potential.

Second, a tree grows if the proper environment is provided, and if such an environment is lacking, the tree becomes arrested in its expansion until the proper environment exists. Each tree, however, does its own 'growing' and has its own unique characteristics. Similarly, we expand from one style of faith to another only if the proper environment, experiences, and interactions are present; and if they are not, then our expansion of faith is arrested. Of course no style of faith is natural to any particular age and everyone can expand into a new style providing the proper interactions with other faithing souls is present.

Third, a tree acquires one ring at a time in a slow and gradual manner. We do not see that expansion, although we do see the results, and surely we are aware that you cannot skip rings, moving from a one-ring to a three-ring tree. The same is true of faith. We expand from one style of faith to another slowly and gradually (it cannot be rushed), adding one style at a time in an orderly process over time.

Fourth, as a tree grows, it does not eliminate rings but adds each ring to the ones before, always maintaining all the previous rings as it expands. It is the same with faith. As we expand in faith we do not leave one style of faith behind to acquire a new style but, on the contrary, each new style is added to the previous ones. We do not outgrow a style of faith and its needs but expand it by adding new elements and new needs. Indeed, if the needs of an earlier style of faith cease to be met, persons have a tendency to return to that earlier style of faith. Once, however, these needs are again satisfied persons return to their farthest expanded style of faith.

Faith is an action which includes thinking, feeling, and willing and it is transmitted, sustained, and expanded through our interactions with other faithing selves in a community of faith. To describe each style of faith is to understand the faith pilgrimage possible for us all. To those styles of faith we turn now.

Experienced faith

No one can determine another's faith and no one can give another faith, but we can be faithful and share our life and our faith with another. Others, regardless of age, can do the same with us, and through this sharing we each sustain, transmit, and expand our faith.

During the preschool and early childhood years, children typically act with 'experienced faith.' That is to say faith is first experienced enactively. To understand this style of faith we need to remember that children initiate action and respond to our actions. The child explores and tests, imagines and creates, observes and copies, experiences and reacts. Children's actions influence those with whom they interact, and the actions of others influence them. Their acts provide a mirror and a test for those with whom they interact. Not only children live by experienced faith, of course, and while this style of faith represents the earliest style, its characteristics are important and foundational to persons throughout their lives. For example, just as children need to be hugged, caressed, and stroked, so do adults. Regretfully, we seem to have forgotten that and, as a result, adolescent and adult 'skin hunger' needs are met by antisocial punching and jabbing. Basic and continuing needs are denied because we have not found socially acceptable ways to affirm hugs between persons of the same and opposite sex. Similarly, throughout our lives, we need to take seriously the needs of experienced faith and, like the child, we need to act in ways that explore and test, observe and copy, imagine and create, experience and react.

Experience is foundational to faith. A person first learns Christ not as a theological affirmation but as an affective experience. For children and adults, it is not so much the words we hear spoken that matter most, but the experiences we have which are connected with those words. Language and experience are interrelated. Experiences of trust, love, and acceptance are important to Christian faith and, regardless of age, the need is always present for experiences consistent with the meanings we attribute to our words. If a person is 'used' whenever the word love is spoken, the word love takes on that meaning for the person. A new definition can be learned, but the power of the word will be related to the experiences of the word. That explains why we are called to be doers of the word and not hearers only. As the apostle James writes: '"Here is one who claims to have faith and another who points to his deeds." To which I reply: 'Prove to me that this faith you speak of is real though not accompanied by deeds, and by my deeds I will prove to you my faith"' (2:18). We experience and express faith through our interactions with others. The meaning of our vocabulary of faith is directly related to our experience with the words spoken to express that faith.

To be concerned about others' faith is to share our faith with them in word and deed, and to permit them to share their faith with us in similar ways. We can share and respond, but the character of another person's faith cannot be determined. What we can do is provide an environment of sharing and interaction between faithing selves. The responsibility of Christian parents is to endeavor to be Christian with their children, and the responsibility of all Christians is to strive to be Christian with all others.

God makes himself known through his word – his actions. God has not waited to be discovered, but has taken the initiative and addressed his word to humankind through his deeds. In Jesus Christ, the word became flesh. God established the criteria by which we may recognize and understand the word and deed of God in many other and unexpected ways; but for Christian faith, word and deed are never separated.

Experienced faith, therefore, results from our interactions with other faithing selves. And thus the question for a parent to ask is this: What is it to be Christian with my child? To seriously address that question is to discover what sort of environments, experiences, and interactions are necessary for our own and another's life in faith. To live with others in Christian ways, to put our words into deeds and our deeds into words, to share life with another, to be open to influence as well as to influence, and to interact with other faithing selves in a community of Christian faith is to provide the necessary environment for experienced faith.

Affiliative faith

If the needs of experienced faith have been adequately met during the childhood and early adolescent years, persons may begin to adopt an affiliative style of faith. During this period persons seek to act with others in an accepting community with a clear sense of identity. All of us need to feel that we belong to a self-conscious community and that through our active participation can make a contribution to its life. Persons with affiliative faith need to participate in the community's activities – for example, serving at a fellowship supper, singing in the choir, having a part in the Christmas pageant, participating in a service project, belonging to a group in the church where they know everyone's name and they are missed when absent. Of crucial importance is the sense that we are wanted, needed, accepted, and important to the community. The character of our actions may change with age, but all of us need to feel that we belong to a community and have opportunities to act like someone who truly belongs.

I recall a young man describing his faith pilgrimage and explaining that one of his most significant experiences was in the year that he didn't go to church school but instead read comics, collected the offering, and maintained the attendance records. Why was this experience so important? Because for the first time he felt that he belonged.

A second characteristic of affiliative faith is seen in the dominance of the religious *affections*. Some of us have forgotten or ignored the primal importance of the religion of the heart. We have become too concerned too early with the activities of thinking in Christian education, and we forget that the intuitional mode of consciousness is of equal importance with the intellectual. Indeed, in terms of faith, actions in the realm of the affections are prior to acts of thinking, which is why participation in the arts – drama, music, dance, sculpture, painting, and storytelling – are essential to faith. We need opportunities to act in ways that enhance the religious affections. Opportunities for experiencing awe, wonder, and mystery, as well as chances to sing, dance, paint, and act, are needed by us all. Events like the annual Christmas pageant *are* important. Far greater attention needs to be given to the religion of the heart and those actions that encourage the development of religious affections.

The third characteristic of affiliative faith is a sense of *authority*. What I mean by authority is a community's affirmation of a story and a way of life that judges and inspires its actions. I recall the many times our children told us that everyone else was doing something and we simply replied, 'That's fine, but that is not the Westerhoff way.' And then we would tell the story of how the Westerhoffs have acted through the years and why that way of life is important to us. Identity and authority go hand-in-hand.

The church must constantly be aware of its story and its way. We need to hear and tell that story, and we need to act so as to internalize it as our story. Child-centered and life-centered education have sometimes forgotten that the story or tradition is of central importance. While faith is first experienced enactively, it is next experienced in images or stories. Learning the community's story is, therefore, an essential for faith.

Throughout our lives, but particularly in the childhood and early adolescent years, we need to belong to and participate in an identity-conscious community of faith. We need to act in ways that nurture our religious affections. And we need to act to internalize, rehearse, and personally own the story which undergirds the community's faith.

Searching faith

Providing that the needs of affiliative faith have been met some time during late adolescence, persons may expand into searching faith. Searching faith also has three characteristics. First, there is the action of doubt and/or critical judgment. Sometimes painful and sometimes celebrative, those with searching faith need to act over against the understanding of faith acquired earlier. We seem to know this, at least in terms of adolescent family behavior, but we have neglected it when considering faith. For example, my teenagers sometimes think I am quite stupid and misguided. And while that is not easy to live with, it is important for them to believe it in order to acquire their own identity. The same is true of faith. In order to move from an understanding of faith that belongs to the community to an understanding of faith that is our own, we need to doubt and question that faith. At this point the 'religion of the head' becomes equally important with the 'religion of the heart,' and acts of the intellect, critical judgment, and inquiry into the meanings and purposes of the story and the ways by which the community of faith lives are essential. Serious study of the story, and engagement with historical, theological, and moral thinking about life become important. The despairs and doubts of the searching soul need to be affirmed and persons need to join others in the intellectual quest for understanding.

A second characteristic of searching faith is *experimentation*. Searching faith requires that we explore alternatives to our earlier understandings and ways, for people need to test their own tradition by learning about others. It is only then that they are able to reach convictions which are truly their own.

And third, searching faith embodies the need to *commit* our lives to persons and causes. Persons with searching faith sometimes appear fickle, giving their lives to one ideology after another, sometimes in rapid succession and on occasion in contradiction. But that is how we learn commitment. How can we know what it means to give our life away until we have learned how to do it? It appears, regretfully, that many adults in the church have never had the benefit of an environment which encouraged searching faith. And so they are often frightened or disturbed by adolescents who are struggling to enlarge their affiliative faith to include searching faith. Some persons are forced out of the church during this state and, sadly, some never return; others remain in searching faith for the rest of their lives. In any case, we must remember that persons with searching faith still need to have all the needs of experienced and dependent faith met, even though they may appear to have cast them aside. And surely they need to be encouraged to remain within the faith community during their intellectual struggle, experimentation, and first endeavours at commitment.

Owned faith

Providing that the needs of searching faith have been met some time in early adulthood, we may expand into an owned style of faith. This movement from experienced and affiliative faith through searching faith to owned faith is what historically has been called conversion. Conversion experiences may be sudden or gradual, dramatic or undramatic, emotional or intellectual, but they always involve a major change in a person's thinking, feeling, and willing – in short, in their total behavior. Due to the serious struggle with doubt that precedes it, owned faith often appears as a great illumination or enlightenment, but in any case it can be witnessed in our actions and new needs. Now people most want to put their faith into personal and social action, and they are willing and able to stand up for what they believe, even against the community of their nurture.

Typically, persons owned by their faith strive to *witness* to that faith in both word and deed. They struggle to eliminate any dissonance between their faith as stated in their beliefs and their actions in the world. The words of St. John: 'Whoever claims to be dwelling in Christ, binds himself to live as Christ lived' (1 John 2:6), confront them with a new challenge. Persons with owned faith want and need the help and support of others in sustaining and in putting their faith to work. Of course, remember, the characteristics of searching faith are never eliminated, doubt and intellectual struggle continue but are dealt with in new ways. Still liberation, wholeness of life, spiritual health, and identity are known and persons can live a life in but not of the world. The radical demands of the Gospel can now be met.

Owned faith, personal identity, is God's intention for every person. To reach owned faith (our full potential) is a long pilgrimage in which we need to be provided with an environment and experiences that encourage us to act in ways that assist our expansion of faith. Let us never forget, however, that while the fulfillment of our potential ought to be the aim of all faithing selves, Christ died for us all, and no matter what style of faith we possess none are outside his redeeming grace.

We who are engaged in the church's educational ministry need to commit ourselves to helping each other fulfill our potential as corporate faithing selves, possessed by the Gospel and living according to its radical demands in the world. To do so we need to provide the experiences and environments which encourage those interactions necessary for the expansion of faith. However, it would be well to remember that these styles of faith are not to be used so much to design educational programs for others as to help each of us to understand our personal faith pilgrimage, establish our own needs, and seek interactive experiences with others so we might sustain and expand our own faith. Still, we need to realize that such efforts will contribute to the expansion of others' faith.

Conclusions

While these four styles of faith, characteristic of the faith pilgrimage of Christians, are important to understand if we are to take seriously enculturation as the means of Christian education, a few comments are in order before I proceed to discuss the implications of this understanding for the educational program of the church.

First, if we take seriously the styles of faith and faith's expansion, we must conclude that no single educational program for any age-group is valid. Consider adolescents in college (the group I know best). Some enter college ready to act with searching faith and we find them enrolled in college religion courses where the intellectual approach to the Bible and faith meets their needs. The chapel program with its experimental worship services, or even adventures into alternatives such as Zen Buddhist meditation, appeal to them. The college chaplain, who in the name of some ideology calls them to commitment, attracts their devotion and energy. However, there is another group of college students who have never had the needs of affiliative faith satisfactorily met and obviously are not found at the chapel or in religion courses. Instead, they are attracted to various Christian groups which emphasize belonging, the religion of the heart, and the authority of the story. These students will give hours to social service projects and they will talk about their beliefs, but little time is devoted to radical social action. Typically, they consider the religion faculty to be atheists and the chaplain in need of conversion. Conversion, in this case, is understood as the kind of dramatic, sudden, emotional experience many of them experienced as their transition into affiliative faith. We must not depreciate the importance of these students' faith pilgrimage, but rather we should celebrate their expanded faith and support them in their continuing quest.

We also need to be aware that few adults have owned faith, and that is why it is difficult to involve many adults in radical community and social action. Typically, adults have had their faith arrested in the affiliative style. In every church, therefore, a variety of educational environments and experiences that make possible the expansion of faith is needed. Remember, we can never offer a single educational program for all adults or all youth.

A second implication: While we need to provide experiences for each style of faith, we also need to provide experiences that help persons move from one style of faith to another. Such a movement is naturally made possible when life presents us with situations we cannot resolve satisfactorily through actions consistent with our present style of faith, and when we are presented with role models of persons acting more satisfactorily in an expanded style of faith.

Expansion of faith can also be aided or retarded by the community's rites of transition. Typically, for example, we have placed confirmation, which asks for a personal commitment of faith and a commitment to discipleship in the world, at the age when persons need to be encouraged to doubt, question, and experiment. The effect appears to be the arresting of faith. Perhaps confirmation should be moved to early adulthood and a new early adolescent rite celebrated on St. Thomas Day developed. This rite should encourage persons to make a covenant with God and the church and to struggle with their faith as Jacob wrestled with the angels.

If we were to take such insights seriously, we would involve ourselves and others in an educational ministry centered on experiences of interaction between and among persons according to their faith needs. For example, in the preschool and early childhood years we would encourage children to experience the word of God by interacting with those who are striving to be Christian with them through shared experiences. The rite of baptism could initiate persons into this style of faith and prebaptismal preparation for expectant parents could enable them to act in ways helpful to those in experienced faith. First communion during first or second grade could initiate a person into affiliative faith. Intergenerational experiences (in a belonging community where the story is expressed, owned, and known) through participation in the arts could frame the church's educational ministry during the childhood and early adolescent years. The Sunday school (at least as it was understood in the nineteenth century) could provide a structure for such experiences between and among children, youth, and adults of all ages.

At some point in early adolescence we need a ritual to affirm persons in searching faith. As such, this ritual should encourage actions which emphasize the importance of intellectual inquiry and interpretation, bless the existential struggle with doubt, support experimentation with alternative understandings and ways, and facilitate commitment to persons and causes. Spiritual life retreats, short-term interest groups, small intensive study groups, and a variety of interactions in and outside the church between adolescents and adults with owned faith are needed to support searching faith. Confirmation is best saved for early adulthood. Extensive (one or two years) and intensive activities are needed to prepare persons for this important initiation into owned faith. Next come experiences and interactions based upon action-reflection or the implication of Christian faith for individual and social life...

To conclude, when we make enculturation the means of Christian education, we turn to faith. That is, we consider its nature and character and the sorts of experiences and interactions, between and among persons within a community of faith, which encourage and support the expansion of faith. Specific activities and resources may not be easily identified, but at least we can be sure that we are struggling with the right questions. Namely: what is it to be Christian together? How can we live our individual and corporate lives under the judgment and inspiration of the Gospel to the end that God's community is come and God's will is done? What can I bring to share with another as a believer in Christ and a member of his church? What are Christian understandings and ways, and how can we express and experience them with others? How can we be open to one another so that as faithing selves in community we might all expand in our faith?

Answers to such questions will not be simple or easy, but they are at the heart of our educational mission and ministry, and they hold some vital resolutions as to whether or not our children will have faith.

From *Will Our Children Have Faith?*, J H Westerhoff, Harper and Row, 1976

A Christian understanding of childhood

Our ideas about what it means to be a Christian relate mostly to adult models. Adults of almost every Christian tradition assume that belonging to the Church is a matter of believing certain things and doing certain things. But the things to believe are mostly things only adults can understand, the things to do are mostly things only adults can do. So these adult categories of faith and conduct do not provide a suitable theological framework for interpreting the place of the child in the church. Childhood requires a theology of its own. This does not mean that there is a different gospel for children, any more than there is a different gospel for women, it does mean that just as we seek to include in a predominantly masculine theology the feminine, so we must include childhood. The task of a theology of childhood is to express a distinctively Christian understanding of the nature and status of childhood. Our concern here is not with what children are to believe and do about Christian faith, but how the Christian faith is to estimate the significance of the child. Too much of our theology has been concerned with an estimation of the male, and especially the adult male...

In the light of the Incarnation, childhood can no longer be regarded as merely a provisional and preparatory episode. The childhood of Jesus does not allow the Church any under-standing of childhood that measures the child by what, not yet being an adult, he lacks. Jesus was a child. This forbids our begin-ning exclusively with some definition of what a Christian should be in terms of what a Christian *adult* should be and then plan-ning only *what* must be done to turn the child into the man. Our theology of childhood concentrates on the 'continuous now' of the child's life, just as we emphasize the 'now' of the adult's life, without neglecting what the child and the adult will some day become. A child at any age may be wholly human and wholly God's. Because Christ was a child, a child can be a Christian...

Children are a gift to the Church. The Lord of the Church sets them in the midst of the Church, today as in Galilee, not as objects of benevolence nor even as recipients of instruction, but in the last analysis as patterns of discipleship. The Church that does not accept children unconditionally into its fellowship is depriving those children of what is rightfully theirs, but the deprivation such a Church will itself suffer is far more grave...

Not to nurture a child in the tradition of his family is to deny him that part of his self-hood which should be given to him. It is to deny him the past, which is his own past, out of which his creation of his own unique selfhood should take place. But if a child is nurtured so as to give him not only his past but his future as well, to determine his future beyond his own power of changing it or creating it, then that part of his personhood which should be his own achievement is denied him. This is one of the most important principles of a truly Christian nurture – to give the past but not to close the future...

The task of the nurturing community

The task of Christian nurture must be seen not only in domestic terms, as something taking place within the families and gener-ations of the Church, but also within the larger context of the Church's universal mission to humanity. The mission of the Church is God's mission. It is the initiative of God towards mankind. The task of the Church is to discover and respond to the mission of God. The Church is certainly not the only agency of divine mission nor are the present, visible, Christian communities the goal of the mission. The image of the Church as the body of Christ could be misleading, because it might suggest that the only access of God through Christ to the world is through the visible Christian Churches. The task of the Church would then be seen as multiplying itself and so 'spreading' the incarnation. But then Christian nurture could easily be thought of as being nothing but religious socialization, inducting the young into the life of the institutionalised churches. Christian nurture should however enable young people (and their elders) to recognise the mission of God wherever He may be active in our world, and to participate in it. It is even possible that thorough socialization into the life of a local church, with perhaps limited horizons and merely parochial interests, might actually hinder young people in responding to God's universal mission...

The Christian way is not something fixed and unchanging. A living way is not a way that never changes, but one which remains true to itself. The mark of a living tradition is not immutability but continuity. Christian growth is thus not a matter of simply taking over the tradition, or of swallowing what it offers us, but rather of *responding* to what is offered. As we grasp it, make it our own, it does something to us. But at the same time *we* do something to *it,* as we interpret it to meet our own needs, and as we put to it the questions which face us now. We become new people by walking in the Christian way, but the way itself is continually renewed by those who walk in it...

If we continue to present the bible to children we ought to examine carefully our motives for doing so. Bible teaching is often given, not because it really helps the child's understanding, but because it makes the teacher feel better. The teacher tells a bible story, and tells it well, and feels a great sense of satisfaction, a conviction that something must have been achieved. This is to assume that bible teaching is somehow self-justifying, an end in itself. But the aim of presenting biblical material is to increase Christian understanding. Where understanding can be more readily promoted by other means, we must cheerfully adopt them...

Nurture for decision
It is all too easy to think of Christian nurture in protective terms, shielding the child from certain experiences and influences and

ensuring others, so that at the end of the tunnel a permanent place in the Christian community is assured.

The aim of Christian nurture, however, is to enable the child in the end to face a radical challenge. The nurturer must have a real choice in mind: belief or disbelief. This choice initially is presented as part of the child's own development when in early adolescence ability to handle abstract ideas enables him to refine his beliefs by critical examination. It is often pointed out that just as the emergence of religious insights become a real possibility, negative attitudes engendered by previous religious upbringing lead to hostility and rejection.

However smooth the passage from birth to adult life, there can be no real personal belief in any depth until it can be called '*my* belief', and this pre-supposes a proper questioning of what has been received. Christian nurture must prepare for this and not try to avoid it...

Nurture as response must have three things in mind.

(a) Experience

The structuring of experience is part of the process of Christian nurture, but the illumination of that experience into an awareness of God's presence is the activity of grace. This is something we cannot teach, and our nurture patterns must be sensitive to children's religious sensitivity so that the gifts of wonder and awe are preserved. Too often we impose our experience patterns and prevent children from finding their own knowledge of God.

(b) World events

If we believe God is pressing in upon us in the events of our time, nurture must prepare us for understanding the events of history. As the prophets related their understanding of God's purpose in history to the events of their time, so must we. This is not an individual function outside the context of the Christian community, but a community function which all share. It is essential for understanding and participating in the Church's mission.

(c) Personal ethics

The area of moral decision-making is also an area of personal response for which Christian nurture must prepare. It is as we are motivated by our belief in Christ, and as we take our knowledge of him and all his insights about the nature of our humanity into our human relationships that we respond to

God's disclosure in Jesus Christ. This is not experienced as a private opinion but happens within the context of the Christian community, yet the decision is personal and constitutes our response. It is not a question of obeying fixed rules, but of responding in given situations as we bring Christian insights to bear on our human behaviour...

Implications for the life and structure of the local church

If Christian nurture is taken seriously, the whole life of the Church must be reappraised. Questions must be asked about its essential ethos and the relationships which form it. Is this a community which proclaims in action the faith of which it speaks in words? How is the stranger, adult or child, received? What natural groupings exist and is there communication between them or could they be described as cliques? How much is this community aware of the real needs of those around it and within it?

Nurturing includes the offering of security and community tradition, but it should not do this to the exclusion of independent or even revolutionary thought and action. To be able to question the norms of the Christian community without breaking the relationship is of prime importance. Children will achieve this balance if in the community where they feel most accepted and at home they find adults who question traditional ways and are capable of responding to new situations with novel actions.

From *The Child in the Church*, a report of the Consultative Group on Ministry among Children, a network of the British Council of Churches, 1976. Part 2, *Understanding Christian Nurture*, was added in 1981. (See the next chapter.)

Let the Children Come to Me
The Story Behind Mark 10:13–16

Whatever meaning was given to the term 'prophet', the crowd met in Jesus an extraordinary rabbi, a divine man. No wonder, therefore, that children were brought to him so that He might touch them.

There was a custom of children asking for the blessing of famous rabbis, just as sons and daughters went to their father to be blessed. In *Soferim*, one of the late minor tracts which are included in some editions of the *Talmud*, the following information is given: 'It was a beautiful custom in Jerusalem to make the little children, boys and girls, fast on the fast-day (that is, on the Day of Atonement), those who were a year old until daybreak, the twelve-year-olds till evening, and then carry or lead them to the elders (the scribes) for them to bless them, strengthen (that is, exhort) and pray for them, that they might one day attain to knowledge of the *Torah* and to good works' (*Soferim* 18.5). As with most rabbinic writings, one can no more ascertain how far back the oral tradition concerning this information reaches. It is quite possible that, in Jesus' day, this custom already existed and that it was followed not only in Jerusalem, but also in the cities and villages of Galilee. One could imagine, therefore, that the scene described in Mark 10:13 ff. happened on the evening of a Day of Atonement, although this is far from certain. If so, it is most revealing to compare what Jesus did and said on that occasion with what is reported about blessing by the elders.

The children were not only brought to be blessed. According to Mark's and Luke's account, they were brought 'that He may touch them'. This request probably meant more than the customary blessing. In the four gospels, almost all of the more than 30 occurrences of the verb 'to touch' are found in stories where Jesus heals lepers, the blind or the sick. The healing touch of this prophet from Nazareth must have become proverbial. Even healthy people expected a special benediction from Jesus' touch, and therefore children were brought to him. Yet the disciples would not let it happen, which provoked Jesus' indignation.

This is the only place in the whole New Testament where it is written that Jesus was indignant. Jesus could be deeply moved (Mark 1:41). He sometimes would sternly rebuke someone (Mark 1:43) or even be full of anger (Mark 3:5). But here, He is indignant, and in his indignation Jesus addresses himself to quite another group than his disciples had expected.

The evangelists do not tell who brought the children. Christian artists usually depict mothers, carrying babies in their arms (Luke in fact writes about *brephē*, the Greek term for babies) together with elder children led by their mother's hand. However, none of the three parallel accounts of the evangelists mentions any women, and the presence of women in the gospels is usually specially emphasized. The children came probably with their fathers or more likely with their elder brothers and sisters. These were rebuked by the disciples.

Again, the evangelists do not specify why the disciples felt it necessary to hinder the children from coming. Were these children ritually unclean? Did the disciples, as typical Jews of their time, consider children too insignificant to take up the time and attention of their master? Was their intention to resist an almost magic belief in the power of the prophet's touch? We do not know. We can be certain, however, that the disciples were astonished about their master's reaction. Instead of being indignant with those who brought the children Jesus became indignant with his well-meaning disciples!

Earlier Peter had been put straight in a similarly harsh manner. When Jesus had announced his coming suffering and death, Peter rebuked his master, presumably advising him not to go the way of the cross. Yet this rebuke was immediately returned: Jesus 'rebuked Peter, and said, "Get behind me, Satan! For you are not on the side of God, but of men"' (Mark 8:33). This was followed up with an important teaching about discipleship. Just as during that crucial conversation near Caesarea Philippi the disciples were not 'on God's side' and had therefore to be taught the true way of discipleship, so it happened now when they hindered the children from coming to him. The whole sequence of events recalls yet another incident where, again, the disciples did not perceive what really mattered and had to be taught through a meaningful gesture and word: In the house of Simon the leper at Bethany a woman came with an alabaster jar of very costly ointment. She broke that jar in order to anoint Jesus. In this case, some of the bystanders, presumably the disciples, became indignant and they reproached the woman (Mark 14:3–5). Yet, just as during the incident with the children, Jesus intervened with literally the same command: 'Let be!' (in Greek *aphete*), 'Let her alone; why do you trouble her? ... She has anointed my body beforehand for burying. And truly, I say to you, wherever the Gospel is preached in the whole world, what she has done will be told in memory of her' (Mark 14:6–9). Indeed, it is in such extraordinary actions and sayings in the midst of everyday scenes of life with seemingly unimportant people like women and children that the very core of the Gospel is revealed.

A prophetic word and act

It is difficult to know exactly what Jesus said when children were brought to him. Mark, Matthew and Luke almost totally agree with regard to the first saying which fits in very well with what had been told so far: 'Let the children come to me, do not hinder them; for to such belongs the Kingdom of God' (Mark 10:14). Matthew then immediately concludes the passage by briefly referring to Jesus' gesture of the laying on of hands. Mark and Luke add another saying of Jesus which interrupts the main line of thought. The passage speaks about Jesus' attitude to children and their relationship to God's Kingdom. The saying of Mark 10:15, however, refers figuratively to the children as an example in discipleship. Moreover, Matthew has used another version of presumably the same saying in the context of a different passage where Jesus does in fact present a child as an example of discipleship (Matt. 18:3). A similar saying of Jesus is reported by John in yet another context (John 3:3, 5). Jesus may, of course, have taught his disciples on different occasions that in order to enter the Kingdom one must receive it like a child. However, He was too good a teacher to make two different points on one and the same occasion. If one attempts to replace the story behind Mark 10:13–16 in its original setting, it is advisable to leave out the second saying of Jesus (Mark 10:15), which was probably inserted later from another context.

With regard to Jesus' actions, we can be almost certain that Mark reports what actually happened. Not all interpreters would agree with this statement. Some believe that the earliest Church originally knew only a saying of Jesus concerning the children (Mark 10:14b, possibly a further development of the saying in Mark 9:37). According to them, it was the Church which, during the period of oral transmission, created for this saying the context of the scene in which the disciples rebuke those who want to bring children to Jesus (Mark 10:13–14a). That incident should not, then, be understood as something which actually happened, but rather as an ideal scene, a biographical note to introduce the saying of Jesus. The same interpreters also believe that Mark later added the end of the story (Mark 10:16).

Contrary to the above understanding of how the story grew, it seems much more likely that the scene, the first saying of Jesus and his actions belonged together from the beginning. Jesus lived and taught in an oral culture, where actions and sayings went together. It was in this way that the Old Testament prophets announced God's will. Similarly, during his last supper, Jesus taught the disciples with both actions and words (John 13:1–20; Mark 14:22–25). He did so earlier, too, when children were brought to him. In all these cases, the deeds are more than mere illustrations of the sayings, and the words much more than explanations of the deeds. In different, yet complementary ways, the two together communicate the message.

Those who brought the children wanted Jesus to touch them. He did so, although the ominous verb 'to touch' is not used again at the end of the story. In fact, the way in which Jesus spoke to the children and sought physical contact with them, far surpassed what was expected, and must therefore have astonished both the disciples and those who had brought the children.

Having set his disciples straight, Jesus made a surprising announcement. In the original setting, He probably did not say: 'To people who are like such children belongs the Kingdom of God'. In this case, the children would serve as a metaphor. Jesus did sometimes use such figurative language with regard to children... Moreover, from the time of Mark onwards, the evangelists have indeed understood Jesus' sayings in this metaphorical way. However, in the original setting, Jesus referred to the actual children which were brought to him. The original Aramaic must therefore have said: 'To these and other such children belongs the Kingdom of God.'

Some interpreters have wondered whether Jesus wanted to say thereby that these children would witness the establishment of God's Kingdom. Would these boys and girls under 13 be the generation of the last times, those 'who will not taste death before they see that the Kingdom of God has come with power' (Mark 9:1)? Nothing in the text itself suggests such a reference to future events. On the contrary, the saying and the actions which followed immediately afterwards confirm that Jesus spoke about a present reality. On the evening of the Day of Atonement, a rabbi might have blessed the children and exhorted them to go to school and learn diligently, so that some time in the future they might know the *Torah* and be enabled to do good works. Jesus also blessed the children. He gave a sermon as well, although that was not addressed to the children, but to the adults. At that very moment, the children received the greatest gift possible, the Kingdom of God, which is both a present and a future reality.

Jesus immediately symbolized this gift by taking the children in his arms. The Greek term used for this occurs only twice in the New Testament, and both times with regard to children (Mark 10:16 and Mark 9:36). It recalls the scene in which Simeon took up the child, Jesus, in his arms (Luke 2:28) and when, in the parable of the two sons, the father embraced and kissed the prodigal son who had returned home. In the story about the children, this gesture of tenderness and protection becomes the counterpart to the indignation of Jesus. There is more than a magic touch here. The symbolic action is deeply significant. According to a rabbinic treatise, the resurrection of the people of Israel will happen when 'God embraces them, presses them to his heart and kisses them, thus bringing them into the life of the world to come' (*Seder Elijahu Rabba* 17). Something like that has happened to the children. They who received the Kingdom were embraced by the messianic king.

How did the children merit such a reception? Absolutely no condition is made. The children have not yet reached even 'the age of the Law', and they therefore have no merit. Nothing is said about their innocence, their childlike confidence or any other such qualities. If anything is suggested at all in the text, it is the children's helplessness and weakness, for they must be brought to Jesus. But the main point of Jesus' prophetic words and action does, not lie here. What He intended to teach was not something about the nature of children. Rather, He wanted to reveal the nature of God. God's will is to present the children with his Kingdom, and against all human calculation this is done in a totally gratuitous way. Thus, children are counted among the poor in spirit who have been called blessed because 'theirs is the Kingdom of Heaven' (Matt. 5:3). It has pleased God to do so, without any reasons being given. His love for children is as 'unreasonable' as the generosity of the steward in the parable of the labourers in the vineyard (Matt. 20:1–20).

This gratuitous love of God, assured to the children in Jesus' prophetic words and action, turns upside down both Greek and Jewish classifications. Children receive a place of preeminence, if human realities are considered from the point of view of God's Kingdom.

From *Jesus and the Children*, H-R Weber, World Council of Churches, 1979

1980s
Faith Development

or forty years much of the emphasis in church education had been on the experience of the child in the church and in society. James W Fowler struck a new note in 1981 in his *Stages of Faith: The Psychology of Human Development and the Quest for Meaning*. Jeff Astley summed up Fowler's work:

> Faith development is a controversial phrase which refers to a controversial theory ... Faith development theory is controversial for three main reasons. First, it greatly broadens our usual idea of faith. For Fowler, *faith is universal* ... Faith isn't just for the religious ... 'The opposite of faith', Fowler writes, 'is not doubt. Rather, the opposite of faith is nihilism.' ... Secondly, Fowler's theory is contentious in concentrating on *the form, rather than the content of faith.* [Many people are interested in what people believe.] Fowler, on the other hand, has as his focus of research the ways in which we have faith, the *how* of faith... The third main area of controversy is Fowler's claim that *the form of faith develops...* Fowler argues that the way we hold our faith can pass through up to six stages. At each stage we 'faith' differently. *[See page 224 for a note on some of Astley's work on Fowler.]*

From *Learning in the Way: Research and Reflection on Adult Christian Education*, J Astley, Gracewing, 2000

From this brief summary it is clear that Fowler's work was no help to those concerned with catechesis. It was and is valuable to Christian educators though major questions remain: why do some people fail to move on from one stage to another, and why do some regress? What difference would it make if instead of teaching and experiencing at the earlier stages, Christian education and church life were conducted at stages five and six?

Again, though it happened only gradually, the content and style of teaching had to be reappraised. Meanwhile the emphasis on the place of children in the church had led to serious discussion in many churches about the place of the child in the celebration of the Eucharist or Holy Communion. Traditionally, the receiving of bread and wine had been reserved for confirmed members of the church who were usually older children, teenagers or adults. Now the voices of children were being raised and the significance of baptism as the entry into the church and as the most meaningful ordination was on the ecumenical agenda.

The report of a World Council of Churches consultation, *And do not hinder them...*, strongly supported the case for children being active participants in the Eucharist. Children had contributed to the Consultation by writing letters, which in many cases were both deeply perceptive and imaginative about their experience and their under-standing of receiving bread and wine. For instance, a nine-year-old Spanish boy had explained in a long letter what he meant by his phrase, 'communion is going with God to meet him'. And a ten-year-old Scot wrote, 'It seems wonderful when a silence falls between everybody in church. The candles spread light so brightly that it almost reminds me of stars on a dark night. When I go up onto the altar it gives me a feeling of gladness, something may have come into the world that hasn't been here before.' The discussion of the place of children in the Church was also taken further by the advocacy of 'all-age worship' in a Church of England Report, *Children in the Way* (1988), and in 'an ecumenical consideration' of *Children and Holy Communion* published by the British Council of Churches' Consultative Group on Ministry among Children in 1989.

One of the dominant themes of the 1980s – part of the teasing out of the implications of earlier insights and developing practice – was that everyone in the Church who held an office, and particularly those working with children and young people, needed appropriate training for the undertaking of specific responsibilities. There was nothing new in the principle; it had been adopted as Methodist Church policy as a result of Youth Department proposals to Conference in 1970. These required all children's and youth workers to submit themselves for a Pastoral Assessment and serve a proba-tionary period of service and training spread over a twelve-month period. Nonetheless, it seemed that the adult Christian population was not eager to learn; questions need only be asked about how adults understood the text of the Gospel for it to become evident that most had heard little or nothing of the biblical scholarship of the past hundred years. In 1985, John Hull asked *What Prevents Christian Adults From Learning?*, and more optimistically Rhoda Hiscox published *Eager to Learn* in 1986. In *Learning and Teaching Together* (Chester House Publications, 1980), I argued that all in the Church, not children only, are learners and teachers: 'In the personal process of finding and maintaining faith and in thinking in a Christian way about living, we are helped by the experience, wisdom, insight, questions, criticism and faithfulness of the whole community.' But I also had to admit that for many adults it is not easy to 'accept the idea that in a community composed of children and adults all are teachers, as well as learners. It has been common practice to appoint adults to teach children, but not the reverse. Sometimes the contribution of adolescents to the church is recognised... But it has not been supposed they have much to teach the church.' (pages 25–26)

The Church's understanding of its creative place in local communities continued to develop (not least provoked by the then Prime Minister's aggressive individualism). Jeff Astley's *A Manual For Action* and *Community Development: Towards a National Perspective* were both published in 1982. The eighties saw the introduction of inclusive language into hymnody, liturgy and Bible readings and, in a minority of churches, into conversation. This led also to a new sensitivity about the role models, and implicit presuppositions about roles, to which girls were exposed.

In the early 1980s there was a reappraisal of the place of story in Christian and religious education, and in 1986 Collins published *Our Faith Story* by Patrick Purnell, with a welcoming foreword by Bishop David Konstant, on behalf of the Department of Christian Doctrine and Formation of the Roman Catholic Church. In the Introduction Purnell writes (he might also have referred to himself in Fowler's terms, as learning to faith differently):

> I came to realise that faith sharing required first of all discernment, a sensitivity to the divine. My task was not to give God to anybody but to help people discover God within themselves as the life-giving and love-giving source of their existence ... my understanding of truth was something that was in the process of growing ... My faith was evolving; I was a pilgrim on the journey of faith. There was no way I could write except within this context.

Purnell begins by telling his own story and sharing his own faith: story is his model. But there are stories which are not faith stories but can still be explored as a source of meaning and purpose – as a theological mine. Children will not develop self-understanding, vision, and faith, and personal and social consciousness by reading only information books or working at a computer. They need the stimulation of ideas and interactions. David Ford, then a lecturer in theology at the University of Birmingham, made a particularly creative contribution by pointing up how story worked at three levels.

Christian religious education, like all education, is a complex enterprise, and no description of it will ever be exhaustive. Statements of its purpose, context, and so on will come later; here I am attempting to name only the nature of this activity as it is carried on in an historical context. Christian religious education is *a political activity with pilgrims in time that deliberately and intentionally attends with them to the activity of God in our present, to the Story of the Christian faith community, and to the Vision of God's Kingdom, the seeds of which are already among us.*

In that description the specificity of what Christian religious educators do derives from the Christian communities' Story, with its primordial expression in Jesus Christ, and the Vision of God's completed Kingdom to which the Story gives rise. But perhaps the most important point for attention is my claim that Christian religious education participates in the political nature of education in general. If few educators advert to the political nature of their educating, Christian religious educators are even more reluctant to recognize the political implications of our activity. The standard argument for refusing to admit such implications arises from the classical (Greek) distinction between the secular and the religious, and more recently from the Enlightenment distinction between the citizen and the individual (Rousseau). When these distinctions are accepted as accurate 'religion' is confined to the private sector, and thus religious educators are to intervene in the lives of individuals to influence them only in 'spiritual' matters, not in social ones.

But the dichotomies at the base of this argument are false. Any kind of educational activity, either immediately or ultimately, influences people in how they live their lives in society. Educational activity of any kind can never have only 'private' consequences, since the individual and the citizen are the same person. Nor can a Christian spirituality ever be 'private'. Far from denying the spiritual task of Christian religious education, I will later argue at length for its importance. If religious educators promote a spirituality that ignores responsibility for the world, they are not promoting a Christian spirituality (nor a Jewish one either). The heart of a Christian spirituality must flow from the heart of the Christian vocation which is to lead a life of *agape* – loving God by loving our neighbor. Love of neighbor is essentially antithetical to a privatized spirituality. Thus Christian religious education, precisely by proposing a spirituality which is Christian, is being political, that is, intervening in people's lives to influence them in how they live out their temporality in social relationships.

When Christian religious educators dichotomize the spiritual/religious from the social/political, we fall into a false dichotomy. Even if a religious community should set itself the task of confining its educational activity to the 'spiritual' in a narrow private sense, it is actually performing a political act, but it is the politics of silence, of nonengagement. By what we reclaim from our past heritage or propose for our future, by what we ignore from our past and refuse for our future, Christian religious educators are being political. We have no choice about whether or not Christian education will have political implications. It is inevitably political and our choice is about the direction in which we should shape the future of society by our present engagement as Christians within it...

Prologue

The first Christians told a story about the risen Christ that Christian educators would do well to remember. It is recounted by the evangelist Luke (24:13–35).

The story goes that on the first Easter Sunday two of Jesus' followers were making their way to Emmaus, a small village about seven miles from Jerusalem. As they went their way, they discussed 'all that had happened' (14) over the previous days, and, as might be expected, it was a 'lively exchange' (15). Who should join them but the risen Jesus, who began 'to walk along *with* them' (15). For whatever reason, they were 'restrained from recognizing him' (16). He entered into their company by inquiring, 'What are you discussing as you go your way?' (17). Somewhat distressed and a little impatient at the stranger's ignorance, they wondered where he had been. Surely everyone in Jerusalem knew 'the things that went on there these past few days?' (18). Rather than seizing this obvious opportunity to disclose his identity (Who knew better than he what had gone on there?), he inquired 'What things?' (19). They told him the story as they knew it and their dwindling hope that 'he was the one who would set Israel free' (21). Now, adding confusion to their disappointment, 'some women' (22) of the group were spreading the 'astonishing news' (22) that 'he was alive' (23).

Jesus cajoled them for not looking at these recent events within a broader context, and in response to their story and hope he told them an older Story and a larger Vision. 'Beginning, then, with Moses and all the prophets, he interpreted for them every passage of Scripture which referred to him' (27). He pointed out that the Messiah had to 'undergo all this so as to enter into his glory' (26). Surely now they would recognize him. They did not, and he continued to resist telling them. But he had obviously aroused their curiosity, for they 'pressed him' (29) to stay the night in their company. He agreed.

At table that evening he blessed and broke bread for them and 'with that their eyes were opened and they recognized him; whereupon he vanished from their sight' (31). Then the pieces of their puzzle fell in place, and they remembered how their hearts had 'burned' inside them as he talked 'on the road.' But instead of spending time in self-reproach for not seeing sooner, they set out immediately for Jerusalem (a hazardous journey by night) to tell 'the Eleven and the rest of the company' (33). They told the story of what had happened 'on the road' and 'how they had come to know him in the breaking of bread' (35).

This story has been much commented on by biblical exegetes and interpreters. I offer an educator's reflection. I see the risen Christ portrayed here as the educator par excellence. He begins by encountering and entering into dialogue with the two travellers. Rather than telling them what he knows, he first has them tell the story of their recent experience and what their hopes had been. In response he recalls a larger Story of which their story is part, and a broader Vision beyond what theirs had been. We might expect the typical educator to tell them now what 'to see,' but he continues to wait for them to come to their own knowing. He spends more time in their company. Surely the dialogue on the road carried over into their table conversation. Eventually, in their table fellowship together, they 'came to see.' Thereupon they set out immediately to bear witness to what they now knew.

Here the risen Christ educates by encountering, entering into dialogue, inviting people to tell their stories and visions, reminding them of a broader Story and Vision. Then still refusing to 'tell them' what to see, he waits gently for them to see for themselves. This story is a fitting memory as we begin Part IV, which suggests one possible approach to doing Christian religious education. It has been a significant influence on my thinking, and I have returned to it many times since I first began to devise such an approach.

As all educators who attempt to practice the art well know, there is no easy and sure way of doing education of any kind. Education is a human endeavor in which, to use Bonhoeffer's phrase, there is no 'cheap grace.' As Whitehead once cautioned, 'I merely utter the warning that education is a difficult problem, to be solved by no one simple formula.'

There can never be a simple formula, technique, nor 'how to do it' for education of any kind. We educators seem to have more than the usual penchant for jumping on new bandwagons that come along promising an easy solution. But easy solutions are sure to disappoint us.

In this Part, I describe a 'shared praxis approach' to Christian religious education. I shudder to think that it could be made to sound like another panacea. In my enthusiasm for it, born of some apparent success in my own praxis, I may sometimes make strong claims for its, possibilities. But I know its limitations, having experienced them, too, in my own praxis.

Some preliminary remarks about a shared praxis approach may help to avoid misunderstandings later. To begin with, the word *approach* is important. I avoid calling shared praxis a theory or a method because, in a definite sense, I intend it to be both. Attempting to avoid the traditional dichotomy between theory and practice and to capture the twin moments of praxis (reflection and action), I call it an approach – in other words, an informed reflective (theory) manner of doing (method) Christian religious education.

I also favor the term *approach* because it has the possibility of pointing toward and questioning the underlying outlook and disposition that the initiator brings to an enterprise. The educator's underlying attitude is perhaps the most crucial variable in shaping the activity of Christian religious education. Our attitude shapes, in large part, our way of being with students, and ultimately education is a way of being with people. How we perceive such foundational issues as the nature, purpose, and context of Christian religious education will decide the basic outlook we bring to the task. That attitude is decisive in determining whether we are 'with' or 'over' people in the educational setting; whether we attempt to educate as leading out people to their future possibility of union with God and each other in Christ, or whether we socialize them into a taken-for-granted world, both ecclesial and social.

If Christian religious education is to lead people out in response to the Kingdom of God in Jesus Christ toward lived Christian faith and human freedom, then our most appropriate underlying attitude is to see ourselves as brother or sister pilgrims in time *with* our students. Whether one favors a shared praxis approach or not, this underlying attitude toward ourselves and our students is most appropriate for our enterprise, however it is done.

I offer what I have come to know about a shared praxis approach because it has the possibility of responding to the nature, purpose, and context of Christian religious education as previously described. However, I hasten to add that what call a shared praxis approach is far from being a new creation *ex nihilo*. On the contrary, it arises, as it should, from my own praxis and from the praxis of many other religious educators. It comes from reflection on what many of us are already doing. In fact, shared praxis is, to some extent, a drawing together of many trends and insights that have been evident in religious education over the past eighty years. There are many shoulders on which to stand even as we attempt to reach beyond them.

To religious educators who are already doing Christian education by shared praxis, or by some variation of it, the statement here should resonate with their own experience and practice. I hope that offering a language to describe what we do and some clarity about it may enable us to be more deliberate, consistent, and effective in our educational praxis. For those who approach Christian religious education very differently, the statement should be sufficiently challenging to cause reflection on and greater clarity about why and how they educate.

The components of a shared praxis approach

Christian religious education by shared praxis can be described as *a group of Christians sharing in dialogue their critical reflection on present action in light of the Christian Story and its Vision toward the end of lived Christian faith.*

To begin with, shared praxis takes place in a situation of group dialogue. Shared in the dialogue is an articulation of critical reflection upon one's present active engagement in the world as a Christian. That present engagement is in fact the embodiment of one's own story and vision, and critical reflection upon it takes place in light of the Christian communities' Story and the response which that Story invites. This requires that the Story and its Vision be made available in the pedagogical context. The telos or end of it all is further Christian praxis that is faithful to the Story and creative of its Vision. Thus I understand there to be five main components in Christian education by shared praxis, each requiring some detailed explanation. These are: 1) present action, 2) critical reflection, 3) dialogue, 4) the Story, and 5) the Vision that arises from the Story.

Present action

Present action here means much more than the overt productive activity of the present moment. It means our whole human engagement in the world, our every doing that has any intentionality or deliberateness to it. Present action is whatever way we give expression to ourselves. It includes what we are doing physically, emotionally, intellectually, and spiritually as we live on personal, interpersonal, and social levels. In a sense, it encompasses any kind of human activity beyond the inevitable metabolic activity of our bodies.

It is this comprehensive reality of present action that is the object of critical reflection. Since the action arises from the self, the *primary* object of reflection is the self who reflects. All reflection is primarily self-reflection because when we reflect upon our activity, we are in fact reflecting upon the self that is expressed in such activity. It is only by reflection on its own objectification in action that a subject can come to appropriate himself or herself. Reflection on the self is also primary in the sense that in a praxis way of knowing one begins with one's own constitutive knowing, with how one makes meaning out of one's own present action. To begin with what 'they say' would be to fall back into a *theoria* epistemology. However ... the self is socially mediated. Thus while critical reflection is *primarily* on the self, it is *ultimately* on the social context by which the self comes to its self-identity. The whole sociocultural context, with its norms, laws, expectations, ideologies, structures, and traditions, constitutes the present action for the participants' critical reflection.

I intend the word *present* here [to mean] the present of things present, the present of things past, and the present of things future. In other words, it is the historical self and society that are reflected upon, since our present action is the consequence of our past and the shaper of our future. By reflecting on present action, we can uncover the 'pasts' that have brought us to such action, and raise to consciousness the 'futures' in that action by becoming aware of its likely or intended consequences. This is why critical reflection on our present action is a way of coming to know and name what I will call our own stories and visions.

Critical reflection

Critical reflection is an activity in which one calls upon 1) critical reason to evaluate the present, 2) critical memory to uncover the past in the present, and 3) creative imagination to envision the future in the present.

Critical Reason to Evaluate the Present. At its first level of reflection critical reason attempts to perceive what is 'obvious' about the present. Very often the obvious is so much part of our given world that it is 'taken' for granted and either no longer noticed or seen as inevitable. Critical reflection, then, is first an attempt to notice the obvious, to critically apprehend it rather than passively accept it as 'just the way things are.' This is why Freire, the most notable proponent of a praxis approach to education, often refers to himself as 'a vagabond of the obvious.'

But while critical reason begins by noticing the obvious in the present, at a deeper level of reflection it must delve below the obvious. By a critical evaluative analysis we can attempt to discover the interest in present action, critique the ideology that maintains it, and recognize the assumptions upon which it is based. This requires returning to the genesis of present action, and so we come to the role of memory.

Critical Memory to Uncover the Past in the Present. With the activity of memory critical reflection becomes a reflection upon one's reflection, a process of remembering the source of one's thinking. If critical reason is to discover the interest of present action, critique the ideology that maintains it, and recognize the assumptions upon which it is based, then the personal and social genesis of our action needs to be brought to consciousness. This is done by remembering.

The remembering cannot be a facile calling to mind. Simply to recall will do no more than maintain the influence of the past upon the present in a reified manner. Rather, *critical* memory is needed to break open the hardened shell of the past in the present, so as to prevent it from determining the present.

A critically remembered past can be a basis from which to choose the present and its future. A 'forgotten' past, on the other hand, holds unconscious sway over the present and thus limits our freedom in shaping the future. Remembering is not only a looking backward to the personal and social biographies of individual and community. It also requires a looking outward, a re-*membering* of our present action with the source of that action in its present social context. It is becoming aware of the world of which we are *members* and how that membership shapes our present action.

By critical memory, then, together with reason, we can discover the personal and social genesis of our present action. In reflecting upon the source of our activity, we come to know our own story and to name our own constitutive knowing, that is, the knowing which arises from our engagement in the world. Without this our own stories are forgotten, and the world is named for us. But critical reflection is incomplete if it rests only on reason and memory. The purpose of naming our present and knowing our story is that we may have some freedom to imagine and choose our future.

Creative Imagination to Envision the Future in the Present. Critical reflection is incomplete without imagination. Imagination is needed as we look at both the present and the past, but its predominant focus is the future. The reason we attend to the present and the past is that we may intend the future. But intending the future requires imagination; otherwise the future will be little more than repetition of the past.

The imagination I am describing here cannot be idle wonderment about the future. Rather, it must be a creative and shaping activity that gives intentionality to the future as it arises out of the present and the past. Imagination involves a refusal to duplicate what is given or to take the shape of the future as inevitable. It looks from the present to the future to envision the consequences of present action and returns from the future to shape the present in the direction of what might be preferred consequences.

In critical reflection on present action (praxis) the exercise of creative imagination is an expression of hope. Hope is what makes the real seem less real than it is, and the imagined more real than it is already. Only humankind has this ability for hope, because we alone can dream, envision, fantasize. If our educating is to promote this essential dimension of being human, then it must encourage imagination.

When education is understood as an activity of 'leading out,' the role of imagination seems even more obvious. The future thrust, essential to all education, demands imagination. But so much of our educational efforts stifle the imagination of the participants, telling them what to think and how to think it. So often what is authentic imaginative activity is dismissed as idle day dreaming or as naive idealism. We tell our students to 'grow up,' and by that we often mean 'join our world and settle for it.' But Jesus did not tell us to grow up. He told us, instead, that unless we become like little children, we cannot enter the Kingdom of God (see Mark 10:15). Little children are still capable of discovery, fantasy, and openness to what is not yet. The invitation of Jesus to become as children is, among other things, an invitation to imagination, creativity, and freedom. For education to lead out to that possibility requires imagination on the part of both students and teachers.

Critical reflection, then, requires the exercise of reason, memory, and imagination. I hasten to add that such are the predominant but not exclusive concerns of each dimension. All three are necessary for attending to the past, the present, and the future. While the focus of attention for our memories is the past, we also need to call on our reason and imagination if it is to be a critical memory that reclaims the past in a new way. In bringing reason to the present, we also need our memories to understand the genesis of the present and our imagination if we are not to settle simply for what we find there. And as we use imagination to envision the future, the images we use come out of our memory and are evaluated by our reason. In other words, a distinction among the functions of reason, memory, and imagination is valid, but a separation is false.

There are two other points about critical reflection that need clarification before we move on. The first pertains to the word *reflection* and the second to the word *critical*. Each word has the possibility of being misinterpreted.

Critical *reflection* engages both the rational and the affective capacities of the human person. In saying this, I am faithful to Aristotle's understanding of praxis as appetitive as well as cognitive. I first became convinced of the affective dimension of critical reflection in my own experience with groups of people in a shared praxis situation. I have found that in such groups emotions often run high. The language of critical reflection tends to mask this dimension and gives the impression of an intellectualistic and strictly cognitive activity. However, I must insist that in the praxis critical reflection is an affair of both the heart and the head.

Two factors explain why the rational and affective are inevitably fused in a praxis way of knowing. First, when we critically reflect on present action, it is primarily our own selves that we come to know, and we cannot know ourselves dispassionately. Head and heart are fused inevitably in self-knowledge. Second, the affective dimension enters into critical reflection because of the components of memory and imagination. Perhaps critical reason alone can be dispassionate (though I doubt it), but when linked with memory and imagination it certainly cannot be so. One cannot remember one's own story dispassionately, nor choose a future action without appetite to move the will. The acts of hoping and choosing not only include, but demand, desire. So when critical reflection is self-critical of one's own lived participation in the world for the sake of choosing further action, then the rational and passional are copartners in the process.

My second clarification pertains to the word *critical*. Critical here is not intended to mean negative criticism that finds only what is wrong in our present action and in the story and vision embodied there. I intend critical, instead, in the sense I have previously described as a dialectical critique. A dialectical critique affirms what is good and true in present action, recognizes its limitations, and attempts to move beyond it. Thus a critical reflection, far from being an exercise in debilitating negativism, is a positive creative activity. This is where imagination plays a vital role. Imagination is essential for the creative and transforming moment of moving beyond. Without it we end up, as Habermas appears to do, with only negative criticism.

It must also be emphasized that in critical reflection the source of discernment, as always, is not solely our own reason, memory, and imagination. It is only by the Spirit's grace of discernment working within our own human efforts that we can come to know reality in light of God's activity and contribute to its transformation according to God's will.

From *Christian Religious Education*, T H Groome, Harper and Row, 1980

In our culture we both celebrate and belittle childhood. We project onto it a false state of happiness and freedom from care. At the same time, we feel compelled to help children become serious and responsible. In other words, children are incomplete human beings in need of being shaped into adults.

It is as if when we became aware of children and ceased to treat them as little adults, we also stopped treating them as full human beings. Now they are *only* children. It was a questionable gain...

Children possess naturally the essential elements for having faith. The Kingdom of God is first perceived in the world children know best. Children, therefore, have as much to offer adults as adults have to offer children – perhaps more. As parents, we are not responsible to give our children faith; faith is a gift from God given to both us and our children. We are called to live faithfully in childlike ways with our children so that we both might know the gift of faith and live in its grace...

It is so easy to lose the gift of creativity and so difficult to get it back. But get it back we must. Our sense of God is so easy to lose, especially in our kind of adult, scientific, technological, affluent world, but get it back we must.

We cannot date when faith begins in human life. Neither can we teach another person faith. It is a gift that we share with each other. The faith of an adult may be different in its expression from that of a child, but it is the same faith...

Faith ... doesn't develop in a vacuum, but in response to our experiences in the world...

I have five guidelines for sharing our faith with our children from birth through childhood:

> We need to tell and retell the biblical story – the stories of the faith – together.

We need to celebrate our faith and our lives.

We need to pray together.

We need to listen and talk to each other.

We need to perform faithful acts of service and witness together...

Our responsibility is not to offer our children information, advice or guidance. But children do deserve a response to their questions, an affirmation of their quest. We need to help them come into touch with the struggles, pains, doubts, and insecurities their questions reveal. The most profound questions of life have no answers; each only opens new questions that lead even deeper into the unspeakable mystery of faith and ultimately to the mystery of God. What our children are really asking is for us to reveal and share ourselves and our faith, not to provide dogmatic answers ... You see, it is in the relationship between us during our shared quest that God is revealed.

From *Bringing Up Children in the Christian Faith*, J H Westerhoff, Harper and Row, 1980

In speaking of models or examples, it is well to remember that, as the gospel stories are retold, hearers identify with those who first heard and responded. We do not identify with Jesus. He is the one who calls, heals, and tells the good news. This point can be made clear by comparing pictures illustrating the story of Zacchaeus. Sometimes the viewer stands with Jesus and the disciples looking up at Zacchaeus. A more accurate interpretation would place Zacchaeus as the central figure, looking down from the tree at Jesus and the disciples. Here the learner identifies with Zacchaeus. Children can appreciate this situation. They, too, are small and cannot see above adults. How wonderful that Jesus noticed Zacchaeus and promised to come to his house! Children also understand Zacchaeus' hidden guilt. What child has not at some time used money intended for some other purpose? 'Salvation' as release from guilt after confession and restitution is good news. Teachers will have no difficulty finding more stories once they become aware of ways in which children identify with characters.

Understanding symbolic writing

Parents and teachers need to ask what symbols children understand. When in doubt, it is best to keep away from the symbolic. Explaining the rainbow story (Gen. 9:12–17), the teacher may say, 'Whenever you see a rainbow, it can remind you of God's promise to take care of everyone.' Or in telling about John the Baptist (Mark 1:4–8): 'When John baptized people he was reminding them that God had washed away their sins.' (Christian baptism, however, has the broader dimension of dying and rising with Christ.) The cross reminds us that Jesus loved people so much that he died for them. This may not have much meaning beyond the idea that the cross in some strange way reveals God's love. Adults also find the idea profound beyond their full comprehension.

Parables are symbolic forms that young children cannot translate. Through the parables of the kingdom Jesus tried to help people see that God's rule was hidden but was worth every effort to uncover. Children, however, understand these as stories about a woman who rejoiced over finding a lost coin or a man who sold everything for a valuable jewel. They can picture the farmer sowing seeds with varying results, but the application of 'sowing the word' is not their way of concrete reasoning. However, the story of the son who left home but was forgiven and restored (and the elder brother who resented this) will remind them of the forgiving love of God. Children cannot be expected to think of themselves as sheep in the parable of the lost sheep, even if they come from places where sheep raising is an industry. No matter how that parable is transformed to show a lost dog or a lost child, young hearers do not put themselves in this place. People who live in industrialized cultures have to make a deliberate effort to identify with the symbol of the sheep. They may do so in reading the Twenty-third Psalm, but the identification doesn't come naturally. Metaphors, similes, parables, symbols, object lessons – all require a cognitive process the young child is not ready to use. In all the pages of the Bible there must be something beyond a few overused stories to evoke the religious response of children.

Teachers and parents need to give serious thought about how to use miracle stories. This is not a matter of one's belief; it is a warning that what adults say might cause children to misunderstand the Bible. When people are healed by the power of God made known through Jesus, children should be able to understand the action as God's work. This is communicated by how the story is written, how it is told, how children perceive it, and how their questions and comments are answered. What the child cannot grasp is better left unexplained until a later time.

If children learn these stories through television, parents and teachers will need to deal with what the children describe, reinterpreting television portrayals of the marvelous into an understanding that these stories aroused a sense of wonder in those who watched, were helped, or wrote down the story. People today echo the astonishment of Jesus' contemporaries, who were 'astonished beyond measure' (Mark 7:37). Children need to hear stories of how Jesus entered into the lives of people: visiting, eating, talking, healing, teaching, and comforting. Often he visited a family home for a meal.

Teachers and parents will not avoid the Passion story. This is part of the total experience of the Christian community. Children are aware that this is a significant event. Since they already know the ending of Easter Day, they do not view the crucifixion simply as a cruel and tragic death. With Christians everywhere, they celebrate these events, participating in the drama of redemption. This is the paschal feast, as the oldest hymns remind us. The connection should be emphasized. It is more important than secular symbols of prehistoric fertility rites that have come from the more recent past. The joy of Easter tells the child that Christ is risen and lives among his people.

The Bible was conveyed to the people of Israel for many generations in oral form, as the first remembrances of the words and works of Jesus were later conveyed to the earliest Christian congregations. The forms of writings in the Bible include story, poem, hymns, prayer, and proclamation. There are also literary forms such as The Song of Solomon and the letters of Paul. Story telling is still a basic method for conveying what the Bible has to say. The competent teacher will take time to become an expert story teller. Stories on records and cassettes will provide models. One will soon enjoy putting oneself into the retelling of a story, using voice, hands, and the whole body to make it vivid, and finding satisfaction in the response of the hearers.

Children who hear Bible stories at home bring an enriched experience to their religious education classes. The stories can be told in class without insisting that they must be linked with a lesson or have some application to child experience. Stories can be told or read to early comers. If there is time for juice and crackers, the children will enjoy listening while they eat. When interest centers are used, a small rug and a collection of story books will invite the children to join a story-telling teacher or helper. Whole units may be built around Bible stories, without the need to find a life parallel or point a moral.

Finally, it is helpful to get acquainted with the riches for teaching to be found in biblical affirmations. Teachers fix their attention so fully on using Bible *stories* that they may fail to see what else there is. If the point is to have the Bible speak to the learner, the material may lie elsewhere. The following passages, for example, are helpful: 'O give thanks to the Lord, for he is good; for his steadfast love endures for ever' (Ps. 136:1); 'When I am afraid, I will put my trust in thee' (Ps. 56:3); 'We love, because he first loved us' (John 4:19); 'Love one another as I have loved you' (John 15:12); 'You are my friends if you do what I command you' (John 15:14).

From *Christian Child Development*, Iris V Cully, Gill & Macmillan, 1980

Infancy and Undifferentiated Faith

In the pre-stage called Undifferentiated faith the seeds of trust, courage, hope and love are fused in an undifferentiated way and contend with sensed threats of abandonment, inconsistencies and deprivations in an infant's environment. Though really a pre-stage and largely inaccessible to empirical research of the kind we pursue, the quality of mutuality and the strength of trust, autonomy, hope and courage (or their opposites) developed in this phase underlie (or threaten to undermine) all that comes later in faith development.

The emergent strength of faith in this stage is the fund of basic trust and the relational experience of mutuality with the one(s) providing primary love and care.

The danger or deficiency in the stage is a failure of mutuality in either of two directions. Either there may emerge an excessive narcissism in which the experience of being 'central' continues to dominate and distort mutuality, or experiences of neglect or inconsistencies may lock the infant in patterns of isolation and faded mutuality.

Transition to Stage 1 begins with the convergence of thought and language, opening up the use of symbols in speech and ritual play.

Stage 1. Intuitive-Projective Faith

Stage 1 Intuitive-Projective faith is the fantasy-filled, imitative phase in which the child can be powerfully and permanently influenced by examples, moods, actions and stories of the visible faith of primally related adults.

The stage most typical of the child of three to seven, it is marked by a relative fluidity of thought patterns. The child is continually encountering novelties for which no stable operations of knowing have been formed. The imaginative processes underlying fantasy are unrestrained and uninhibited by logical thought. In league with forms of knowing dominated by perception, imagination in this stage is extremely productive of long-lasting images and feelings (positive and negative,) that later, more stable and self-reflective valuing and thinking will have to order and sort out. This is the stage of first self-awareness. The 'self-aware' child is egocentric as regards the perspectives of others. Here we find first awarenesses of death and sex and of the strong taboos by which cultures and families insulate those powerful areas.

The gift or emergent strength of this stage is the birth of imagination, the ability to unify and grasp the experience-world in powerful images and as presented in stories that register the child's intuitive understandings and feelings toward the ultimate conditions of existence.

The dangers in this stage arise from the possible 'possession' of the child's imagination by unrestrained images of terror and destructiveness, or from the witting or unwitting exploitation of her or his imagination in the reinforcement of taboos and moral or doctrinal expectations.

The main factor precipitating transition to the next stage is the emergence of concrete operational thinking. Affectively, the resolution of Oedipal issues or their submersion in latency are important accompanying factors. At the heart of the transition is the child's growing concern to know how things are and to clarify for him- or herself the bases of distinctions between what is real and what only seems to be.

Stage 2. Mythic-Literal Faith

Stage 2 Mythic-Literal faith is the stage in which the person begins to take on for him- or herself the stories, beliefs and observances that symbolize belonging to his or her community. Beliefs are appropriated with literal interpretations, as are moral rules and attitudes. Symbols are taken as one-dimensional and literal in meaning. In this stage the rise of concrete operations leads to the curbing and ordering of the previous stage's imaginative composing of the world. The episodic quality of Intuitive-Projective faith gives way to a more linear, narrative construction of coherence and meaning. Story becomes the major way of giving unity and value to experience. This is the faith stage of the school child (though we sometimes find the structures dominant in adolescents and in adults). Marked by increased accuracy in taking the perspective of other persons, those in Stage 2 compose a world based on reciprocal fairness and an immanent justice based on reciprocity. The actors in their cosmic stories are anthropomorphic. They can be affected deeply and powerfully by symbolic and dramatic materials and can describe in endlessly detailed narrative what has occurred. They do not, however, step back from the flow of stories to formulate reflective, conceptual meanings. For this stage the meaning is both carried and 'trapped' in the narrative.

The new capacity or strength in this stage is the rise of narrative and the emergence of story, drama and myth as ways of finding and giving coherence to experience.

The limitations of literalness and an excessive reliance upon reciprocity as a principle for constructing an ultimate environment can result either in an overcontrolling, stilted perfectionism or 'works righteousness' or in their opposite, an abasing sense of badness embraced because of mistreatment, neglect or the apparent disfavor of significant others.

A factor initiating transition to Stage 3 is the implicit clash or contradictions in stories that leads to reflection on meanings. The transition to formal operational thought makes such reflection possible and necessary. Previous literalism breaks down; new 'cognitive conceit' (Elkind) leads to disillusionment with previous teachers and teachings. Conflicts between authoritative stories (Genesis on creation versus evolutionary theory) must be faced. The emergence of mutual interpersonal perspective taking ('I see you seeing me; I see me as you see me; I see you seeing me seeing you.') creates the need for a more personal relationship with the unifying power of the ultimate environment.

Stage 3. Synthetic-Conventional Faith

In Stage 3 Synthetic-Conventional faith, a person's experience of the world now extends beyond the family. A number of spheres demand attention: family, school or work, peers, street society and media, and perhaps religion. Faith must provide a coherent orientation in the midst of that more complex and diverse range of involvements. Faith must synthesize values and information; it must provide a basis for identity and outlook.

Stage 3 typically has its rise and ascendancy in adolescence, but for many adults it becomes a permanent place of equilibrium. It structures the ultimate environment in interpersonal terms. Its images of unifying value and power derive from the extension of qualities experienced in personal relationships. It is a 'conformist' stage in the sense that it is acutely tuned to the expectations and judgments of significant others and as yet does not have a sure enough grasp on its own identity and autonomous judgment to construct and maintain an independent perspective. While beliefs and values are deeply felt, they typically are tacitly held – the person 'dwells' in them and in the meaning world they mediate. But there has not been occasion to step outside them to reflect on or examine them explicitly or systematically. At Stage 3 a person has an 'ideology,' a more or less consistent clustering of values and beliefs, but he or she has not objectified it for examination and in a sense is unaware of having it. Differences of outlook with others are experienced as differences in 'kind' of person. Authority is located in the incumbents of traditional authority roles (if perceived as personally worthy) or in the consensus of a valued, face-to-face group.

The emergent capacity of this stage is the forming of a personal myth – the myth of one's own becoming in identity and faith, incorporating one's past and anticipated future in an image of the ultimate environment unified by characteristics of personality.

The dangers or deficiencies in this stage are twofold. The expectations and evaluations of others can be so compellingly internalized (and sacralized) that later autonomy of judgment and action can be jeopardized; or interpersonal betrayals can give rise either to nihilistic despair about a personal principle of ultimate being or to a compensatory intimacy with God unrelated to mundane relations.

Factors contributing to the breakdown of Stage 3 and to readiness for transition may include: serious clashes or contradictions between valued authority sources; marked changes, by officially sanctioned leaders, or policies or practices previously deemed sacred and unbreachable (for example, in the Catholic church changing the mass from Latin to the vernacular, or no longer requiring abstinence from meat on Friday); the encounter with experiences or perspectives that lead to critical reflection on how one's beliefs and values have formed and changed, and on how 'relative' they are to one's particular group or background. Frequently the experience of 'leaving home' – emotionally or physically, or both – precipitates the kind of examination of self, background and life-guiding values that gives rise to stage transition at this point.

Stage 4. Individuative-Reflective Faith

The movement from Stage 3 to Stage 4 Individuative-Reflective faith is particularly critical for it is in this transition that the late adolescent or adult must begin to take seriously the burden of responsibility for his or her own commitments, lifestyle, beliefs and attitudes. Where genuine movement toward stage 4 is underway the person must face certain unavoidable tensions: individuality versus being defined by a group or group membership; subjectivity and the power of one's strongly felt but unexamined feelings versus objectivity and the requirement of critical reflection; self-fulfillment or self-actualization as a primary concern versus service to and being for others; the question of being committed to the relative versus struggle with the possibility of an absolute.

Stage 4 most appropriately takes form in young adulthood (but let us remember that many adults do not construct it and that for a significant group it emerges only in the mid-thirties or forties). This stage is marked by a double development. The self, previously sustained in its identity and faith compositions by an interpersonal circle of significant others, now claims an identity no longer defined by the composite of one's roles or meanings to others. To sustain that new identity it composes a meaning frame conscious of its own boundaries and inner connections and aware of itself as a 'world view'. Self (identity) and outlook (world view) are differentiated from those of others and become acknowledged factors in the reactions, interpretations and judgments one makes on the actions of the self and others. It expresses its intuitions of coherence in an ultimate environment in terms of an explicit system of meanings. Stage 4 typically translates symbols into conceptual meanings. This is a 'demythologizing' stage. It is likely to attend minimally to unconscious factors influencing its judgments and behavior.

Stage 4's ascendant strength has to do with its capacity for critical reflection on identity (self) and outlook (ideology). Its dangers inhere in its strengths: an excessive confidence in the conscious mind and in critical thought and a kind of second narcissism in which the now clearly bounded, reflective self overassimilates 'reality' and the perspectives of others into its own world view.

Restless with the self-images and outlook maintained by Stage 4, the person ready for transition finds him- or herself attending to what may feel like anarchic and disturbing inner voices. Elements from a childish past, images and energies from a deeper self, a gnawing sense of the sterility and flatness of the meanings one serves – any or all of these may signal readiness for something new. Stories, symbols, myths and paradoxes from one's own or other traditions may insist on breaking in upon the neatness of the previous faith. Disillusionment with one's compromises and recognition that life is more complex than Stage 4's logic of clear distinctions and abstract concepts can comprehend, press one toward a more dialectical and multi-leveled approach to life truth.

Stage 5. Conjunctive Faith

Stage 5 Conjunctive faith involves the integration into self and outlook of much that was suppressed or unrecognized in the interest of Stage 4's self-certainty and conscious cognitive and affective adaptation to reality. This stage develops a 'second naïveté' (Ricoeur) in which symbolic power is reunited with conceptual meanings. Here there must also be a new reclaiming and reworking of one's past. There must be an opening to the voices of one's 'deeper self'. Importantly, this involves a critical recognition of one's social unconscious – the myths, ideal images and prejudices built deeply into the self-system by virtue of one's nurture within a particular social class, religious tradition, ethnic group or the like.

Unusual before mid-life, Stage 5 knows the sacrament of defeat and the reality of irrevocable commitments and acts. What the previous stage struggled to clarify in terms of the boundaries of self and outlook, this stage now makes porous and permeable. Alive to paradox and the truth in apparent contradictions, this stage strives to unify opposites in mind and experience. It generates and maintains vulnerability to the strange truths of those who are 'other'. Ready for closeness to that which is different and threatening to self and outlook (including new depths of experience in spirituality and religious revelation), this stage's commitment to justice is freed from the confines of tribe, class, religious community or nation. And with the seriousness that can arise when life is more than half over, this stage is ready to spend and be spent for the cause of conserving and cultivating the possibility of others' generating identity and meaning.

The new strength of this stage comes in the rise of the ironic imagination – a capacity to see and be in one's or one's group's most powerful meanings, while simultaneously recognizing that they are relative, partial and inevitably distorting apprehensions of transcendent reality. Its danger lies in the direction of a paralyzing passivity or inaction, giving rise to complacency or cynical withdrawal, due to its paradoxical understanding of truth.

Stage 5 can appreciate symbols, myths and rituals (its own and others') because it has been grasped, in some measure, by the depth of reality to which they refer. It also sees the divisions of the human family vividly because it has been apprehended by the possibility (and imperative) of an inclusive community of being. But this stage remains divided. It lives and acts between an untransformed world and a transforming vision and loyalties. In some few cases this division yields to the call of the radical actualization that we call Stage 6.

Stage 6. Universalizing Faith

In order to characterize Stage 6 we need to focus more sharply on the dialectical or paradoxical features of Stage 5 faith. Stage 5 can see injustice in sharply etched terms because it has been apprehended by an enlarged awareness of the demands of justice and their implications. It can recognize partial truths and their limitations because it has been apprehended by a more comprehensive vision of truth. It can appreciate and cherish symbols, myths and rituals in new depth because it has been apprehended in some measure by the depth of reality to which the symbols refer and which they mediate. It sees the fractures and divisions of the human family with vivid pain because it has been apprehended by the possibility of an inclusive commonwealth of being. Stage 5 remains paradoxical or divided, however, because the self is caught between these universalizing apprehensions and the need to preserve its own being and well-being. Or because it is deeply invested in maintaining the ambiguous order of a socioeconomic system, the alternatives to which seem more unjust or destructive than it is. In this situation of paradox Stage 5 must act and not be paralyzed. But Stage 5 acts out of conflicting loyalties. Its readiness to spend and be spent finds limits in its loyalty to the present order, to its institutions, groups and compromise procedures. Stage 5's perceptions of justice outreach its readiness to sacrifice the self and to risk the partial justice of the present order for the sake of a more inclusive justice and the realization of love.

The transition to Stage 6 involves an overcoming of this paradox through a moral and ascetic actualization of the universalizing apprehensions. Heedless of the threats to self, to primary groups, and to the institutional arrangements of the present order that are involved, Stage 6 becomes a disciplined, activist *incarnation* – a making real and tangible – of the imperatives of absolute love and justice of which Stage 5 has partial apprehensions. The self at Stage 6 engages in spending and being spent for the transformation of present reality in the direction of a transcendent actuality.

Persons best described by Stage 6 typically exhibit qualities that shake our usual criteria of normalcy. Their heedlessness to self-preservation and the vividness of their taste and feel for transcendent moral and religious actuality give their actions and words an extraordinary and often unpredictable quality. In their devotion to universalizing compassion they may offend our parochial perceptions of justice. In their penetration through the obsession with survival, security, and significance they threaten our measured standards of righteousness and goodness and prudence. Their enlarged visions of universal community disclose the partialness of our tribes and pseudo-species. And their leadership initiatives, often involving strategies of nonviolent suffering and ultimate respect for being, constitute affronts to our usual notions of relevance. It is little wonder that persons best described by Stage 6 so frequently become martyrs for the visions they incarnate *(see* Life-Maps: Conversations on the Journey of Faith, *Fowler & Keen, Word Books, 1978, pages 87–89).*

Stage 6 is exceedingly rare. The persons best described by it have generated faith compositions in which their felt sense of an ultimate environment is inclusive of all being. They have become incarnators and actualizers of the spirit of an inclusive and fulfilled human community.

They are 'contagious' in the sense that they create zones of liberation from the social, political, economic and ideological shackles we place and endure on human futurity. Living with felt participation in a power that unifies and transforms the world, Universalizers are often experienced as subversive of the structures (including religious structures) by which we sustain our individual and corporate survival, security and significance. Many persons in this stage die at the hands of those whom they hope to change. Universalizers are often more honored and revered after death than during their lives. The rare persons who may be described by this stage have a special grace that makes them seem more lucid, more simple, and yet somehow more fully human than the rest of us. Their community is universal in extent. Particularities are cherished because they are vessels of the universal, and thereby valuable apart from any utilitarian considerations. Life is both loved and held to loosely. Such persons are ready for fellowship with persons at any of the other stages and from any other faith tradition *(see 'Perspectives on the Family from the Standpoint of Faith Development Theory', Fowler, in* Perkins Journal *volume 33/1, Fall 1979, pages 13–14).*

See overleaf for a table describing the Faith Stages by aspect.

From *Stages of Faith: the Psychology of Human Development and the Quest for Meaning,* J W Fowler, Harper and Row, 1981

Fowler's Faith Stages by Aspects

ASPECT:	A. Form Of Logic (Piaget)	B. Perspective Taking (Selman)	C. Form of Moral Judgment (Kohlberg)	D. Bounds of Social Awareness	E. Locus of Authority	F. Form of World Coherence	G. Symbolic Function
STAGE:							
I	Preoperational	Rudimentary empathy (egocentric)	Punishment – reward	Family, primal others	Attachment/ dependence relationships. Size, power, visible symbols of authority	Episodic	Magical – Numinous
II	Concrete Operational	Simple perspective taking	Instrumental hedonism (Reciprocal fairness)	'Those like us' (in familial, ethnic, racial, class and religious terms)	Incumbents of authority roles, salience increased by personal relatedness	Narrative-Dramatic	One-dimensional; literal
III	Early Formal Operations	Mutual inter-personal	Interpersonal expectations and concordance	Composite of groups in which one has interpersonal relationships	Consensus of valued groups and in personally worthy representatives of belief-value traditions	Tacit system, felt meanings symbolically mediated, globally held	Symbols multi-dimensional; evocative power inheres in symbol

IV	Formal Operations (Dichotomizing)	Mutual, with self-selected group or class – (societal)	Societal perspective, Reflective relativism or class-biased universalism	Ideologically compatible communities with congruence to self-chosen norms and insights	One's own judgment as informed by a self-ratified ideological perspective. Authorities and norms must be congruent with this.	Explicit system, conceptually mediated, clarity about boundaries and inner connections of system	Symbols separated from symbolized. Translated (reduced) to ideations. Evocative power inheres in *meaning* conveyed by symbols
V	Formal Operations (Dialectical)	Mutual with groups, classes and traditions 'other' than one's own	Prior to society, Principled higher law (universal and critical)	Extends beyond class norms and interests. Disciplined ideological vulnerability to 'truths' and 'claims' of outgroups and other traditions	Dialectical joining of judgment-experience processes with reflective claims of others and of various expressions of cumulative human wisdom.	Multi-systemic symbolic and conceptual mediation	Postcritical rejoining of irreducible symbolic power and ideational meaning. Evocative power inherent in the reality in and beyond symbol *and* in the power of unconscious processes in the self
VI	Formal Operations (Synthetic)	Mutual, with the commonwealth of being	Loyalty to being	Identification with the species. Transnarcissistic love of being	In a personal judgment informed by the experiences and truths of previous stages, purified of egoic striving, and linked by disciplined intuition to the principle of being	Unitive actuality felt and participated unity of 'One beyond the many'	Evocative power of symbols actualized through unification of reality mediated by symbols and the self

153

5. In *The Child in the Church* (Chapter 4) we distinguished Christian nurture from secular education, instruction and indoctrination. 'Instruction may be to do with learning the skills which will get you a job; secular education is to do with becoming a reflective person; Christian nurture is to do with becoming a Christian person'. We found Christian nurture to be compatible with secular education but incompatible with indoctrination. It has a difference in aim from secular education since it is concerned to further enquiry and personal development in accordance with a Christian understanding of personhood. Indoctrination, however, seeks to deprive a person of his personhood. It is concerned with conformity to correct ideas, not open to rational argument and persuasion, and must override individual judgment. However, this position poses a number of questions. Believing Christian nurture is about nurturing children into a received tradition (a Christian past) how can this be effected while avoiding the dangers of indoctrination? Is it possible to nurture into a tradition with a dogmatic basis and yet be open? What is the rationale in theology for a Christian nurture which would be non-authoritarian and open to other views? These were the kinds of questions posed by our previous work and which led us to make the recommendation B.5: 'We recommend that, since the renewal of the Churches' ministry in nurturing both children and adults requires for its support a theology which sees critical openness as springing from Christian commitment, the attention of the British Council of Churches Division of Ecumenical Affairs be drawn to this area of theological construction'... In other words we saw 'critical openness' as the central idea in the resolution of these problems. It is the main feature which distinguishes the faith-fostering activities of the mainstream churches from those of the sects. Without an understanding of this there is no satisfactory way in which Christian upbringing in open, plural societies can be defended against the charge that it is indoctrinatory, and without the practice of critical openness there is no way whereby Christian adults can be formed so as to live freely and creatively in plural societies...

6. This second report, therefore, is namely a response to one particular recommendation contained in the first. In the first two chapters an attempt is made to develop a theology of critical openness as an important part of an understanding of Christian nurture and growth. We do not pretend this is a full treatment of the nature of Christian nurture and we do not think 'critical openness' is at all times and in all places its most important aspect. Love is greater. But we do believe it has great significance for the process of Christian growth in modern Western societies and it is because we have found ourselves asking what it means to foster Christian faith in such societies (especially in Britain) that our attention has been drawn to 'critical openness' as a vital key in unlocking the problems and in opening the way to a renewed and more confident policy of Christian nurture for the churches...

19. Critical openness is also related to the New Testament image of the Christian life. 'The prophets who prophesied of the grace that was to be yours searched and inquired about this salvation. They inquired what person or time was indicated by the Spirit of Christ within them' (1 Peter 1:10–11). The prophets are certainly not thought of here as examining the evidence of their prophecies to see if it was credible or not. Rather, they made a spiritual and perhaps mystical search into the inner meaning to discover what was discoverable, the truth hidden there. The sense is similar to John 5:39, where the Jews are spoken of as searching the scriptures. The Beroean Jews (Acts 17:11) displayed a spirit of enquiry which was possibly closer to that which we meet today, when they 'received the word with all eagerness, examining the scriptures daily to see if these things were so'. When the Spirit of God or Christ is described as 'searching' the reference is to a searching out and bringing to light of what is already known, a probing or testing, as when Christ searches the minds and hearts of men (Revelation 2:23), or 'The Spirit searches everything, even the depths of God' (1 Corinthians 2:10), but when this searching Spirit dwells in the hearts of believers, he enables them to search out what they did *not* know before, giving them spiritual insight and discerning power. So 'The spiritual man judges all things, but is himself to be judged by no one' (1 Corinthians 2:15). The penetrating power of the Spirit is spoken of in Romans 8:26–27, where human ignorance of what to pray for is overcome by the searching knowledge of the Spirit, too deep for words. This power of penetrating enquiry is to be turned outwards, as when Christians are advised to 'test the spirits, to see whether they are of God' (1 John 4:1) and inwards, as when the Corinthian Christians were told 'Examine yourselves, to see whether you are holding to your faith. Test yourselves' (2 Corinthians 13:5). The gift of discrimination is impelled by the knowledge of God's discrimination (his judgment) between men. 'If we judged ourselves truly, we should not be judged. When we are judged by the Lord we are chastened, so that we may not be condemned along with the world' (1 Corinthians 11:31f). It is because the judgment of the Lord is expressed through his giving of himself in the bread and the wine (1 Corinthians 11:27) that Christians are not only to examine themselves before they partake but also to discern the body of the Lord (vv 28f). We can see that the critical and discriminating spirit of the early Church sprang thus not only from the Old Testament doctrine of the all-searching eye of God but also from the peculiar tension of the early Christian community, caught between a given salvation and a not yet given vindication. It is this situation of being poised on the brink of a great crisis, of being granted complete certainty, yet enjoying it in uncertainty, which gave the Christian critical spirit its essential flavour. On the one hand, 'there is no condemnation' (Romans 8:1) and on the other hand, 'the time has come for judgment to begin with the household of God' (1 Peter 4:17). Certainly, there are times when this critical spirit of testing is to be suspended. When the Corinthian Christians sit down to dinner, they are not to ask questions about the food set before them, just for conscience sake, but to eat it up in the name of faith (1 Corinthians 10:25, 27), and Paul acknowledges the limits of self-knowledge and self-criticism. 'It is a very small thing that I should be judged by you or by any human court. I do not even judge myself' (1 Corinthians 4:3). The key thought is that it is ultimately God who is the supreme tester and validator of hearts. 'It is the Lord who judges me' (1 Corinthians 4:4).

20. This inquiring spirit of the early Church may be called 'eschatological criticism'. It springs from a knowledge that the goal has not yet been grasped (Philippians 3:12), the future not yet known (1 John 3:2), the true and the false grow side by side (Matthew 13:30). Everything therefore was to be tested, and that which survived the test was to be held fast...

Summary: *The concept of Christian criticism although related to and affected by many modern trends, springs essentially from the New Testament where it is one mark of the eschatological people of God...*

85. The biblical basis for Christian childhood is rather stronger than it is for infant baptism, since the arguments for the latter often depend upon inference or even silence. Christian childhood is a somewhat more general concept than baptised childhood, and more general evidence will be relevant. But we wish to emphasise that we are not immediately concerned with the sacramental question. Most of the modern discussions about infant baptism have been motivated by a concern for the meaning of baptism rather than for the meaning of childhood in the church.

86. The child had an accepted place in Israel. The children were present at the passover meal, and took an active part in the ritual (Exodus 12:26). Children were within the covenant and received circumcision as a sign of their participation in the relation with God (Genesis 17:7). Several prophets were regarded as sacred from their birth (1 Samuel 1:11; Judges 13:5; Luke 1:15) and began their ministries in childhood (1 Samuel 2 and 3) or were full of the Holy Spirit from or before birth (Luke 1:15).

87. The teaching of Jesus is clear on the point, provided we do not expect to find direct references to expressions such as 'being Christian'. The child 'in the midst' is the representative of Christ and of God (Mark 9:36f) and the little ones believe in Christ (Mark 9:42). Children receive the blessing of Christ who describes them as not only belonging to the Kingdom (or rather, the Kingdom belongs to them) but adds that the Kingdom can only be received as a child (Mark 10:14–16). In Matthew's account (18:3) repentance, necessary in order to enter the Kingdom, is associated with becoming a child. This verse alone would be sufficient for us to ask not whether a child can be a Christian but whether an adult can. The various references to family churches and family baptism in the Acts and Letters although perhaps inconclusive for infant baptism are surely quite convincing on the more general point of child membership in the church and their status as Christians. Paul speaks of the faith which had been in Timothy's grandmother and his mother and is now in him (2 Timothy 1:5) who from childhood had known the scriptures (2 Timothy 3:15).

88. The childhood of Jesus himself is important for this question. When Paul tells children to obey their parents in everything (Colossians 3:20), adding 'for this pleases the Lord' we may well be reminded of the obedience of the child Jesus to his own parents (Luke 2:51). His infancy is venerated (Matthew 2:11) and we have no reason to exclude his childhood from the general instructions to imitate Christ. The infant John the Baptist may be regarded as the first who responded to the infant Christ – a favourite subject of medieval art – hearing the voice of Mary and leaping in his mother's womb (Luke 1:41 and 44). The expression 'in the Lord' which is used by Paul to describe the relation of the Christian to Christ is used of children, who are to obey their parents 'in the Lord' (Ephesians 6:1) and it is continually 'in the Lord' that their upbringing is to take place (Ephesians 6:4). The very fact that children are addressed in the ethical sections of the letters along with fathers, mothers, masters and slaves shows that the children were thought of as an accepted part of the church, subject to its discipline, incorporated within it, not as 'junior members' but as sharing fully in the life of the congregation. There seems little doubt then that the teaching and practice of both Jesus and the early church was such that the church received children into its midst, and that this is the origin of the church's practice which continued until the individualism of the Renaissance and the Reformation created the modern ambiguity, which is mainly confined to Protestantism.

Summary: *The practice of ancient Israel, the teaching and practice of Jesus, as well as his own childhood, and the custom and teaching of the early church are unanimous in the belief that children may be members of the church as fellow Christians, sharing with adults the life of the spirit and being 'in Christ'...*

257. It is important that young Christians should learn to appreciate the traditional ways of worship, traditional expressions of Christian thought and feeling, and the traditional language of worship. Only if each generation in its turn is prepared to treat with respect and pay serious attention to the contribution of previous generations can we maintain the continuity of the people of God and the continuity of the gospel which we preach and the faith we affirm. But, especially in a time of rapid cultural change, older Christians must be prepared for the fact that ways of expressing Christian thought and feeling which they have found meaningful and satisfactory may not be equally meaningful and satisfactory to their children. They must therefore be prepared to look for the virtues in those forms of expression which come more naturally to the young.

258. If in a Christian community we do not find this readiness to accept or to take seriously each other's preferred styles, both in worship and in other aspects of community life, then the Christian nurture going on in that community is in some ways defective. Christian nurture can never be an entirely one-way traffic. We must learn *from each other* or we are not learning well. We must grow *together* or none of us will grow as we should. One of the marks of Christian maturity itself is a willingness to accept each other in spite of differences of culture. If there is in Christ 'neither Jew nor Greek, bond nor free, male nor female', then there is in him neither young nor old. If there is a 'generation gap' in our society, the church ought to be one of the places where that gap is most readily bridged. In finding ways of worshipping satisfactorily together we are both exploring and expressing our unity in Christ...

Summary: Some of the difficulties of worshipping satisfactorily together are due to the cultural differences between the generations. It is important that children learn to value the traditions of worship in their church. It is also important that older Christians respect the forms in which younger ones prefer to express their faith. Learning to accept each other's cultural preferences is a concomitant of our growth together towards Christian maturity.

From *Understanding Christian Nurture,* a report of the Consultative Group on Ministry among Children, a network of the British Council of Churches, 1981

The vision of community

The admission of children to the eucharist is based on a deepened understanding of the community which Christians share in Christ. A new emphasis on the Church as *communio* has contributed to inviting children to the Lord's supper. The reverse is also true. The admission of children to the eucharist has implications for the understanding of the nature of the Church. The Church is seen as the community which reflects God's determination to gather people from all cultures, races, classes and ages. The community which God wills is inclusive, and by its very nature it transcends human barriers. Therefore, the admission of children is not simply a marginal change in the worship life of the Church. It poses a far-reaching question to the churches as they exist today: Are you as inclusive and comprehensive as you are called to be? ...

Eucharist and conditions for participation

Holy communion is a meal of the community, the community with the risen Lord, in two ways: it is the community of the participants who accept and support each other because Christ has linked them together in his body and has died for them; it confirms and helps them to discover afresh the general experience that each person needs the other and that all depend on the help of others. Communication/communion requires understandable symbols. Communion becomes the children's communion if their own signs are accepted and included in the celebration and it becomes accessible to them as an unbroken whole. Liturgical traditions need to be examined to see whether they do not rather obstruct than facilitate the understanding of what this sacrament means for the congregation (meal character, bread, table, feast, relationship between word and action). It is important that the natural symbols (signs and action) regain the natural context in life and that abstractions and ossifications which have accrued in the rites of different sacramental traditions be removed.

The image of *oikos* means that the various members can find ever new ways of living, believing and celebrating together. Thus tradition (continuity) and renewal (reform relevant to the situation) are always kept in balance. For example the following aspects need to be kept in mind:

- the Church must develop a variety of ways of celebrating the eucharist and of making evident its many-faceted meanings;
- it may be appropriate to encourage family or group celebrations;
- in some families preparation for the service contributes much to the children;
- the eucharist itself is a learning experience; attitudes and action often communicate concepts to children, e.g. forgiveness, praise, thankfulness, devotion, contrition.

We see no theological reasons for excluding any baptized persons from communion, whatever their age... *(G Müller-Fahrenholz)*

Order of experience

From all that children have written about their experiences and from what adults have said about those who, having received holy communion from early childhood, have become confirmed or been received into Church membership, there seems to be no doubt that for many the order of their experience is that first, through birth and baptism they belong to Christ. Second, they experience that they belong and grow to believe it to be so. And third, they acknowledge and profess and, maybe, understand their belonging. Such a progress of growth must have been observed by many who have taken seriously an experiential approach to education... (J M Sutcliffe)

When I began to work on the communion of infants several years ago I came fairly quickly to this working hypothesis: the practice of the communion of young children and infants varies directly with the sense of community within the church. That is to say, where the Church sees itself as a community that takes seriously the importance of the individual in the corporate whole, then infants and young children will receive the eucharist...

What does all of this say to us today? First, I believe it serves as a rule by which we can measure our present experience. In large parts of the Church young children and infants are coming to the eucharist in ever increasing numbers. The familial model for the eucharist which has become increasingly common has had much to do with that. Pastors are giving the eucharistic elements to these children, often without official sanction. The effect is two sided. At the level of acted catechesis the children feel themselves a part of the community as they had never done before. Their own words witness to that. Yet, at the same time, pastors and lay people who have talked more about community during the past two decades than they have for a very long while are suddenly struck by an aspect of community life that they had long overlooked. It comes like a conversion. Never more can they go back to their old ways.

The communion of the young has some very profound things to say about the nature of our communities. It pushes us to examine aspects of our community life that are often left unquestioned. In the developed West, where we have become too accustomed to dry cerebral Christianity, it opens the possibility for the irrational and the childlike. To the extent that true worship demands the participation of the whole self and not just the mind, the communion of the young helps us to recover a worship that is truly catholic.

While claiming to have vanquished Pelagius, we require people to exercise a religious character that is always adult, always self-contained. We need to admit Augustine's image of the sucking child. We must admit that sometimes we can only come to God as a helpless infant throws himself on his mother's breast. At the same time we need badly to break the link between chronology and Christian maturity.

Seeing children being fed at the Lord's Table pushes the adult communicant to examine anew why Jesus thought that children belonged at the centre of the Christian scheme of things. How can Jesus see the child as the model for Christian believers? If men and women hope to find healing and fulfilment in the kingdom of God, they must begin by becoming 'like children'. Mere unrecon-structed adults have no hope of entering that kingdom.

When confronted with the child as a model for the Christian, we experience anew some oft-hidden realities of our faith. We can see the child, the perfect receiver, unembarrassed and graceful, receiving the unmerited and unearned gift of God's grace. We can see in the child, ever launching himself out, unafraid, into a perilous world, the model of perfect trust. We can see in the child infectious, effervescent joy, the model of the delight of the saints. And week by week, as the pastor passes along the altar rail seeing upstretched hands, looking into wondering eyes, and hearing small voices say 'amen', he knows the model is before him, and with God's grace he too will become like those whom he feeds. *(D R Holeton)*

From the papers by G Müller-Fahrenholz , J M Sutcliffe and D R Holeton in *And do not hinder them...*, G Müller-Fahrenholz (ed), World Council of Churches, 1982. The paper by David Holeton is a very useful 'overview of some of the historical and theological questions that help to illuminate the question of the communion of young children and infants as a sacrament of community.'

Three types of story

I have found one helpful simplification of the weave of stories is to see them basically operating at three levels. The first is the 'overarching story': those big stories like progress, evolution, the Marxist view of history as class-warfare heading for the classless state, the world from creation to consummation, cycles of reincarnation, universal history, the thousand-year Reich or many others. Such stories have had immense influence in history and still have today, and their very vastness and comprehensiveness make them extremely difficult to assess or compare. They are often called 'myths', especially by their opponents. One very important point to note about any religion or ideology is what weight it places on this level. Some, like Marxism, place a great weight on it. Others, among which I see Christianity, are far less concerned about having a reliable, detailed overview of all history, and so are compatible (on certain conditions) with a variety or mixture of overarching stories. This has been specially important for Christianity in the modern world, as realized with considerable agony in the controversies over evolution.

The second level is that of 'middle distance' stories. These embrace everything from national history to personal relationships: the usual scope of the 'historical'. There can be many types of story under this heading, from academic history and most novels to myths and parables, and most of the stories that make up such a large part of every religious tradition are found here.

The third level is that of the inner self, consciousness, or soul (not that each of these means the same). Psychic and spiritual history can be amazingly rich and deep even in most unpromising historical circumstances, and intensity of concentration on the inner world and its processes has produced a wealth of spiritual, psychological and literary work.

From 'Narrative in Theology', David Ford, in *Learning for Living* Volume 4 number 3, 1982

Christian faith and Man's salvation are rooted in the facts centred on the incarnation of the Son of God and his death and resurrection. These divine deeds become the substance of faith through revelation by the understanding of scripture. From the day of Pentecost, the fruit of this revelation, the truth, is contained in the one, holy, catholic and apostolic church, which the Orthodox Church believes itself to be. The truth, however, is not a static abstraction, but the divine person of the Son of God who, revealed by the third person of the Holy Trinity, the 'Spirit of Truth' (John 16.13) is the Lord of history...

The gift of divine life to man is experienced in the church, first and foremost in the Lord's Supper, the Eucharist. The other sacraments, instituted by Christ and the church, highlight significant moments in the life of individual Christians and the life of the community as a whole. The Orthodox view of the sacraments, as mysteries of the kingdom already apparent and operative, witnesses to an essential acceptance of the world which never loses its first destiny of being good. This, in principle, postulates the theological worth of human activity and personal life: human life, labour, marriage, family, is transfigured as reflecting total communion with God. This view places infinite confidence in man as a living person in the exercise of repentance and forgiveness, the avoidance of evil and the furtherance of good, to become, like the disciples on the eve of Christ's crucifixion, a friend of God...

Patristic thought defines the goal of man's life as *deification* after the pattern of Christ's humanity seen transfigured. In the light of this theology, Christian education is formulated within the complementary dimensions of personal and corporate life.

The infant and his parents. In the early stages a child's whole existence is coloured by its family, it learns fundamental lessons of life and its spirit first awakes to the realm of religious experience. What will in later life become man's longing for the Father's house, is already offered vicariously to the child, from the early days of his life on earth, by the wonderful, all-pervading presence of his mother and father. In the words of Saint John Chrysostom, the Christian family is a 'little church', an *ecclesioula*.

The child and the church. The parents' prayers need to be their own genuine communication with God, not a lesson intended for the child. The central task of the Christian educator is to instil the sense of God's loving presence into the child. The Orthodox tradition offers a variety of means and allows the child to exercise all his senses: kissing the icons over his cot and his baptismal cross; singing prayers, noticing the living flame throwing light on to the saints represented on the ikons; kissing these saints as he kisses his mother; tasting the bread and wine of holy communion, the Body and Blood of Christ, the food of God.

The specifically Christian ingredient in the life of the home depends on parental faith and worship in and membership of the church. Early exposure to the worship and activity of the church prepares the child for personal and corporate lifelong membership. The child will first express his internal perceptions and needs in the midst of the community, and in order to share them he will then learn the accepted, historical language of the group, its symbols and customs; he will finally reabsorb the experience which will bring him to enter conscious, personal membership of the church. This integration into the church relies on the involvement of the senses of the growing child, interacting as it does with the world of symbols of the church tradition, word, ikon, and sacraments. Having been admitted into the sacramental body of the church in baptism, the baby, growing, developing child is a full communicant member...

Christmation is given early by the baptizing priest, and no subsequent commitment by the adolescent is prescribed.

From 'Orthodox Church', Michael Fortounatto, in *A Dictionary of Religious Education*, J M Sutcliffe (ed), SCM Press, 1984

The approach to the construction and content of this syllabus has seven aspects:

1. Beginning with God, Creator and Redeemer

Our approach to our educational task in the Church, whether in the preparing of a syllabus like this or in a specific programme on a specific occasion in a local church, must begin with God, Creator and Redeemer. The living God draws us to Himself, and into His future for the world, through His revelation of Himself and His presence in the world. Our ability to recognize Him alive in His world depends on prophetic insight, on theological and personal sensitivity; and on a deep sense of our being personally addressed by Him. It is in God, and ultimately for Him, that the Church engages in Christian education. Where He is and what

He is are much more important than the nature and presence of the Church with regard to the content and style of Christian education.

2. The Community of Faith

Against that all important background the next most important thing to say about the approach to Christian education is that it can have no other location than the community of faith. By no means all congregations perceive this; in many, perhaps in a majority, the patterns of church life are certainly not designed from the basis of such a perception. In recent years, however, some congregations have developed new styles of community life which have involved people of all ages in learning, worshipping, serving, and witnessing together. These are the congregations which will most readily find the value of this syllabus and the annual programme material based upon it. The syllabus is, however, addressed perhaps even more firmly to those other churches whose pattern of life does not yet embody a conviction that Christian education can have no other location than the community of faith. The Joint Publications Board offers it, and the annual material, as a stimulus for change.

3. We learn from people

There are two implications in recognizing that learning takes place within, and as a consequence of, the whole life of the church. One is that a major resource for Christian education is people. This derives partly from an understanding of the nature of persons. They are the children of God, made in His image and called to be priests, partners with Christ in His body the Church. Their role, in keeping with the biblical understanding, is active. More particularly, people bring experience – from daily life, knowledge and so on – as a resource: no one person fully participates in the vast range of experience open to humanity and therefore, if all available experience is to be used as a Christian resource, all available people must be used. This requires openness to new ideas and to people, a willingness to question, listen, adapt, change. It requires imagination in finding ways of enabling people to contribute and in enabling them to feel secure and accepted.

4. We all Teach, We all Learn

The other implication is that the task of Christian education should not and cannot be left to a few individuals who are identified as teachers. All are teachers, whether they recognize it or not, and equally all are learners, whether they recognize it or not. On the one hand those churches which devolve their educational responsibility for the young as a burden on a few individuals not only neglect their responsibility but also fail to appreciate that church life itself is an effective educational medium. The hidden agenda, the values and attitudes of people in their own relationships with one another and in their own way of life, the quality of worship and service – all these are at least as powerful as are specific 'lessons' in deciding what young people learn.

The image of school (or Sunday School) is unhelpful and there is urgent need to search for alternative patterns for expressing the corporate life and tasks of the church. On the other hand, while it is recognized that adults do not consciously go to worship in order to be taught, it is quite certain that in worship and the other activities of the common life of the church they do in fact learn, just as younger people do, whether consciously or not, whether constructively or not. Throughout the whole of life there is always more to be discerned in the Bible and its teachings, in the doctrines and traditions of the Church, in the implications of the Gospel for individual and corporate action in the world; while the demands of contemporary life, and the patterns of hopes and fears, of joy and sadness, mean that however competent we may be we are all learners.

5. Theology and Education

A fifth dimension of the approach of this syllabus concerns the relationship between theology and education. It has to be recognized in all teaching that content and method, substance and process, interact with one another. What we wish to teach conditions to a greater or lesser extent, depending on the circumstances, the way in which we teach. Conversely, the way we teach places some limits on what we are able to teach and further, the method itself is part of what is learned. The methods chosen as a vehicle for Christian communication are not therefore a matter of indifference from a theological point of view. The content of any particular programme and the methods used for expressing it interact on one another. Even more fundamentally, however, our theological presuppositions, and in particular what we believe about God and the way He deals with His creatures, affect both what it is we understand we have to communicate and the methods we adopt in order to communicate it. A clear example of these relationships can be seen if we consider the importance of areas of experience other than the cognitive – or to put it another way, the importance in Christian education of feelings and of commitment, of will, as well as of thought and knowledge. A procedure for Christian education which consists only or mainly of formal instruction by way of an address from the front, the audience remaining at best receptive, at worst passive, heavily stresses the transfer of information at the cost of a failure to develop aesthetic or any other feelings or value commitments. It also fails to feed the emotional or other dimensions of personality, or to represent a biblical and Christian understanding of human nature. Such a method is therefore at fault on theological and social as well as on educational grounds.

This syllabus, the Joint Publications Board firmly believes, can be used with integrity by programme-writers with quite widely different theological views and using different methods. Its authors have their own views, both theological and methodological, and these must inevitably find expression to some extent in the syllabus itself...

6. Experience and learning

A sixth aspect of the approach of this syllabus concerns the relationship between experience and learning. Previous syllabuses have stressed the crucial necessity to take into account the experience of the learner in devising both the content and method of education; and from its inception *Partners in Learning* has been based on what is called the experiential approach – beginning in experience and working through experience to experience. Where properly understood and used this approach has transformed and enormously enriched Christian education and we would wish to build on it. The term experience is used in a number of different ways, none of them easy to delineate and all of them running into one another. It can be used to mean that of which the individual learner is conscious and in which he or she is actively participating at a given moment; in that sense the experiential approach means using whatever the individual is thinking or feeling at that moment as the point of departure for an educational exercise. The term experience is also used to indicate the store of knowledge and insight, or the degree of maturity of emotional response, which the individual has acquired from all his or her previous 'experiences' in the earlier sense of the term. An alert teacher will always be sensitive to the very different 'experience' of individuals in this context. A child brought up in a sparsely populated country area will have a very different experience from that of a child brought up in an inner city. If people are to learn effectively the teacher must start from where they each are.

To be effective the experiential method has to be aware of these and of other different usages of the term and also of the relationship between thee different kinds of 'experience'. For one thing, it is not entirely accurate to speak of 'experiences' as individual, separate events. On the contrary for all of us our experience is a living, continuous whole. Partly, but not wholly, for that reason, every part of our experience is what it is partly by what has gone before, and itself modifies the nature of 'experiences' which come later. Furthermore, the individual is practically never in the state of simply passively receiving impressions from outside, but on the contrary is actively involved in experiencing. Perception is an amalgam of what happens to me and what I do with, or how I react to, what happens to me. My previous experience may be so conditioned, and may so condition me now, that I have a distorted view of, or attitude to, myself or the world, by which I am, to a greater or lesser extent, disabled from learning constructively and healthily from present experience.

The approach then is to recognize that, for everyone, previous experience conditions what they are able to learn and how they are able to learn it; that we learn more quickly and deeply by experiencing than by hearing about, or by being told; and that the goal of Christian education is to enable individuals to grow into the experience of faith – an experience which is, or should be to a significant extent, already the possession of the teacher. This approach gives a content and style of Christian education which is richer than can be provided by any partial approach – the imparting of a body of knowledge, approach through 'life themes', child centred, and so on. It also enables us to recognize that the term experience does not limit us to one narrow dimension of life. Our experience is compounded of a complex of acquired knowledge (part of a body of knowledge which exists irrespective of the individual), of acquired skills, and of reflection which includes as an important element the use of the imagination. It is recognized that the effectiveness of experience, as a basis for the learning process, depends upon the quality of experience, and its meaning, and that it is not possible to provide a fully personal experience for all that must be learned. The Church, in its Christian education function, must think in terms of 'educative experience' as much as of 'experiential education'.

7. The Social Context

Seventh, the approach of this syllabus recognizes that the church is not isolated from the world and Christian education must take account of its social context. The local community, as well as national and international issues, contributes to the church syllabus. Furthermore, the church must take account of the changing environment which conditions education and learning. Technological developments can be either a gift to the church or a threat to it. The moral, personal and social questions which are raised by technological developments must be recognized and faced seriously. At the same time developments like microprocessors, video, and cable television can radically enlarge the educational capacity of the churches if they have the foresight to take advantage of them in the collaborative use of ideas and financial resources.

From *Being God's People*, Methodist Division of Education and Youth and the National Christian Education Council, 1987

The 'Pilgrim Church' model

3.22 The image of the Church as a pilgrim community adds new dimensions which may be helpful. While the school model can all too easily be interpreted as teacher and taught and the family model may feel too restricted, the pilgrim community comprises a band of people all sharing in and learning from common experience.

3.23 Imagine a group of people of all ages going for a long walk together. At times the children and adults will walk along together, talking as they go, sharing stories with first one person and then another, each observing different things and sharing their discoveries. At times the children will lag behind and some of the adults will have to wait for them or urge them on. Sometimes the smallest children may ask to be carried. At other times, though, the children will dash ahead making new discoveries and may, perhaps, pull the adults along to see what they have found. Some adults may well behave like these children, of course. For all there will be times of progress and times of rest and refreshment, time to admire the view, and times of plodding on, and the eventual satisfaction of arrival at their destination.

3.24 Of course, a pilgrimage is something more than a hike. Traditionally it is a group of people of all kinds and ages united in reaching a common goal. They stop at significant places on the way. They exchange their own stories, and share past experiences and memories of those who have gone before them. They look forward to the rest of the journey and to reaching their ultimate destination.

3.25 When we apply this image to the community of the Church we see that there are still those who teach and those who learn – but the teaching comes from all members of the community and the learning just as much from informal as formal situations...

The pilgrim model suggests learning from shared experience and shared stories. It implies developing new skills, adapting and changing attitudes, and looking for new visions. We are all slow to recognise as adult Christians that this sort of learning is a life-long process. The success of adult Christian Education courses is a step in the right direction; the pilgrim community suggests this is not an optional extra but a real necessity for all.

3.26 We are learning, as we have seen, a great deal from the family model of Christian nurture. But families can become inward-looking, can concentrate solely on their own internal lives, can be too restrictive for the growing life of children and adults. These are dangers we need to guard against, just as we must recognise the numbers of children who do not find the family image a source of security and comfort, and who may also need a wider community to which to relate. At best the pilgrim Church provides just such a wider grouping; people of different styles and ages, people of widely ranging sympathies and ideals, people whose experience and concerns are of use to the children travelling with them, and with whom the children can share their insights and skills. Yet how often do we create the situations where the two may meet and share?

3.27 What comes through time and again in the pilgrim model is that all those involved on the journey are inextricably bound up one with the other. All are in some sense responsible one for the other, all are learning and sharing in the communal life. The whole body is impoverished by the loss of any of its members. All learn from each other. All need more than one kind of knowledge, experience or skill. Nurture which does not include experience and worship as well as learning will always fail to create real growth. At the same time we need to be sensitive and supportive to those adults who are apprehensive about this kind of involvement.

3.28 Any programme of Christian nurture focused solely on knowledge – biblical, doctrinal or moral – is inadequate without an equal concentration on worship, prayer and growth in the spiritual life. So it is as important to say 'Our children are not taught to pray' as the much more frequently heard 'Our children aren't getting taught Bible stories today'. It would also be good to hear the complaint 'Our children don't get real experience of what being a Christian is all about'. Some difficult questions follow. Is our Church an environment where children can absorb the importance of all these elements of the Christian life? What opportunities do we provide for children to work alongside adults in a joint venture? What quality of experience of worship, Christian learning and the Christian life does your church provide for its children? And the question is not just about what your Sunday school or family service provides, but about what is provided by your church in all its variety and life.

3.29 The same sort of questions apply to the content of our course materials. Some critics believe that children are not getting a real diet of Christian teaching on which to feed and grow. Sadly what they often mean by this is a heavy dose of random Bible stories, the geography of first-century Palestine and Church history. We would agree that children often do not get a sense of the cutting edge of Christianity, the strength of its ideals and the reality of its demands. We need to establish from the beginning the essence of the great salvation story as it is lived out in the Bible, and as it shapes our understanding of our journey.

We would also argue that children are not given sufficient opportunity to become instruments of their own learning, to share in discussion, to match their stories to the stories of God's people, to contribute to joint activity, to make real contributions to worship. Throughout we are arguing for a better diet of learning, experience and worship in the lives of our children, in a community where all are valued for themselves, where it is leader and fellow-learners rather than teacher and taught, where all are involved in the enterprise, all partners on the journey, all seeking to grow through greater understanding, deeper worship and a wider experience of Christian living.

From *Children In the Way,* a Church of England Report, National Society and Church House Publishing, 1988

1990s
Spirituality, Context
and Integration

The 1989 Children Act led to Social Service Departments and social workers becoming specifically attentive to the religious persuasion of children in care and generally to a more holistic approach among those working with children. These developments contributed to the thinking behind the United Reformed Church's publication *Towards a Charter for Children in the Church*. The unfolding debate was later reflected in John Bradford's *Caring for the Whole Child: a Holistic Approach to Spirituality*, published by the Children's Society (1995). *Towards a Charter for Children in the Church* was the first of a number of publications and programmes which emphasised the rights of the children and the need for greater care to be taken by those leading children's groups to respect the child and guard against any form of abuse, including spiritual abuse. *Unfinished Business*, a summation by the Consultative Group on Ministry among Children of the major agenda issues of earlier reports and of issues facing the Churches, was published in 1994.

As each of the mainstream denominations published new service books, it became evident how close the study of liturgy and the Lima texts (*Baptism, Eucharist and Ministry*) had brought the Churches. The same can be said of Christian education. For the first time in four hundred years, a *Catechism of the Catholic Church* (to be used universally) was published, but a *General Directory for Catechesis* followed this in 1997. That the Churches have much in common in their educational approaches is particularly evident in the section on 'Elements of Methodology'. The imaginative material produced by the Roman Catholic Diocese of Liverpool, for instance, sets out a developmental understanding of children and aims that could have been written ecumenically. The introduction to a programme on prayer reads:

> Children have a natural aptitude for prayer. They are open to God. They respond in joy, wonder, anger, disappointment and elation to the world around them. The whole of creation is new to them and their days are full of endless exploration and discovery.

Other publications also reflected the respect which had developed for the spiritual insight of children, for instance, Coles' *The Spiritual Life of Children* (HarperCollins, 1990), Hull's *God Talk With Young Children* (Christian Education Movement, 1991) and most particularly the Chichester Project's *The Education of the Whole Child,* edited by Ericker, Ericker, Sullivan, Ota and Fletcher (Cassell, 1997).

The published discussion of Fowler's *Stages of Faith* continued unabated. See for instance, *How Faith Grows: Faith Development and Christian Education* (J Astley, National Society and Church House Publishing, 1991), *Stages of Faith and Religious Development: Implications for Church, Education and Society* (SCM Press, 1992), and *Learning in the Way* (J Astley (ed), Gracewing, 2000).

The exploration of the innate spirituality of children found an echo in the considerable interest shown by adults in spirituality, but in some centres there was a more gritty approach to adult theological education. In part this grew out of thinking about mission and community development. It was inspired by examples of theological education in other parts of the world and, for instance, by work pioneered in Birmingham and reported in *Doing Theology* (L Green, Mowbray, 1990). It reflected the greater emphasis placed on theological reflection (see *The Art of Theological Reflection* (K P O'Connel and J de Beer, Crossword Publishing Company, 1994)). The contextualising of theological education was based on the understanding that all theology originates from and bears the marks – strengths and limitations – of a particular context and particular biographies. It was argued that theology and the work of the Church must take account of social, economic, gender, ecclesial and other contexts. This was said to be done most effectively by facilitating the development of local, temporary and partial theological expressions in much the same way as, earlier, Base Community and Minjung Groups in Latin America and Korea and more recently Dalit and Black African groups in India and South Africa had developed theologies which had been both liberating socially and politically and the source of renewed liturgical celebration. The educational emphasis on integration was based on the recognition that neither one theological discipline, nor any one human experience, can stand apart from any other. There was need, in spite of a pervasive postmodernism, to look at theological education and Christian life holistically. That the emphases on contextualisation and, to a lesser extent, on integration were stimulated by work done in churches in other parts of the world also pointed to the growing contact between members of the world

Christian community and to the influence of books such as *Transforming Mission: Paradigm Shifts in Theology of Mission* (J D Bosch, Orbis, 1991), *Images of Jesus* and *Europe: Was it Ever Really Christian?* (both A Wessels, SCM Press, 1990 and 1994 respectively), *Feminist Theology: A Reader* (A Loades, SPCK 1990), and *'Voices from the Margins'* (R Sugirtharajah (ed), SPCK, 1992).

Towards a Charter for Children in the Church

1. Children are equal partners with adults in the life of the church.
2. The full diet of Christian worship is for children as well as adults.
3. Learning is for the whole church, adults and children.
4. Fellowship is for all – each belonging meaningfully to the rest.
5. Service is for children to give, as well as adults.
6. The call to evangelism comes to all God's people of whatever age.
7. The Holy Spirit speaks powerfully through children as well as adults.
8. The discovery and development of gifts in children and adults is a key function of the church.
9. As a church community we must learn to do only those things in separate age groups which we cannot in all conscience do together.
10. The concept of the 'Priesthood of all Believers' includes children.

Could you nail this to the door of your Church?

Towards a Charter for Children in the Church, The United Reformed Church, 1990

In *The Measure of Mission* there is an extended description of how the word 'evangelism' should be understood. The heart of the section is contained in the following sentences:

Evangelism is the making known of the gospel of the Lord Jesus Christ, especially to those who do not know it ... We are charged to communicate that the life, death and resurrection of Jesus Christ is good news from God. Evangelism usually involves the use of words, but not inevitably so. Identification and solidarity with people are indispensable and may themselves be forms of evangelism if they evoke a response which enables Jesus Christ to be named. Much communication takes place at a non-verbal level and even the verbal has a visual aspect and can have other forms of expression added to it: drama, music, dance, mime or symbolic action. It is essential in evangelism that the dignity of human beings is affirmed by giving them freedom to choose, without pressure ... Certainly it is the hope of evangelists that their hearers will be persuaded and come to faith...

(The Measure of Mission, *Church House Publishing, 1987*)

The first strength of this definition is that it focuses upon the story to be told and the telling of it. Some definitions speak too much of what is held to be the object of the exercise (such as conversion and incorporation into the Church). Here the stress is truly upon the *evangel* – the life, death and resurrection of Jesus Christ (cf. 1 Cor. 15.1–8). This is what, in this report ... is called 'the story'. In children's evangelism the concept of evangelism that is most satisfactory is 'story-orientated' rather than 'response-orientated'. So much of what we may be doing is investing in the future – building in lasting memories of the story and the people who told it.

The second strength of this definition is that it avoids a commitment to any particular means of communication. Rather than talk of 'proclaiming the gospel' – with all the associations of preaching *at* people – it settles for 'making known ... the gospel'. The Lambeth Conference Resolution 43 concerning the Decade of Evangelism also uses this helpful form of words. The value of this terminology is that one can focus at least as much on how people *receive* the information as on how others may *impart* it. Too much discussion of evangelism is weighted on the 'retailer' end of the equation rather than the 'consumer' end. In children's evangelism (and surely this ought to apply to any type of evangelism) it is important to reflect upon *how people discover the gospel for themselves*. In the majority of cases the discovery is made as a result of a process of experiences and encounters – of which direct story telling is usually but not always one component.

The third strength of this definition lies in its emphasis upon 'identification and solidarity' as indispensable and as having an evangelistic effect in themselves. We are talking here about the incarnational aspect of evangelism. Disembodied messages can never replace the presence of message bearers. In children's work this is especially important. It is often Christ seen in the person of a leader that communicates and remains in the memory. Again 'solidarity' matters. An ill-resourced club or Sunday gathering staffed by a lone enthusiast or two, is no evidence of the congregation's solidarity with children. The plea of the Working Party is that the body language of the congregation should speak of the welcome and the importance given to the children of the neighbourhood.

The fourth strength of this definition lies in its respect for the dignity and vulnerability of those being evangelised. This should always be the case but it is a particularly crucial matter when we contemplate evangelising children and especially the children of those who do not attend church. It is very easy to sway children – particularly when they are members of a crowd. Manipulation is all too easy and very often it is completely unintentional. An enthusiastic young adult talking attractively to a group of children who have just laughed and sung heartily can evoke a response to whatever he or she is angling for, that may seem genuine at the time, but soon afterwards will be seen to be spurious. More seriously, some ways of handling themes like judgement can disturb sensitive children for prolonged periods of time.

The fifth strength of this definition is that, in spite of fully recognising the danger of exerting false pressures, it acknowledges the great hope that lies behind all evangelism. The 'hope of evangelists' is that 'their hearers will be persuaded and come to faith'. That hope should be the foundation of their prayers but it needs to be informed by a realism. The reality is that while children can easily 'make decisions', these, while sincere, are often fleeting. What children's evangelisers need to keep in mind is a longer term scenario. Rather than seeking to achieve an adult type response now, what we long for is *an adult type of response to Christ when the children are adults*. There are appropriate responses for children to make and these will be discussed in the next chapter, but many of these relate to identification with the group or community in what it is saying or doing.

From *All God's Children?*, a joint report of the Church of England's Boards of Mission and Education, National Society and Church House Publishing, 1991

The power of a concrete theology

How can children understand the concept of God when it is so abstract? Should the idea of God be introduced to young children when it is beyond their understanding? When are children ready for talk about God?

These are some of the questions which frequently occur to parents and teachers whether at home, in church or at school.

What is an Abstract Idea?

The question whether children can understand the idea of God raises a problem about abstract ideas. We must not assume that children, even very young children, cannot understand abstract ideas. After all, what is an abstract idea?

If an abstract idea is an idea about something which you cannot touch or see, then let us consider words like 'tomorrow', 'darkness', 'big' and 'heaven'. None of these are available to sense perception. 'Big', for example, refers to a relationship. The same thing can be big when compared to this but not big when compared to that. You cannot tell whether something is big just by looking at it or touching it. Let us take the familiar children's puzzle about why tomorrow never comes. Children will laugh at the idea that when it comes it is not tomorrow any longer. There is something amusing about a reality which never quite comes within reach. In spite of this, children can use the word 'tomorrow' at quite an early age. So in this first sense of 'abstract idea', children seem to be able to cope quite well.

Perhaps an abstract idea is simply a generalisation. Children can generalise at a very early age. When your child asks, 'Is that a dog?' there is surely a general or an abstract idea of dogginess which is being fitted to this particular image or likeness of a dog.

The idea of God is abstract in both of these senses. In the first place, you cannot touch or see God any more than you can touch or see tomorrow. That does not mean that young children cannot talk quite sensibly about God. Secondly, the word 'God' is a kind of generalisation by which we refer to 'the ground and source of everything', 'the power of all life', 'the ground of being'. The word 'God' is certainly more difficult than the word 'dog'. Children see lots of particular dogs and can thus form a general idea of dogginess. They do not see lots and lots of particular gods, unless they are from the Hindu tradition. On the other hand the word 'God' is not only an abstract generalisation but is also the name of an actual God. He is the God of Abraham and the God and father of our Lord Jesus Christ, the God who brought up Israel out of bondage, who did these particular things...

There are many stories about limitations of the concrete thinker, but you seldom hear stories about the power and flexibility of concrete thinking. The child, for example, asks what God had for supper. The parent replies that God doesn't eat because he has no body. 'What?' asks the surprised child. 'Do his legs go right up to his neck?' Many people hearing this familiar anecdote conclude that children cannot understand the concept of God. Here is a story which illustrates the expressive power and flexibility of the concrete or indeed the pre-concrete thinker, since the child in question was 3½ years old.

Example 1

CHILD:	Was that man's name Mr Bird?
PARENT:	Yes.
CHILD:	Was he a bird? *(Laughs)*
PARENT:	Was he like a bird?
CHILD:	No.
PARENT:	Why not?
CHILD:	Birds have feathers. *(Laughs)*
PARENT:	And the man didn't have feathers did he? He had clothes. *(Both laugh)*
CHILD:	And birds have wings.
PARENT:	Yes.
CHILD:	Birds die.
PARENT:	So do people.
CHILD:	*(Silence)*
PARENT:	What does 'die' mean'?

CHILD: You go to be with God.

PARENT: Where is God?

CHILD: Up in the sky.

PARENT: But up in the sky there are clouds.

CHILD: *(Laughs)* No but I mean when you go up and up and up past the clouds and you go *(speaking in a little high thin voice)* up and up and up and then you come *(whispering)* to a teeny cottage and in that cottage there's God.

Interpretation

This young child knew perfectly well that there was something odd about the literal location of God in a place in the sky, but could not express that oddity in the form of a structure of sentences arranged so as to reason from one sentence to the next. In other words, the child could not say 'when I say "sky" I am referring to a symbol for that which stands over against this earth and our lives. I am trying to say that God is transcendent, and that the dead are likewise translated somehow into this other plane of reality.'

No, the child cannot say that or think in those terms, but the child laughs at the question about clouds. Why? The child knows that in asking the question the parent has playfully and perhaps deliberately misunderstood. The child responds not by moving from concrete to abstract thinking, but by using concrete pictures in literal ways. Moreover. the child dramatises the situation by speaking in a higher, smaller voice, suggesting that this is something beyond the ordinary plane which is half comical and yet very serious and important, like a shared secret...

... What distinguishes abstract from concrete thinking is not that the former makes use of concepts, but that the concepts are related in abstract patterns whereas in concrete thinking the concepts are related in practical, immediate, or experienced contexts. Older children can relate to concepts within the domain of speech alone, which may not be confined to story, while younger children relate most easily to concepts when they are encountered in immediate experience including narration.

By claiming that abstract thinking is conceptual, the impression is given that conceptual thought is the goal of the developmental process, and that pre-abstract thinking is not really thinking at all. This idea is false in several ways. We have already seen that there is conceptual development at every stage of language development, and we need also to realise that conceptual thought is not the only kind of thinking.

There would be some advantages if instead of speaking of concepts we spoke of constructs. A construct is a combination of idea, picture and attitude towards some aspect of experience, which has developed through experience and will continue to develop. The word construct emphasises the tentative and the changing nature of thought, and the fact that it is assembled through connecting several bits and pieces of experience. The word concept tends to suggest something more absolute, more finished and coherent, something against which our thinking can be judged rather than something which we are actually thinking. The young child's construct of fatherhood may undergo rearrangement when it is discovered that other children call their male parents 'Daddy', and the child's construct 'car driver' will develop when it is discovered that there are fathers as well as mothers who drive cars.

One of my own children came back from an outing with the remark 'And you know, Daddy, there was a man sitting in mummy's seat' i.e. in the driving seat.

Constructs would be related to each other in concrete ways in middle childhood and in more abstract and theoretical ways in later childhood, just as appears to be the case when we speak of concepts. The pre-concrete child would think intuitively, in the sense that the constructs are less well developed, more impressionistic, liable to rapid swings and changes, and several constructs of a similar reality may exist with little apparent integration. It is that which gives the thought of very young children its delightfully fanciful and creative qualities to the adult ear.

It may also be helpful if we speak of thinking in images. Let us take the thinking which is done in dreams. There is no doubt that dreams do represent a form of thinking, and experiences of insight and even illumination occur to many people when their dreams are interpreted, i.e. translated from dream-thought into conscious thought. The processes of dream-thought are profoundly different from those of conscious thought.

Dream-thought is expressed in images. These may include audible as well as visual images, as when one dreams of hearing someone shouting. It is not that we think in words during waking life and in pictures at night, but that the words and pictures are associated in a different way. With the pressures, dangers and realities of the external world withdrawn, the sleeping thinker draws upon both recent and remote memories to fashion processes of thought in which emotion is usually dominant. We often sense in our dreams that one thing leads to another with a kind of strange mysterious logic which we find both trivial and sometimes strangely impressive when we consider it from the vantage point of consciousness.

Images are also important in our waking thoughts. This is true in all sorts of trivial ways e.g. I only recognise you because I have an image of you from yesterday, and our language is studded with metaphors which help us to understand each other. When we speak of a very complicated climatic change affecting the whole of our planet, we speak of the 'greenhouse effect', using the homely, concrete image of the greenhouse not only as a convenient shorthand but as a way of enabling us to grasp something of the immense and complex significance of the thing.

The Power of Images

Images are important in our thinking in ways which are far from trivial. There is today a far greater realisation of the role of the imagination in scientific thought and discovery than was the case one hundred or even twenty years ago. Scientific thinking is not the cold, rational process of thought it was once imagined to be, but is often experienced as a series of flashing insights, of imaginative leaps, of solutions which just seem to come from nowhere, often driven by stirring new images which relate situations in new and unexpected ways.

Moreover, it is often through our images that we are moved to develop our patterns of thought. Although images always have a specific content, they also seem to have a power to re-pattern our thinking processes. Many adults have found that during times of crisis in their lives, the various phases of re-adjustment have been marked by a certain compelling image which came to the forefront of the mind, and which gradually (or suddenly) gave way to another image that seemed to represent a solution to the problem. The more far-reaching the crisis, the more likely it is that it will be expressed and resolved in images. If a problem is mainly administrative and can be handled in a compartment of life as a contained problem, it can often be sorted out through conceptual thinking, but if the problem is systemic, affecting the whole person, then progress through images seems more common. Perhaps this is why images appear to be most powerful in politics, religion and in literature.

The reason for this power seems to be the way in which images combine thought, feeling and experience in a certain vivid, perhaps even concrete way...

My Heart Told Me

Example 7

CHILD *(aged 5¼)*: I've got four invisible friends.

PARENT: Who are they?

CHILD: Well, there's Mary, Jesus, God and the Holy Spirit.

PARENT: *(Laughing)* Who told you that?

CHILD: My heart told me that *(pause)* my brain told me that *(laughs)* Does my brain talk to me? Does it say hello (child's name)?

Interpretation

This child is attending a Catholic infant school. It is possible that the image of the 'invisible friend' was remembered from something said at the school, and the fact that the three Persons of the Trinity are referred to correctly together with Mary supports this suggestion. It is also possible that the 'heart' as the locus of religious devotion has come from the school. Be that as it may, this is a useful image for the child, and it is noteworthy that it was repeated spontaneously and happily at home.

Perhaps more interesting is the way in which the image and the question 'Who told you that?' seems to stimulate the child into an awareness of image-making processes. Is it the heart or the brain? Are there two? Where do thoughts and images come from? Are we in charge of our own thoughts?

The idea of God as resident within human thoughts, ideas and speech does not lessen the transcendent power of these ideas, but enables the child to begin a process of constructive criticism. If attention is never drawn to speech itself and to imagery in particular as the context of God, if attention is always upon God and never upon God-talk, there is a danger that God becomes too much a part of the external world and insufficiently a bridge for the child's inner and outer experiences.

A Very Big Idea

It is better for children to have too many images than too few. Indeed, I am not sure that a child can have too many images of God. It is certainly far more common for a child to be starved of images or even fixated on one image into which every other aspect of God must fit.

Sometimes it is right to contradict an image: usually, however, the child's images should be confirmed and extended. It is best to follow the lead of a child and to encourage the child as theological image-maker.

Example 8

FIRST CHILD *(aged 5.2)*: Is God the air?

PARENT: No. God's not the air but he's a bit like the air.

SECOND CHILD *(aged 3.9)*: Is God the ceiling?

PARENT: No, God is not the ceiling, but he is a bit like the ceiling.

FIRST CHILD: Is he a round baby?

PARENT: No, he's not a round baby, but he's a bit like a little baby because he's new and fresh.

SECOND CHILD: Is he invisible?

PARENT: Yes he is.

FIRST CHILD: Is he like a round baby with wings flying through the air? *(general laughter)*.

PARENT: God is a bit like lots of things but he's not exactly like anything.

SECOND CHILD: Why not?

PARENT: Because God is unique. God hasn't really got a shape at all.

FIRST CHILD: Why hasn't he got a shape?

PARENT: Because God is a sort of idea. Have ideas got shapes?

FIRST CHILD: *(Pause, then laughs)* No.

PARENT: Well, God is a bit like a very big idea.

Interpretation

The 18 months difference between these two children is evident. The older child identifies God with the air, the younger child with the ceiling. The ceiling is visible, and the younger child goes on to the quality of invisibility later in the discussion.

The parent's intention is to move from ideas of identity to ideas of likeness. In this way the conversation moves from the nature or essence of God to images or models of God. If children can be helped to use the expression 'like' when speaking of God, the way is open for many comparisons. The parent agreed that God was a bit like a ceiling partly in order to avoid discouraging the younger child, and partly because God might indeed be thought of as being above us, higher than us, arching over us in protection and so on. There is, of course, a whimsical aspect of the younger child's observations. The child will ask about the first thing its eyes happen to rest on, and in this case the ceiling was possibly suggested by the comment about the air.

With the image of the round baby, the next step is taken; the parent begins to suggest aspects of the image which may be like God. Even if an entire image is not applicable, aspects of it may be. With the thought of invisibility, the discussion moves from images to qualities. Of course, it would once again have been possible to have said that in some senses God is invisible and yet he is also visible in all beautiful things and so on. The younger child, however, needs more affirmation. She needs to know that she is on the right track, whereas the older child has a richer fund of images to draw upon and can make more distinctions. No doubt the image of the winged cherub has been seen in religious art, whether in books or on Christmas cards.

The pause that follows laughter is often a good moment to introduce a new idea or to sum things up. Hence the change in the discussion at this point. It doesn't matter if the children don't know the word 'unique'. This may be their first introduction to the word, but its meaning is clear enough in context and they will return to it later. The discussion concludes with the parent suggesting a new image, that of an idea. Like the other images, there are only certain aspects of this which apply, hence the concluding thought that God is a bit like this, but only a bit...

Example 24

Both children were helping to look for mummy's glasses. The younger child suddenly found them.

FIRST CHILD (aged 4.2): I've found them! I've found them!

PARENT: *(from downstairs)* Oh, you are a good girl. Bring them down to me.

SECOND CHILD (aged 5.8): I was helping too because I was praying to God. I was praying to God that you would find them sooner or later.

Example 25

The child woke up about 11 p.m. crying. Father went upstairs to comfort her.

CHILD (aged 4.6): I want mummy to come up and talk to me too.

PARENT: Mummy is sewing. She'll come up later.

CHILD: Grandma was sewing. She was sewing a new jumper for me for next year.

PARENT: That was kind of grandma. Aren't you lucky to have two grandmas and two grandpas?

CHILD: Yes. I've got everything I need.

PARENT: Yes, you have.

CHILD: I've got plenty of toys and ... games to play with.

PARENT: Yes, and you've got a nice warm bed to sleep in, and clothes to keep you warm.

CHILD: Is God really everywhere like (older brother) says he is?

PARENT: Yes, he is everywhere.

CHILD: Is he even on my head?

PARENT: Yes. He's everywhere, but especially when we are talking about him.

CHILD: Like when we are praying.

PARENT: Yes. But also when we are just talking.

CHILD: Like we're talking about him now.

PARENT: Yes, and in all our talking. It's nice to talk isn't it?

CHILD: Yes.

PARENT: You go to sleep now then.

Prayer presents rich possibilities for developing images of God. Questions about God's way of life, his daily routine and so on are often evoked by the context in which he is about to be addressed. The following example is a young child's first spontaneous theological observation, and it took place in the context of preparing to go to sleep. although there had been no particular invitation to pray.

Example 26

CHILD (aged 2.6): Does God go to bed when he's sleepy'?

PARENT: God never gets sleepy. He always stays wide awake.

CHILD: Doesn't he have a bed then?

PARENT: Well, he always stays wide awake, to look after things and to love us.

CHILD: Oh *(goes to sleep).*

Interpretation

This child had been taken by a neighbour to a school mass only a few days earlier where he had, for the first time, spontaneously joined in the prayer time. His prayer, which he made up, was simply 'Help, God'.

Prayer Conversations

Prayer is based upon images of speaking and listening. In prayer, human relationships with God are constructed on the basis of the human experience of conversation. As with all images of God, this should be placed beside other images. Proliferation of images enriches the child's conversational repertoire and helps to prevent rigidity in thinking about God. Metaphors based on God as seeing and listening should be placed alongside language which refers to God as knowing or as being. The tendency of prayer to suggest that God is like a person doing things also needs to be supplemented (not corrected) by images of God as the sustainer rather than the intervener. Both these points are illustrated in the following examples...

Example 33

PARENT: Would you like to say the Lord's Prayer?

CHILD (aged 4.2): Yes.

PARENT: Say after me then: Our Father

CHILD: Our Father

PARENT: Which art in heaven

CHILD: *(No reply)*

PARENT: Which art in heaven?

CHILD: (Child's name) doesn't know which are in heaven.

PARENT: OK. Miss that bit out then. Hallowed be Thy name.

CHILD: *(No comment)*

PARENT: Hallowed be Thy name?

CHILD: (Child's name) doesn't know hallowed be Thy name.

PARENT: OK. Thy kingdom come.

CHILD: (Child's name) doesn't know that bit.

PARENT: OK.

CHILD: Daddy (child's name) knows Our Father, Amen.

PARENT: *(placing hand on child's head)* O.K. That's fine. Our Father, Amen

Often it is best to let children take the initiative in requesting prayer. Sometimes this will come from church or school. Individual styles will, of course, vary widely from one religious tradition to another, but I have always found it best to avoid the 'God bless mummy and daddy' pattern. In general children should not be encouraged to offer petitions in prayer, since this easily establishes a magical aura around prayer, feeds the child's fantasies of omnipotence, and establishes God as being a magical giver of all bounties, leading inevitably to disappointment and rationalisation. It is far more creative to encourage the child to express gratitude; it is better to be thankful for what has happened than to lay out magical words against fear. The use of memorised liturgical prayers is often the most satisfactory. If the child is taught the Lord's Prayer, there are endless opportunities for conversation and reflection. The child will understand the words, since they will be in the context of a trusted relationship at the close of the day. They will be enjoyed for their sound and their familiarity, while as conversational gambits they can gradually be extended so as to create networks of meaning. It does not matter that a child cannot all at once offer an adult understanding of a prayer. The great liturgical prayers, whether it is 'lighten our darkness' or 'Hail Mary, full of grace' offer the child a rich religious vocabulary and an opportunity for image-formation. It does not matter if there are weeks or months when there is no prayer. The presence of God can be realised in many ways, and the child must not be conditioned into believing that the passage from wakefulness to sleep is dangerous or sinful unless accompanied by prayer. This turns prayer into a talisman against the dark. Whether we wake or sleep, we are the Lord's, and whether we pray or not His presence is with us. Prayer can be the realisation of that presence, but only if it is entered into creatively and flexibly.

Prayer can often be introduced in the context of ordinary conversation. The typical final conversations of the day often involve laughter over something which happened, recollection of a happiness, and anticipation of something which will take place tomorrow, or a shared memory. In these little exchanges, when the child has the parent all alone, there is a first encounter with self-criticism, with life-review, and with the selective evaluation of the day. 'What is worth remembering? What is worth looking forward to?' This is the unspoken agenda of these last conversations. God as the participant in these conversations is the natural bond of sympathy and of value. The God whom we present to our children in Christian nurture must, however, always be the God who calls our children up out of the house of bondage, out of slavery into freedom. Let us therefore give our children a rich repertoire of symbols which will enhance their creativity and which will lead them into a lifetime of security and risk-taking but let us not inflict upon them rigid patterns of obligation charged with magical hopes and guilty fears.

From *God Talk With Young Children*, J Hull, Christian Education Movement, 1991

According to the popular Sunday school chorus, Jesus is 'the friend of little children'. And, of course, from the viewpoint of the Christian believer, who could complain about that? Very properly the words convey the sense that the gracious love of God revealed in Jesus is not exclusive, that fellowship with God through Jesus is open – even, and especially, to children, who serve as a kind of 'focal instance' of the breadth of the divine mercy. Nevertheless, a survey of the gospels shows that the picture of Jesus as the children's friend cannot be arrived at straightforwardly. To put the matter more precisely, the claim that Jesus is 'the friend of little children' may be a theological and christological *intuition of Christian faith* which is perhaps only tenuously linked to the gospels' stories of Jesus's actual dealings with children or teaching about them.

Among the grounds for caution are the following considerations. First, it is important not to come to the gospels expecting too much. Like the Bible as a whole, the gospels are – in some sense at least – products of their time and patriarchal social setting. Note, for instance, Matthew's ending to the story of the miraculous feeding: 'And those who ate were about five thousand, *not counting women and children'* (Matt 14:21; cf also 15:38). The additional mention of the women and children in Matthew's version doubtless expresses the evangelist's conviction that women and children belong to the people of God and are recipients of the divine grace revealed in Jesus. At the same time, however, the way they are mentioned presupposes a patriarchal social structure in which the male household head held precedence and the identity and roles of women and children were defined in relation to him.

Second, like the Bible as a whole, the gospels were written by male adults for male adults and their dependants, who included children. This helps to explain why much of the biblical (and gospel) material on children in relation to morality has to do with the obligation upon children – including adult children – of *obedience* to their parents, in accordance with the fifth commandment (eg Mk 10:19). As Duncan Derrett puts it: 'After a child reached the age of 5 he began to learn that society was duty-orientated, not right-orientated'. Elsewhere, as we shall see, the child and children are used in metaphorical ways to express what is incumbent, religiously and spiritually, upon *adults*. Only in one or two instances is attention drawn to children in their own right. It is difficult to escape the general conclusion – unappealing to liberals perhaps – that biblical morality works 'from the top down'; and therefore that Jesus's friendship of children (the sick, the poor, etc) is an act of *condescension*.

Third, it is worth pointing out that two of the four canonical gospels have no material whatsoever on Jesus as a child. For Mark and John it is Jesus's adult, public ministry, culminating in his death and resurrection, which constitutes 'the gospel'. And in none of the gospels does the adult Jesus refer to his own childhood in his teaching. Matthew and Luke contain birth and infancy narratives, and in Lk 2:41–51 there is a story about 'the boy *[ho pais]* Jesus' at the age of twelve attending the Passover with his parents in Jerusalem and revealing in the temple signs of his great wisdom. But it is impossible to be confident about the value of this material as historical evidence pertaining to Jesus as a child. Its value lies, rather, in the testimony it bears to the post-resurrection faith of the respective evangelists that Jesus, the son of Mary and Joseph, was also the Son of God (cf Matt 1:18–23; Lk 1:30–35; 3:23–38). Only later, from the mid-second century onwards, do we have *apocryphal* stories about Jesus's 'hidden years' prior to his baptism, the earliest and most important of which are the so-called *Protevangelium of James* and the *Infancy Gospel of Thomas*. But these stories are pious fictions produced, in the absence of controlling, canonical tradition, for the purpose of satisfying curiosity and defending christological dogma.

Fourth, the claim that Jesus is the children's friend has to cope with certain rather uncomfortable facts about Jesus himself. One is that Jesus himself apparently did not marry and so had no children of his own. Like Paul after him, and contrary to the prevailing social expectations of the time, Jesus understood his vocation as requiring the renunciation of marital and family ties (cf Matt 19:11–12; 1 Cor 7:7). Another is that Jesus called on his disciples to subordinate their own familial obligations for his sake. This included obligations to children: 'If anyone comes to me and does not hate his own father and mother and wife and children *[ta tekna]* and brothers and sisters ... he cannot be my disciple' (Lk 14:26 par Matt 10:37; cf Mk 10:29–30). Yet again, Jesus warned his disciples of serious enmities between parents and their children on his account (Mk 13:12 par Matt 10:21; Lk 21:16). Further, Jesus is nowhere depicted as a teacher of children, except insofar as they were present in the crowds of men and women who thronged to hear him. Children at play provide the stuff of just one of Jesus's parables (Matt 11:16–19 par Lk 7:31–35) – but the parable itself is addressed to adults, and depiction of the fickle, immature children in the parable itself is hardly flattering. In sum, children *per se* were not at the heart of Jesus's message. What *was* central was the prophetic summons of *the people of Israel* to repentance and to a renewed obedience to the will of God in view of the imminent coming of God. In response to this summons, children are expected to obey their parents, in accordance with the commandments (eg Mk 7:9–13; 10:19). Similarly, the various accounts of the miraculous healing of children (eg the healing of Jairus's twelve-year-old daughter, in Mk 5:21–43) are expressions of the power and character of God's coming rule over all people already at work through Jesus.

A fifth and final reason for caution has to do, not with the setting of Jesus and the gospels, but with the setting of *the readers* of the gospels in the modern period. The 'discovery' of child-hood, as a recognized developmental stage of importance in its own right, is a modern phenomenon, as Philippe Ariès and others have shown. And Robert Raikes's Sunday schools for children were not begun in England until the late eighteenth century. In other words, the modern, western fascination with children and the sentimentalizing of childhood ought not to be read back into the gospels. It is possible, of course, that this modern 'discovery' of childhood leads us quite properly to ask questions and to make discoveries of Jesus and the gospels which it was not possible to do before, when the readers' (and writers') conceptual and experiential horizons were different. On the other hand, it is possible that the psychological, social and institutional *investment* in children so characteristic of modernity may lead us to see in the gospels little more than the reflection of our own needs and to interpret them only in ways which justify our prior investment. To what extent, for example, is the Jesus who is the friend of little children a coded way of *idealizing* children (by associating them with Jesus) the consequence of which is, by so distancing ourselves from children, to avoid acting responsibly toward them as actual human beings? Or is it a way of idealizing *Jesus* (by associating him with 'little children') in order to keep at a distance the claims that he makes upon our lives as adults? Alternatively, does the picture of Jesus as the children's friend express a desire to find in Jesus the friend of the child *in us*? Such possibilities are no less real for being hidden. Potentially they are part of what we bring as readers to the gospel material about Jesus and children.

Jesus and children

There are two noteworthy gospel traditions relevant to the study of Jesus's attitude to children: Mk 9:33–37 and Mk 10:13–16 (and parallels). These have received attention in the commentaries and in the works of, among others, Simon Légasse and Hans-Ruedi Weber. Commentators agree that the sayings of Jesus about children have a complex tradition history. In general, the tendency of the tradition is to develop the metaphorical potential of the child for teaching about Christian discipleship. As Hans-Ruedi Weber says, with not a little exasperation: 'Already Mark, Matthew and Luke seem to have been more interested in what a child symbolizes than in Jesus's attitude to actual children'. But it may be that Weber is looking for something which is not there, and that for Jesus, as well as for the evangelists, it was the child as metaphor which was most important in his teaching. Nonetheless, several findings about Jesus's attitude to children are highly probable.

First, Jesus held that children have a share in the kingdom of God. The saying of Jesus in v 14 of Mk 10:13–16 makes this clear: 'Let the children *[ta paidia]* come to me, do not hinder them; for to such belongs the kingdom of God'. In this episode Jesus angrily countermands the disciples (who show their characteristic obtuseness), welcomes the children and, as a sign of blessing – reminiscent, perhaps, of the blessing of Ephraim and Manasseh by Jacob in Genesis 48 – lays his hands upon them. We would be surprised to discover otherwise concerning the attitude of Jesus. The covenantal religion of Israel embraced children. The teaching of the rabbis did likewise. And the Qumran community augmented its ranks by adopting male children. Fundamentally, therefore, Jesus's attitude to the children is in strong continuity with that of his confrères in Judaism. Children belong in the people of God. God's eschatological grace, proclaimed by Jesus, is an inclusive grace, open to the 'little people' of all kinds, including children.

Second, Jesus taught that the kingdom of God was to be received 'as a child *[hos paidion]*' (Mk 10:15 par Matt 18:3; Lk 18:17; cf Jn 3:3,5). Here, in a surprising and powerful simile, Jesus makes the child the model for receiving or entering the kingdom. Many suggestions have been made as to precisely *how* the child is a model. For Matthew it meant humility, for he adds: 'Whoever humbles himself like this child, he is the greatest in the kingdom of heaven' (Matt 18:4). But the very quality of the saying as metaphor suggests that a variety of meanings is possible and legitimate. Nevertheless, it is most unlikely that the Gnostic interpretation in terms of sexual innocence, in *Gospel of Thomas* 22 (cf 37), bears any resemblance to the understanding of Jesus. The interpretation of Matthew is much more likely to be closer to the mark. Differences of status or rank have no bearing on membership of the kingdom. That is what marks off the kingdom of God from normal patterns of social organization, including even the family!

Third, Jesus placed special importance on receiving hospitably and with kindness the least important members of society, including the children: for in the kingdom of God even children can serve as divine representatives, just as Jesus is the representative of God. This seems to be the sense underlying the heavily reworked tradition of Mk 9:33–37 and parallels. According to E. Best: 'The so-called *shaliach* principle is employed here to suggest that Jesus is encountered and helped when the child, who is the least important of all humans, is encountered and helped.'

These three aspects of Jesus's attitude to children are important. Above all, they provide a firm basis in history and the tradition for the Christian theological and ecclesiological claim that Jesus *is* – now, in the present – the friend of little children. Note that debates about baptism are not the point so far as Jesus and the gospels are concerned – which is not to say that such debates may not benefit from reflection upon the gospel stories. The point, rather, has to do, on the one hand, with the inclusiveness of the grace of God revealed in Christ, of which Jesus's acceptance of the children is a marvellous focal instance; and, on the other hand, with the challenging novelty of the values of the kingdom of God over against the values of normal social patterns and structures, such that a child can be used as a type of the model disciple.

The gospels

Study of the history of the gospel tradition shows that these few stories and sayings about children were important for the first followers of Jesus in their various attempts to work out what it meant to be God's new covenant people in the period after Jesus's death and resurrection. Invariably the child becomes a metaphor of discipleship, a way of talking about God and the shared life of faith in the light of Christ.

From 'Jesus – Friend of Little Children?', S Barton, in *The Contours of Christian Education*, J Astley and D Day (eds), MacCrimmons, 1992

Kaleidoscope's guiding principles

Children and adults are loved unconditionally by God. They are affirmed in the life and ministry of Jesus. God's love is made real through human life and relationships. The implications for the Christian community are:

* Children and adults are of equal value.
* All need to experience what it means to belong.
* All need to contribute and all need to receive.
* Children need recognition as people of faith.
* Worship and celebration are key elements in the growth of faith.
* All need to be changed by the love of Christ and to share the good news in the wider community.
* Christian nurture and growth are for all and are the responsibility of all.
* All Christian communities belong to the universal Church and need to share, support and learn from each other in serving the world.

Kaleidoscope's aims and objectives

Aim 1: the worker

To provide the participants with the opportunity to explore and express their own experience of faith and Christian life.

Objectives: to help participants to...

* express, reflect on and enrich their own faith story;
* develop a reflective, enquiring approach to the Bible and its use in faith and life;
* broaden their experience of worship, celebration and spiritual life;
* recognise the role of and deepen their involvement in the shared life of the Christian community, local and universal.

Aim 2: the worker and the children

To help participants to develop an understanding of children and the skills required to nurture children in their journey of faith.

Objectives: to help participants to...

* experience and understand the process of how people develop, learn and grow in faith;
* learn to listen and get alongside children as partners in faith;

- evaluate their own skills, gifts, strengths and weaknesses and devise strategies for development;
- present the Bible as a living, personal and on-going story;
- work creatively with children using various active methods, eg drama, music, art and craft;
- develop skills which awaken children to their own spirituality and capacity to make their own response of faith.

Aim 3: the worker and the children within the church community

To help participants capture and share a vision of a Christian community in which the child's faith is expressed and valued.

Objectives: to help participants to...

- encourage the church to value the participation of children in worship;
- encourage the church to be alert to opportunities for children to play an active part in its fellowship and mission;
- encourage everyone within the church to be involved in learning opportunities.

From *Kaleidoscope*, by members of the Consultative Group on Ministry among Children, National Christian Education Council, 1993

Christian Nurture Revisited

4.4 In focusing not only on the role of the home but of the congregation Westerhoff stresses the significance of liturgy in the formation of Christians and in building up the Church to achieve its mission and vocation. Liturgy is seen as the work of the Church both in its worship as the community of faith and in its daily witness as the body of Christ. From this dual activity stems the Church's engagement in mission. Because enculturation through liturgy, understood in this broad sense, is intentional and implicit in the life of the faith community, and because Westerhoff regards a schooling or institutional model to be inappropriate to personal and community development in the congregation, he adopts the term catechesis to describe the means of achieving growth.

The use of the term *catechesis* is for some Christian traditions problematic. Westerhoff offers a wide and embracing definition when he describes *catechesis* as 'the process by which persons are initiated into the Christian community's faith, revelation and vocation; the process by which persons, throughout their lives, are continually transformed and formed by and in the community's living tradition.' Whether the use of the term *catechesis* helps or hinders our appreciation of the broad experience of Christian nurture is an open question. The Greek verb from which it comes, *katecheo*, stems in turn from the root *echein*, to 'sound' or 'ring'. The history of these words is bound up with notions of instruction and teaching and it is for precisely this reason that a recent Church of England report on an integrated approach to Christian initiation, in referring to the 'catechumenal process', proposes the adoption of the term *enquirer*.

Westerhoff's concept of *catechesis* is a model of Christian nurture which embraces a number of features including home and church, worship as a learning experience (although it is rather more than that), the provision of opportunities for people to prepare for *participation* in the whole worship, life and witness of the congregation, and a process which encourages personal development through experience reflection, commitment and action. Whatever semantic confusion surrounds his notion of catechesis, it represents a rich and promising framework within which we may be encouraged to develop our ministry among children.

Learning and the Development of Faith

4.5 The last twenty years or so have seen a number of advances in the understanding of how the individual's faith develops. The extensive research project into the development of faith undertaken by James Fowler in the United States during the 1970s and 1980s has opened up a whole new field of study and debate. Fowler's earlier work culminated in the publication of *Stages of Faith* in which he identified six possible stages of faith in the human life-cycle. The discussion on the nature of these stages and of how the individual moves from one stage to another is fairly technical and draws extensively on the work of psychologists, educationists and theologians such as Erik Erikson, Jean Piaget, Laurence Kohlberg, H. Richard Niebuhr and Paul Tillich. Fowler has demonstrated convincingly that faith is by no means static but is subject to change, whether as an experience of growth or regression. The idea that faith develops through a sequence of stages somewhat like a stairway is not without its difficulties and Fowler himself has been careful not to make excessive claims but simply offers it as a working model. (An accessible introduction to Fowler's work can be found in *How Faith Grows*.)

Another academic to pursue Piaget's ideas of stage development as applied to religious and moral judgements is Fritz Oser of Switzerland. Whereas Fowler has focused more on faith development in the faith communities of the churches, Oser has concentrated on the development of religious judgment in the context of school and in the sphere of religious education. Like Fowler, Oser and his colleagues have stimulated a rich and productive discussion on religious development through the life-cycle and have prompted others to apply their findings to a range of practical concerns including those relating to Christian nurture and religious education. The American Catholic writer Gabriel Moran has brought his concern for precision of language and of analysis to bear on the work of Fowler and has expressed considerable unease over the whole conception of faith development where the impression is given of progression from lower stages to higher stages. He enquires whether the 'religiously developed' consider themselves 'higher' than others. He is also critical of some of the theological assumptions (such as the distinction made between faith and belief) made by Fowler and the experimental design employed in gathering data. At the same time, Moran has emphasized the desirability of lifelong learning and has defined adulthood as a *process* of maturation.

4.6 Theories of stage development such as those propounded by James Fowler and others, for all the difficulties accruing to them, have the considerable merit of emphasizing the dynamic character of faith. Faith is a process. It is subject to change and development and so is transitional in nature. Precisely how and under what conditions these transitions take place is the subject of continuing study at the present time. What is of immediate consequence is the reinforcement of the insight, if such be needed, that childhood is not a static entity, just as there is nothing fixed or final about adulthood. How individuals manage their own personal development and how they may be assisted and enabled to develop meaningfully and creatively is the concern of the related disciplines of nurture and education. Lifelong learning must become more than a slogan in the Church if individuals are to be helped in managing the transitional process in the life-cycle that brings the fulfilment and maturity that foster the realization of the Kingdom of God within them.

4.7 In addition to the interest in faith development, other areas relating to the theory and practice of Christian education have received attention in the past two decades. These might be summarized as the relationship between worship and learning; the movement away from school-based models and toward liturgical and all-age (i.e. inter-generational) models; the greater appreciation of the catechetical and nurturing responsibilities of the faith community and the role of the community as educator; the growing awareness of the spiritual insights and capacities of children; the significance of task-orientated learning and action/reflection ways of learning in faith and, in some denominations, the place of the liturgy as the context for nurture.

From this activity among theorists and in the churches themselves it is possible to discern four main strands of methodology in contemporary church-based education.

Four Main Approaches

4.8   An Instructional Approach

It is clear that in many congregations across the denominational spectrum in Britain and Ireland the legacy of practice in recent centuries is evident in the continuing preference for an instructional approach to teaching 'the faith handed down'. This somewhat misnamed 'traditionalist' approach begins with the disciplines of knowledge. It is an informational model through which knowledge essential for the moral and spiritual well-being of the child is passed on from teacher to pupil. Despite the fact that the notion of learning by doing is as old as education itself, the heritage of our immediate past has bequeathed to us an approach based upon the notion that knowledge should lead to action rather than arise from it. Faith commitment was reckoned to result from an understanding of the content of faith as presented by the teacher.

Although there has been a considerable shift in educational theory in the churches over the past fifty years, it is obvious that in many places the practice is still one of a highly didactic, knowledge-driven approach. Contemporary syllabuses now in use among Sunday Schools and other church groups may offer much that is child-centred and activity-related, yet the mental set of those who teach remains often at the level of instruction and the reality is that the possession of information and the retention of knowledge are perceived as major criteria. The problems created by the persistence of such an attitude are exacerbated by the reality that many people's experience of children in church is limited to their own recollection of the Sunday School system of their own childhood.

4.9 The Experiential Approach

John Dewey wrote that 'the child's own instincts and powers furnish the material and give the starting point for all education'. He saw also the need for the child's experiences to be so organized as to enable reflection, insight and understanding. Experience does not inevitably give rise to knowing, but experience that is carefully guided is the basis of effective education. In contemporary church curricula used in our congregations the programmes usually assume an experiential approach. 'From experience, through experience, to experience' is a well-known dictum. In congregational programmes this takes the form of an activity-based approach with much connection-making between human experience and the insights and concepts of the faith found in the Bible and in tradition. This amounts to rather more than just starting 'where they are'. It affirms that experience itself is the teacher and vehicle for communicating God's truth and influence. Practical methods range from the formal to the informal across a spectrum of activity in which imagination, discussion, reflection, story and artistic self-expression are all important. In well-organized groups the methodology can be elaborate and the investment of resources most impressive. Even so, the results do not always match expectations.

4.10 The Community as Educator

As noted earlier, the faith community has a vital part to play in the education and nurture of those within its sphere of influence. Where the Church as the people of God lives out what it believes, the possibilities for building up faith in individuals and in the group are awesome. It is in the community of believers, in its life, rites and rituals, activities and worship that faith is found, developed and owned. Because the possibilities for learning are rooted in the community itself, there is a growing tendency to explore and develop strategies whereby people of all ages are encouraged to learn together. Although the patterns of learning range from all-age Sunday School to inter-generational learning and worship, sometimes using liturgical models, the essential insights hold good. Learning together is both a means of strengthening the community and of enhancing the faith experience of the individual. Children have something to bring to the learning group from their own experiences and perceptions which, when shared, benefit and inform the whole group. In the true community of faith all have something to learn and each has something to give.

4.11 Learning as Liberation

Focus on a theology of the Kingdom of God which calls for liberation from oppression, whatever form this takes, and which promotes justice and peace is a crucial component in any serious contemporary attempt to develop children or adults in the Christian life. Following the seminal influence of the work of Paulo Freire in 'conscientizing' impoverished people in Brazil to the oppressive social realities of their existence, and the emergence of a vast literature on liberation theology, the attention of Christian education has turned increasingly toward 'humanization'. In this respect the work of Thomas Groome in North America has attracted much attention and interest. Groome has developed an approach to the faith tradition which takes account of interactions between an individual, the learning group and the situation in which they find themselves. Experience and action are followed by reflection, which leads on to further action. Thomas Groome describes this approach as 'Shared Praxis'. The shared praxis approach has many applications and holds much promise for further development, especially in terms of envisioning God's purpose for his people and of target-setting for specific action and discipleship.

4.12 Another area of investigation to develop over the past two decades, and one of great interest to those engaged in the Christian nurture of children and young people, centres on the spirituality of children. The insights of the Religious Experience Research Unit based in Oxford, under the leadership of Edward Robinson, merited much interest and stimulated further research. By analysing the accounts of childhood experiences recounted in later life by many adults, Robinson concluded that a child has a picture of human existence peculiar to him/herself which can so easily be forgotten – what he termed 'the original vision'. The experiences associated with it are essentially religious. He concluded that childhood is not just a chronological period of human development but a continuing and influential element of the whole person. 'In childhood we may be wiser than we know.'

4.13 Any consideration of the process of faith development is incomplete and inadequate without frank and full acknowledgement of the possibility and increasingly common reality of the faith journey that is arrested or abandoned. A moment's reflection on the statistical trends in the mainstream churches is sufficient to bring home the sorry truth of declining numbers in the Church in these islands. There are fewer people attending church, fewer communicants, fewer confirmations and fewer baptisms compared with twenty years ago. Among children in Sunday Schools and other church groups and organizations the problem of declining numbers is acute. This can no doubt be accounted for in large measure in terms of the social changes which have brought about what has been described earlier as 'the erosion of childhood'. Even so, the churches should ask themselves just how seriously they have taken the paramount question of the nurture of children. With the first publication of *The Child in the Church* came the message, 'the child is the Church of today'. This message quickly assumed the nature of a slogan in Church committees. What is less clear is the extent to which it became the basis for policy and practice in local congregations. One reason for the failure of the churches to hold young people has been the inability and even the unreadiness of their adult members to make a place for children and teenagers within congregational life. The Church's concern for children is by no means restricted to those affiliated to the institution. The second of two influential Church of England reports on ministry among children, *All God's Children? – Children's Evangelism in Crisis*, expressed concern over the Church's perceived role towards the 85% of children who do not go to church or associate with it and for whom the major influences in terms of religion will be the home and the school. The comment: 'It only takes two generations to de-Christianize a nation' is both arresting and challenging.

A Church Rejected by the Young

4.14 Attention to a deeper understanding of the processes of Christian nurture in general, and faith development in particular, will help us to understand the dynamics of rejection. We need to come to a fuller estimate of why it is that young people abandon the Church, its ideas and beliefs, its lifestyle and subculture. Many see it as an irrelevant failure. Is it the Gospel or the institution that they abandon? Contemporary theories of nurture, of which Westerhoff's is a prime example, focus on *nurture for decision*. These acknowledge a process of critical openness, of discourse between the individual and the Church. At appropriate times in the life-cycle, choices will be made with regard to the Church and the faith to which it testifies. Of the four styles of faith identified by Westerhoff – experienced faith, affiliated faith, searching faith and owned faith – it is the third faith style that deserves particular attention when considering why young people reject the Church.

It must be acknowledged frankly that congregations in the main have not been particularly good at enabling young people to question the values, beliefs and activities of the Church. It seems almost as though while it is acceptable for children to be given a sense of belonging in the congregation and so have experience of faith, however unexamined, and while they may be encouraged to affiliate to the life of the congregation by joining in the worship and other activities of the church, and while it is hoped for and prayed for that these same children will progress to the point of making personal commitments in faith, yet there is a nervous reluctance to encourage any form of doubt or questioning. If our young people do not have our 'permission' to doubt, to ask, to probe and search and test the claims of the Gospel, then we must consider the realism of our approach. The questioning or searching style of faith is a necessary antecedent to owned faith. Young people need 'space' in which to examine the gospel and its relevance for today. Too often their intolerance of much within the institutional Church stems from a perceived discouragement to explore in an open-minded way the basic tenets of biblical faith and the doctrinal traditions of the Church. The search for meaning in life remains an essential quest for young people today. It is important that they should be encouraged to engage on this search from within the household of faith. To this end Christian nurture is a process requiring patience, love and a non-patronizing appreciation of the young person's quest for faith, meaning and identity within the frame of reference which the Church at its best is so wonderfully able to provide.

4.15 Young people live in a world of confusion in which conflicting signals are received about what is important and what is unimportant, about what is acceptable behaviour and what is unacceptable, about what is harmful or destructive and what is not. They have to come to terms with a system of values often characterized more by inconsistency and nonconformity than anything else. This applies to such basic standards as always speaking the truth, the appropriation of possessions, the use and abuse of natural resources and concern for the environment, the sustaining of relationships, the coming to terms with one's own sexuality and the assuming of responsibility for the general well-being of others and oneself. In the eyes of the young the world does not always practise what it preaches and, for that matter, neither does the Church. Such confusion is compounded by the cognitive dissonance experienced by young people as they attempt to bridge the gap between *propositions* they are expected to accept and their own inner *feelings* about the subject matter of these propositions.

The formation of attitudes is a highly sensitive area of nurture and one which must necessarily involve young people in a degree of experimentation with ideas and trial-and-error learning. Their quest is all the more difficult in an age in which there is a blurring of the boundaries between the world of the child and the world of the adult. Increasingly, and especially in the sphere of leisure, our young people are to be seen as 'adult-children' interacting with 'child-adults', that is to say with those of mature years who have not realized their potential in terms of personal maturation. This is a breeding ground for much uncertainty over values, standards and beliefs and one which requires to be addressed by the claims of the Christian gospel. Perhaps for too long we have relied upon a method that expects the adoption of Christian beliefs to issue in right behaviour. Perhaps there is more hope of success through an approach which commends 'right behaviour' in terms of a Christian lifestyle which in its turn, and by its efficacy as a fulfilling way to live, will inculcate in the young person an acceptance of basic Christian beliefs.

4.16 In connection with the search for meaning on the part of young people, the Church may do well to pay greater heed to what might be termed *vocational dissonance*. This is the conflict and distance between ideals, visions and potential on the one hand and actual limited achievements on the other. This may be evidenced in under-achievements in terms of career, academic studies, sport or even in the realms of building relationships, and where failure leads to premature withdrawal from any encounter or engagement. There may be good reason for the Church to recover an adequate theology of vocation in which true fulfilment may be conceived as the courageous and adventurous response to the call to discipleship. It is perfectly possible for young people to recognize the validity of the spiritual 'life in the Spirit' and the possibilities that this offers, yet to reject a Church that is judged to have failed and with it the God of the Church, branded as 'the God that failed'. Perhaps these forms of dissonance are also part of the searching process. Yet they call in question the Church that would seek to recruit to its ranks the up and coming generation but only on the terms of those adults already secure within the Church. The nurture process is double-edged. It not only responds to the very question, 'How shall we prepare our young people for Church?' It is required to take with the greatest possible seriousness the question 'How shall we prepare the Church for our young people?' In plain language: what do we have to offer?

4.17 Children and young people need help in working through the searching periods in their lives. Too many churches, keen on receiving those who have 'worked things through' and come to some measure of personalized or owned faith, leave to their own devices those who continue to toil and struggle. Yet are there not among older children and younger teenagers visionaries whose very idealism speaks a prophetic word to the Church? The Church needs to take seriously the journey of faith, the processes whereby individuals develop and progress, and the significance of the stages and phases through which they pass. While the Church has one eye on the potential of the young person, what he or she might become in the future, it must have the other eye on the actuality of what he or she is now, a child or young teenager to be accepted, affirmed and listened to. Just as the child is encouraged to be open to the Church, so the Church is called to be open to the child.

Children in the Community of Faith

4.18 If we are to take seriously the possibility of children *in* the Church, then a child-centred approach to Christian nurture is not fully adequate. Christian nurture has its locus in the faith community. Effective nurture is possible only where there is an appropriate environment and where there is a system of support. Congregations need to heed the warnings that the preparation of children for life in the Church may come to nothing unless they are prepared to receive and accommodate them and to meet the needs of the young.

4.19 There is urgent need in our congregations for a 'whole-church' approach to development and education, children, youth and adults together. This in itself constitutes the basis for a massive programme of awareness education and reorientation of policy and practice in many congregations. Congregational development seeks to establish a vibrant, active faith community at the core of the congregation which will work to widen its sphere of influence throughout the congregation as a whole and to deepen the faith, understanding and commitment, the witness and service of those engaged in the life of the church, whatever their age, whatever their stage on the journey of faith. This requires of the local church vision, careful planning and good management. Above all, it requires a sense of wholeness, togetherness, a commitment to mutual support and the cherishing of a distinctive corporate identity. From such characteristics there emerges the confidence to be the Church and the faith to accomplish great things. In a word, we need in our congregations a sense of *koinonia*.

From *Unfinished Business,* by a Working Group of the Consultative Group on Ministry among Children, CCBI Publications, 1994

- To fulfil its tasks, catechesis avails of two principal means: transmission of the Gospel message and experience of the Christian life. Liturgical formation, for example, must explain what the Christian liturgy is, and what the sacraments are. It must also however, offer an experience of the different kinds of celebration and it must make symbols, gestures, etc. known and loved. Moral formation not only transmits the content of Christian morality, but also cultivates active evangelical attitudes and Christian values.
- The different dimensions of faith are objects of formation, as much of being given as received. Knowledge of the faith, liturgical life, the following of Christ are all a gift of the Spirit

which are received in prayer, and similarly a duty of spiritual and moral study and witness. Neither aspect may be neglected.

- Every dimension of the faith, like the faith itself as a whole, must be rooted in human experience and not remain a mere adjunct to the human person. Knowledge of the faith is significant. It gives light to the whole of existence and dialogues with culture. In the liturgy, all personal life becomes a spiritual oblation. The morality of the Gospel assumes and elevates human values. Prayer is open to all personal and social problems.

As the 1971 Directory indicates, 'it is very important that catechesis retain the richness of these various aspects in such a way that one aspect is not separated from the rest to the detriment of the others'.

The baptismal catechumenate: structure and progression

88. Faith, moved by divine grace and cultivated by the action of the Church, undergoes a process of maturation. Catechesis, which is at the service of this growth, is also a gradual activity. 'Good catechesis is always done in steps'. In the baptismal catechumenate, formation is articulated in four stages:

- the *pre-catechumenate*, characterized as the locus of first evangelization leading to conversion and where the kerygma of the primary proclamation is explained;
- the *catechumenate*, properly speaking, the context of integral catechesis beginning with 'the handing on of the Gospels';
- a time of *purification and illumination* which affords a more intense preparation for the sacraments of initiation and in which 'the handing on of the Creed' and 'the handing on of the Lord's Prayer' take place;
- a time of *mystagogy*, characterized by the experience of the sacraments and entry into the community.

89. These stages, which reflect the wisdom of the great catechumenal tradition, also inspire the gradual nature of catechesis. (This gradual nature is also apparent in the names which the Church uses to designate those who are in the various stages of the baptismal catechumenate: *sympathizers*, those who are disposed to the faith but do not yet fully believe; *catechumens*, those who have firmly decided to follow Jesus; *elect*, those called to receive Baptism; *neophytes*, those just born into the light by the grace of Baptism; the *Christian faithful*, those who are mature in the faith and active members of the Christian community.) In the patristic period properly, catechumenal formation was realized through biblical catechesis, based on recounting the history of salvation; immediate preparation for Baptism by doctrinal catechesis, explaining the Creed and the *Our Father* which had just been handed on, together with their moral implications; and through the phase following the sacraments of initiation, a period of mystagogical catechesis which help the newly baptized to interiorize these sacraments and incorporate themselves into the community. This patristic concept continues to illuminate the present catechumenate and initiatory catechesis itself. This latter, in so far as it accompanies the process of conversion, is essentially gradual and, in so far as it is at the service of one who has decided to follow Christ, it is eminently christocentric.

The baptismal catechumenate: inspiration for catechesis in the Church

90. Given that the *missio ad gentes* is the paradigm of all the Church's missionary activity, the baptismal catechumenate, which is joined to it, is the model of its catechizing activity. It is therefore helpful to underline those elements of the catechumenate which must inspire contemporary catechesis and its significance.

By way of premise, however, it must be said that there is a fundamental difference between catechumens and those being catechized ... between the *pre-baptismal* catechesis and the *post-baptismal* catechesis, which is respectively imparted to them. The latter derives from the sacraments of initiation which were received as infants, 'who have been already introduced into the Church and have been made sons of God by means of Baptism. The basis of their conversion is the Baptism which they have already received and whose power they must develop'...

91. In view of this substantial difference, some elements of the baptismal catechumenate are now considered, as the source of inspiration for post-baptismal catechesis.

- the baptismal catechumenate constantly reminds the whole Church of the fundamental importance of the function of initiation and the basic factors which constitute it: catechesis and the sacraments of Baptism, Confirmation and Eucharist.

The pastoral care of Christian initiation is vital for every particular Church.

- The baptismal catechumenate is the responsibility of the entire Christian community. Indeed 'this Christian initiation which takes place during the catechumenate should not be left entirely to the priests and catechists, but should be the care of the entire Christian community, especially the sponsors'. The institution of the catechumenate thus increases awareness of the spiritual maternity of the Church, which she exercises in every form of education in the faith.

- The baptismal catechumenate is also completely permeated by the *mystery of Christ's Passover*. For this reason, 'all initiation must reveal clearly its paschal nature.' The Easter Vigil, focal point of the Christian liturgy, and its spirituality of Baptism inspire all catechesis.

- The baptismal catechumenate is also an initial locus of inculturation. Following the example of the Incarnation of the Son of God, made man in a concrete historical moment, the Church receives catechumens integrally, together with their cultural ties. All catechetical activity participates in this function of incorporating into the catholicity of the Church, authentic 'seeds of the word', scattered through nations and individuals.

- Finally, the concept of the baptismal catechumenate as *a process of formation and as a true school of the faith* offers post-baptismal catechesis dynamic and particular characteristics: comprehensiveness and integrity of formation; its gradual character expressed in definite stages; its connection with meaningful rites, symbols, biblical and liturgical signs; its constant references to the Christian community.

Post-baptismal catechesis, without slavishly imitating the structure of the baptismal catechumenate, and recognizing in those to be catechized the reality of their Baptism, does well, however, to draw inspiration from 'this preparatory school for the Christian life', and to allow itself to be enriched by those principal elements which characterize the catechumenate...

Catechesis of young people

Pre-adolescence, adolescence and young adulthood

181. In general it is observed that the first victims of the spiritual and cultural crisis gripping the world are the young. It is also true that any commitment to the betterment of society finds its hopes in them. This should stimulate the Church all the more to proclaim the Gospel to the world of youth with courage and creativity. In this respect experience suggests that it is useful in catechesis to distinguish between pre-adolescence, adolescence and young adulthood, attending to the results of scientific research in various countries. In developed regions the question of pre-adolescence is particularly significant: sufficient account is not taken of the difficulties, of the needs and of the human and spiritual resources of pre-adolescents, to the extent of defining them a *negated age-group*. Very often at this time the pre-adolescent, in receiving the sacrament of Confirmation, formally concludes the process of Christian initiation but from that moment virtually abandons completely the practice of the faith. This is a matter of serious concern which requires specific pastoral care, based on the formative resources of the journey of initiation itself. With regard to the other two categories, it is helpful to distinguish between adolescence and young adulthood even though it is difficult to define them strictly. They are understood together as the period of life which precedes the taking up of responsibilities proper to adults. Youth catechesis must be profoundly revised and revitalized.

The importance of youth for society and the Church

182. The Church, while regarding young people as 'hope', also sees them as 'a great challenge for the future of the Church' herself. The rapid and tumultuous socio-cultural change, increase in numbers, self-affirmation for a consistent period before taking up adult responsibilities, unemployment, in certain countries conditions of permanent under-development, the pressures of consumer society – all contribute to make of youth a world in waiting, not infrequently a world of disenchantment, of boredom, of angst and of marginalization. Alienation from the Church, or at least diffidence in her regard, lurks in many as a fundamental attitude. Often this reflects lack of spiritual and moral support in the family and weaknesses in the catechesis which they have received. On the other hand, many of them are driven by a strong impetus to find meaning, solidarity, social commitment and even religious experience.

183. Some consequences for catechesis arise from this. The service of the faith notes above all the contrasts in the condition of youth as found concretely in various regions and environments. The heart of catechesis is the explicit proposal of Christ to the young man in the Gospel; it is a direct proposal to all young people in terms appropriate to young people, and with considered understanding of their problems. In the Gospel young people in fact speak directly to Christ, who reveals to them their 'singular richness' and calls them to an enterprise of personal and community growth, of decisive value for the fate of society and of the Church. Therefore young people cannot be considered only objects of catechesis, but also active subjects and protagonists of evangelization and artisans of social renewal.

Characteristics of catechesis for young people

184. Given the extent of this task, the Catechetical Directories of particular Churches and national and regional Episcopal Conferences must, taking into account different contexts, determine more specifically suitable measures for these areas. Some general directions, however, may be indicated.

- The diversity of the religious situation should be kept in mind: there are young people who are not even baptized, others have not completed Christian initiation, others are in grave crises of faith, others are moving towards making a decision with regard to faith, others have already made such a decision and call for assistance.
- It should also be remembered that the most successful catechesis is that which is given in the context of the wider pastoral care of young people, especially when it addresses the problems affecting their lives. Hence, catechesis should be integrated with certain procedures, such as analysis of situations, attention to human sciences and education, the co-operation of the laity and of young people themselves.
- Well organized group action, membership of valid youth associations and personal accompaniment of young people, which should also include spiritual direction as an important element, are useful approaches for effective catechesis.

185. Among the diverse forms of youth catechesis, provision should be made, in so far as circumstances permit, for the youth catechumenate during school years, catechesis for Christian initiation, catechesis on specific themes, as well as other kinds of occasional and informal meetings.

Generally youth catechesis should be proposed in new ways which are open to the sensibilities and problems of this age group. They should be of a theological, ethical, historical and social nature. In particular, due emphasis should be given to education in truth and liberty as understood by the Gospel, to the formation of conscience and to education for love. Emphasis should also be placed on vocational discernment, Christian involvement in society and on missionary responsibility in the world. (Other important themes include: the relationship between faith and reason; the existence and meaning of God; the problem of evil; the Church; the objective moral order in relation to personal subjectivity; the encounter between man and woman; the social doctrine of the Church.) It must be emphasized, however, that frequently contemporary evangelization of young people must adopt a *missionary dimension* rather than a strictly *catechumenal* dimension. Indeed, the situation often demands, that the apostolate amongst young people be an animation of a *missionary or humanitarian nature*, as a necessary first step to bringing to maturity those dispositions favourable to the strictly catechetical moment. Very often, in reality, it is useful to *intensify pre-catechumenal activity within the general educational process*. One of the difficulties to be addressed and resolved is the question of 'language' *(mentality, sensibility, tastes, style, vocabulary)* between young people and the Church *(catechesis, catechists)*. A necessary 'adaptation of catechesis to young people' is urged, in order to translate into their terms 'the message of Jesus with patience and wisdom and without betrayal'.

From *General Directory for Catechesis: Congregation for the Clergy,* Catholic Truth Society, 1997

The danger in a narrow and prescriptive approach to learning and the curriculum is that we will yet again miss out on the opportunities to gain insight from what children bring to our schools and classrooms. They will remain persuaded that the thoughts, feelings, ideas and excitement of their inner lives and world are not for sharing with others – particularly adults. Through the project we have learned to respect this inner life and world of children and have come to see it as deeply spiritual in the widest possible sense. And yes, this spirituality has connected them to a sense of morality as the use of story has shown.

'Somewhere inside me
the jasmine continues to blossom'

Etty Hillesum was a young Jewish woman who, like so many Jews, found herself in a concentration camp during the Second World War. She kept diaries, just as did Anne Frank, though Hillesum's diaries were only discovered in the 1980s. Her diaries reflect a person of remarkable resilience and a spirit who knew the fate which awaited her – she died in the camp. She retained a belief that, however awful the outer world which confronted her and her fellow Jews, there was an inner world, an inner space which could not be captured or taken away by anyone.

Thus she wrote in her diaries:

> The jasmine behind my house has been completely ruined by the rain and storms of the last few days; its white blossoms are floating about in muddy black pools on the low garage roof. But somewhere inside me the jasmine continues to blossom undisturbed, just as profusely and delicately as it ever did.

> I bring you not only my tears and my forebodings on this stormy, grey Sunday morning, I even bring you my scented jasmine. Even if I should be locked up in a narrow cell and a cloud should drift past my small window then I shall bring you that cloud, oh God, while there is still the strength in me to do so.

> *(Hillesum, 1984, p.188)*

Etty Hillesum gives voice to the potential within all of us to confront the harsh realities of life at times and yet maintain an inner peace and balance. Such an approach to our world and everyday concerns and struggles would be echoed by those from all religious traditions and also those from no religious tradition at all. It is something to do with the essence of the human spirit and the capacity of human beings to rise above the most challenging situations and environments. Young children, as much as adults, have this capacity. They move in and out of different worlds. They have the capacity to adapt to and cope with the world of adults while at the same time protecting an inner world which fascinates and enthrals them. Violet Madge in her book *Children in Search of Meaning* (1965) described the children she worked with thus:

A sense of mystery often accompanies the exercise of curiosity and there seem occasions when the mysteries may cause children to become conscious of eternal realities beyond phenomena.

Madge is writing about the children we meet in the ordinary day-to-day life of the classroom: those children who can drive us to distraction as well as inspire us with their insights and awareness; those children to whom we have to deliver all manner of curriculum and who discover within themselves varieties of attainments and level descriptors. Yet these very same children have deep inner reserves and a capacity to show to us and teach us things we, as adults, have perhaps long forgotten. This is not to glorify or idealize childhood or children but simply to remind us that, as Etty Hillesum shows, there are many layers to the human condition and spirit.

Working within a group of children

Over a considerable period of time I worked with a group of children from a Roman Catholic school. The school, being a church school, was served by a wide catchment area and thus the children came from a variety of backgrounds. There were parents from comfortable backgrounds. There were parents who struggled with the realities of unemployment. Pupils at church schools reflect our contemporary society in their family make-up and this was also reflected within the group. One boy in particular had seen a variety of male adults pass through his relatively short life. The school is warm, friendly and welcoming and there is a clear commitment to the well-being of the children. There is a contemporary religious education programme which teachers plan and prepare together. All teachers see it as a central aspect of the life of the school. Close links are maintained with the local parishes and with parents.

Hallowed ground

The first exploration with the group was to establish if they had a special place where they retreated to, and if so what was it that made it special. Within school we often ask children to explore this concept, though perhaps we do not always have the time to dig deeply with them as to their thoughts and feelings about their special and/or secret places. John Bowker (1993) in the chapter 'Remembered places' from his book *Hallowed Ground* describes this concept of space and place in the following way:

The poetry of place, therefore, has the power to make us, not simply travellers in space, but travellers in time as well. It creates the possibility of our healing and our hope – first because it renews the days of our peace; but second also, because it can take us back to the places of our hurt in the past, and there, through the cleansing of our memory, it can start the process of our completion and cure. In that way it creates in us a better chance by far of becoming a hood of care and protection for others.

When we explored special places, S told us that he found the garage a good place to escape to, somewhere he could find something to do but where he didn't have to think. Notice that he *escapes* to the garage. Children, just like adults, have a desire and need to escape from the stresses and strains of life. As Bowker pointed out, places often have a poetry all of their own which enable us to reflect and think through aspects of our life. Not so for S. He simply wants to be, to do something practical and release his mind from thinking about whatever it is he has escaped from.

J simply went under her bed when she wanted space. The most important aspect of this was not to let on to others that she was there and she filled her time either by 'thinking about things' or 'playing little games in my head'. Again, we have the sense that she was taking control of her world and by retreating to her own private place she was giving herself the clear message that she had the right and freedom to opt into her world. Margaret Donaldson (1976) in *Children's Minds* comments: 'They can learn to be conscious of the powers of their own minds and decide to what ends they will use them' (p. 256).

T escaped into the wardrobe in his bedroom. Here it was dark and secret and he felt free. No fear of the dark, no fear of being enclosed. Absolute freedom to think, to be himself, to have a break from others, were the feelings he vigorously expressed.

The two remaining children had trees for their special places. For C, it was climbing a tree with his favourite friend, sitting high up in the branches where they could not be seen and carving little models from branches with their penknives. As they sat and watched 'the adults go by' C said they often felt no need to talk. It was just good to be there.

L went to a horse chestnut tree near her home with a friend. Again, they climbed far enough into the tree not to be seen. This was where they went to be quiet, and it was special because they knew it had probably been a private place for many people for hundreds of years.

All the children thus recognized a need within themselves to escape from the burly-burly of day-to-day living. Yet deep within themselves they also had a sense of sacred space and hallowed ground, that sense of mystery and eternal realities referred to by Madge. The challenge within the school environment is how we are able to nurture and develop within children this openness to sacred space and hallowed ground. Crowded classrooms and schools within limited space boundaries do not make it easy for adults and children alike to have a sense of inner space. Yet Etty Hillesum in her diaries shows that inner space *can* be nurtured and developed within the most confined spaces. A primary school in Dorset set aside part of its field as a quiet area. Children and teachers planted flowers and shrubs, benches were set around it and it was there for all to use, the only condition being that silence was to be maintained and respected. The children highly value the 'sacred space' and it is often the first place they will take visitors to see. In *Children's Minds* (1976) Donaldson suggests that perhaps the challenge for adults is to place ourselves imaginatively at the child's point of view. Thus we might see our world differently and through fresh eyes.

The Whales' Song

One of the ways of relating to children's sense of story and narrative is to use the medium of story itself in exploring with them their thoughts, ideas and experiences. Using story in an open-ended and sensitive way allows children to bring their own depth and insights into the characters, the emotions, the purpose of the narrative.

The Whales' Song (Sheldon and Blythe, 1990) is a captivating tale beautifully illustrated. In it, Cathy's grandmother recalls how whales have been around long before humans and that if you listened to them, respected them, put a present in the seas for them they might call your name. This had happened to Cathy's grandmother but her uncle, much more the rationalist, describes this as utter rubbish and warns that grandmother should not be filling Cathy's head with such nonsense. Cathy, however, is entranced by her grandmother's tale and slips out one evening to lay a flower on the seas for the whales. She sits until sunset but sees or hears nothing of the whales. But she awakes during the night to hear the whales call 'Cathy, Cathy', and when she looks out of the window she sees the whales dancing in the moonlight.

In using this story with my group of children I asked them first to concentrate on it and then to try and hold in their minds whatever they responded to most about it. When we had finished I asked them to hold in their closed hands what they had responded to most and then as we went round the group in a circle to open their hands as they spoke of what had struck them or touched them most. This seemed to create an atmosphere of quiet expectation as we progressed with the story.

S said he simply loved the whole story but that the ending was magic when the whales called Cathy's name. He said that the trouble with adults and even some older children is that as they do not believe in magic anymore they end up missing the chance to relate to our animal and sea world. D thought the singing of the whales sounded very real, even though she knew what S meant about it being magical.

J said she was struck by how much Cathy believed that if she left her flower on the seas the whales would find it and would come and call her name. She called this 'Cathy's faith' and said that children often believe things that adults think are silly. This made her sad for adults as it meant they missed out on so many things.

C was very amused by the uncle who, at one point in the story, joins Cathy and her grandmother, stamps his feet and declares that whales are only good for blubber. C also found the story both 'fantastic' and 'realistic'. He saw that within it there were two perceptions of whales – one, the possibility of a relationship with humans; the other, that they are simply there for humans to kill. He felt that the grandmother wanted Cathy to tell her children the story of the whales. C became agitated at this point and said that all children should hear this story and that when they grew up they should tell it to their own children. In that way whales might become our friends, and human beings – especially children – would still be able to hear them call their names.

Earlier in my research with this group of children they had been somewhat despairing about the state of the world. They felt that we adults had let them down badly by our neglect of it. We had made the world a poor environment for both human beings and animals. L even offered the suggestion that adults should not presume to know all the answers to the world's problems and should be willing to listen to and learn from children and animals.

The Whales' Song seemed to return the group to a sense of hope, to a belief that we could rediscover the peace and harmony and balance in our world. John Westerhoff III (1980) has commented:

> Children do not fret about the past or fear the future unless they are taught to do so. They live in the joy of the present. Children live in a world of dreams and visions; they take chances and create. They find miracles believable and desirable.

Sometimes, they also throw light on areas of experience, emotion and feeling which adults have long since forgotten or failed to nurture. As Donaldson (1976) points out in *Children's Minds*:

> Some kinds of knowledge are in the light of awareness. Others are in the shadows, on the edge of the bright circle. Still others are in the darkness beyond.

Children move around and between these different worlds. Through narrative and story they can give full expression to their hopes and dreams. They can see that the world is fragile and fractured yet they have a belief that we can make it whole again, that we as human beings can be reintegrated with each other and, above all, with the animal kingdom. They wonder what the animals make of us humans. This is not to suggest that they are over-serious or lack a depth of humour. Donaldson tells us the story of the father trying to show off his 3-year-old to visiting friends:

FATHER:	Stephen, are you a little boy or a little girl?
STEPHEN:	I'm a little doggie.
FATHER:	Come on now, Stephen. Be sensible. Are you a little boy or a little girl?
STEPHEN:	Gr-rrr! Woof!

(Donaldson, 1976, p. 86)

Children are capable of learning – and do learn – much more than what we choose to tell them. In our crowded curriculum and classrooms we may need to remind ourselves of this.

The Mountains of Tibet

As the group of children settled down remarkably well on the occasions when we met and had become used to the sessions being recorded, I decided to use another story with them. This story, The Mountains of Tibet (Mordicai, 1993), is a children's story about the Buddhist concept of reincarnation. It begins with the death of an old man who loves flying kites. It then follows the process of reincarnation – choices about places and worlds and people are put before him. Each time choices are made and the tale progresses – a land is chosen, as are parents who appear as if they will be warm and loving. Finally in a village in the mountains of Tibet, a baby girl is born and as she grows up she becomes known as the girl who loves to fly kites.

I wondered what this group of Catholic children would make of a story rooted in a different culture and set of beliefs from their own. First, they loved the story and C welcomed the way it talked about dying and death and what happened after death. L responded in a lively fashion to the many choices faced in the 'process' of reincarnation. She thought the illustrations were 'stunning' and reflected a way of seeing the world and its peoples somehow from beyond it. She was moved by the sense of being 'out of the world' yet able to make choices about coming back into it. This was exciting. Everyone in the group felt that reincarnation was a reasonable belief, though no one wanted to come back as the opposite sex! When asked how reincarnation differed from Christian belief, L explained the word 'resurrection', but said she thought there was room for both beliefs in the world. Nor did she feel that both sets of beliefs were necessarily all that different. The whole group, through the narrative of the story *The Mountains of Tibet*, engaged with its ideas and meaning and appeared at ease with exploring what it had to say in its own right. They appeared to be captivated by the sense of mystery and excitement about reincarnation. To them it was believable and possible. It was also interesting to discover that it was through the use of this Buddhist story that the group began, for the first time, to use explicitly religious language and ideas. They began to make references to some of their work in religious education.

Encounters with lapwings

Sylvia Anthony in her book *The Child's Discovery of Death* (1940) commented:

> The child approached may close up, like a sea anemone or a wood-louse or he may display himself, like a lapwing when her nest is approached, who of course, does not display her nest but cleverly conceals it.

In one sense in our research we do not do anything that teachers do not do. We spend time with children, we listen to them, we share story and narrative with them. We invite them to take us into their 'special', 'secret' or 'sacred' places, whether these places are within themselves or in the world outside and which we adults very often fail to notice. What we have had in our research project with children which teachers today do not have enough of is *quality time*. We have had the time, space and facilities to explore with them their responses, their insights, their deep-seated feelings and emotions. That has been our privilege.

In return, we can only indicate to the world of adults what we are hearing. When C, with some passion, told me that 'adults just don't listen', it was a despairing statement of fact and not an implied criticism. He was simply frustrated that in our madly active world there appears to be little time to engage with real questions, issues and experiences. He desperately wanted to be able to do that.

The research team is constantly aware of the education debates about curriculum, child-centred learning, standards, expectations and league tables. Interestingly, Donaldson, in *Human Minds* (1993), argues against extremes: 'Both the centred extremes in education – the child-centred and the cultural-centred have serious disadvantages.' She suggests that the cultural-centred extreme underestimates children's ingenuity, imagination and initiative. It overvalues the conveying of information. On the other hand, the child-centred extreme can overestimate the validity of children's judgements and underestimate their fitness for the role of the novice. Donaldson calls for a balance between the intellectual and the emotional. All of us adults may be in danger of losing this sense of connectedness with the inner self and the inner world. In sharing stories with children we may make the mistake of simply sharing and forget how to enter into their world. For teachers in recent years the curriculum has often become so crowded that it has marginalized the opportunities to nurture the affective in children. And who has nurtured the affective in teachers?

Yet the children in the project seem to be identifying the real significance of the spiritual, of the inner world to their lives and give the impression that adults are missing out on a great deal. However, in their wisdom they watch adults and come to their own conclusions. A group of children ('weans' in Scotland) in a very deprived part of Glasgow were moved to write about the Bosnian conflict. One wrote with profound insight and not a little warning to us adults:

> Castlemilk kills war.
> youth against Bosnia.
> weans hate conflict
> war means waste.
> Common people hate war
> weans wait for freedom
> weans watch and wait
> weans do watch
> adults walk by
> weans *do* watch adults.

Children need to have all that is *within* them nurtured and teased out in the most human of ways. Thus they would be free to echo the sentiments of T.S. Eliot in 'Little Gidding':

> We shall not cease from exploration
> And the end of exploring
> Will be to arrive where we started
> And know the place for the first time.

From 'Children's spirituality and our contemporary culture', Danny Sullivan, in *The Education of the Whole Child*, Ericker, Ericker, Sullivan, Ota and Fletcher (eds), Cassell, 1997

Reflection
The Past and the Future

The century began with children of all ages sitting together in Sunday Schools being taught the Bible as the holy word of God; it ended with children having a place in the Church and the recognition that they had insights that could both illuminate the text of the Bible and enrich the life of the community. In some places children were given an active role in the life of the Church and in the work of the Church in society, in the same way that young adults had earlier been welcomed into the Councils of the Churches. Issues of justice for the world's hungry and oppressed people and care about the environment concerned children every bit as much as adults. At the beginning of the 1980s a nine-year-old child had written, 'When we gave our 1% appeal money so that people in poor countries could grow food I thought it was like sharing communion. When the bread and wine are shared I think of sharing in the world.'

If, however, it remains true that children learn more by seeing than by hearing and more by doing than by seeing, deeply disturbing questions remain about the nature of the liturgy and the place of children in it, and about the Christian presence in the world. Whether children will be attracted in significant numbers to the life of faith until the Church becomes a much more action (love)-orientated movement, more seriously engaged in society than it is at present, remains an open question. We have yet to discover what it means for the praxis of the ordinary daily life of the churches to believe that the gospel is for the transformation of society as well as of individuals. The reign of God is elusive. Perhaps in the way that a new appreciation of the figure of Jesus has come from some of the poorer countries of the world, they will also help us to answer this conundrum.

More basic still is the problem of belief. In the 1970s it had become clear that though the emphasis on nurture was important, nurture needed to be balanced by a strong emphasis on equipping children to think critically about faith if they were to cope with the questions posed by contemporary life, and the apathy and antagonism to their faith of many of their peers. It has been suggested that children are innately spiritual, but they can also see that very many people live apparently happy and fulfilled lives without any evident – or active – belief in God. Why then should children take notice of those who speak about belief in God? Cannot children and the world at large get on very nicely – even more peacefully – without God? Jesus may or may not provide useful insights into a way of life lived in relationship, but God? 'Why believe?' The Churches will have to find a persuasive answer to this question, which will have to be expressed in worldly rather than theological terms, before many of our children will be enabled to have faith.

Though there is much that is seriously engaging about Church life and the education it offers children, there is also much triviality and banality. Serious theological conversation has almost disappeared. Perhaps a renewed understanding of oikoumene could be a beginning point. The concept can be spoken about in both theological and 'secular' language. It holds in a united whole the physical world and all its people; it gives individuals and communities – local and world-wide – identity; it points to living with an acceptance of diversity and plurality; it demands seeking the end of exploitation and violence; it suggests meaning and a mega-story in which everyone is respected and has a part to play; it is a concept of vision and hope and love which supersedes all lesser loyalties. In Christian education oikoumene is an integrating concept. Integration implies not only that Christian teaching should be about the world and its people, using the Christian story as the key to interpretation and meaning, but that it should draw on the world's resources as the basis for theological thinking. It points to Fowler's Stages 5 and 6 and to our being undeterred by Jeff Astley's warning (*Learning in the Way: Research and Reflection on Adult Christian Education*, Gracewing, 2000):

> Much of the history of Christianity, including perhaps its earliest years, may be interpreted in part as a series of conflicts between Stage 5 (and indeed Stage 6) perspectives, over against those Christians who possessed rather more circumscribed ways of being in faith.

Indexes

indicates an extract from the listed publication

Publications

Names and Organisations

Acknowledgements

The Publishers would like to thank the following for permission to reproduce copyright material. Every effort has been made to trace and contact all copyright holders but we apologise for any errors or omissions and, if informed, would be glad to make corrections in future editions.

Extracts from *All God's Children?: children's evangelism in crisis* (National Society/Church House Publishing 1991) and *Children in the Way: New Directions for the Church's Children* (National Society/Church House Publishing 1988) are copyright © The National Society (Church of England) for Promoting Religious Education and are reproduced by permission.

Specified excerpts from *Bringing Up Children in the Christian Faith* by Revd Dr John H Westerhoff III copyright © 1980 the Winston Press, *Christian Religious Education: Sharing our Story and Vision* by Thomas H Groome copyright © 1980 by Thomas Groome, and *Stages of Faith: the Psychology of Human Development and the Quest for Meaning* by James Fowler copyright © 1981 by James Fowler, are reprinted by permission of HarperCollins Publishers Inc., New York, USA.

Extracts from *Child Psychology and Religious Education* by Dorothy Wilson, 1928, *Religion and the Growing Mind* by Basil Yeaxlee, 1939, and 'Orthodox Church' by Michael Fortounatto in *A Dictionary of Religious Education*, ed. John M Sutcliffe, are reproduced by permission of SCM Press, a division of SCM-Canterbury Press Ltd, London, England.

Excerpts from *Children in Search of Meaning* by Violet Madge, 1965, are reproduced by permission of SCM-Canterbury Press Ltd, London, England.

'Children's Spirituality and our contemporary culture' by Danny Sullivan, from *Education of the Whole Child* by C Erricker, J Erricker, D Sullivan, C Ota and M Fletcher, published by Cassell, 1997, is reproduced by permission of Continuum International Publishing Group Ltd, The Tower Building, 11 York Road, London, England.

The excerpt from *Christian Child Development* by Iris V Cully (1980) is reproduced by permission of Gill and Macmillan Publishers, Dublin, Eire.

Excerpts from *The Church and Young People*, 1971, are reproduced by permission of the United Reformed Church.

'Conscientizing as a Way of Liberating' from a taped version of a talk by Paulo Freire in Rome, 1970, published in the Mexican quarterly *Contacto* March 1971, from the LADOC Keyhole Series 1 and included in *Liberation Theology: a documentary history*, Hennelly (Orbis, 1990), is reproduced by kind permission of the United States Catholic Conference.

The extract from *Education and Religion* by A Victor Murray, 1953, is reproduced by permission of James Nisbet & Co Ltd, Hitchin, Hertfordshire, England.

Excerpts from *General Directory for Catechesis: Congregation for the Clergy* (1997) are published by kind permission of the Catholic Truth Society, London, England.

The extract from *Jesus and the Children* by Hans-Ruedi Weber (1979) is reproduced by kind permission of the World Council of Churches, Geneva, Switzerland.

The excerpt from 'Jesus – Friend of Little Children?' by Stephen C Barton, from *Contours in Christian Education*, ed. J Astley and D Day (1992), published by McCrimmons, Great Wakering, Essex, England, copyright © Dr Stephen C Barton, is reproduced by kind permission of the editors and author.

The extract from 'Liturgy and Christian Formation' by Neville Clark, from *Worship and the Child*, ed. E C D Jasper (1975), is reproduced by kind permission of SPCK, London, England.

The excerpts from *Readiness for Religion* by Ronald Goldman (1965) are reproduced by permission of Routledge, London, England.

The extract from 'Report of the Joint Commission of the Three Methodist Churches on Sunday-school Work' to Conference, 1931, copyright © The Trustees for the Methodist Church Purposes, is used by permission of the Methodist Publishing House, Peterborough, England.

Towards a Charter for Children in the Church, Rosemary Johnston, published by the United Reformed Church, 1990, reproduced by permission.

The excerpt from *Vision and Tactics – Towards an Adult Church* by Gabriel Moran FSC (1968) is reproduced by permission of Burns and Oates, an imprint of Continuum International Publishing Group Ltd, The Tower Building, 11 York Road, London, England.

Material from *Will Our Children Have Faith?* by Revd Dr John H Westerhoff, 1976, revised and republished 2000 (Harrisburg PA: Morehouse Publishing), is reproduced by permission of the author.

Notes